THE
SECRET AGENT'S
BEDSIDE READER

THE
SECRET AGENT'S
BEDSIDE READER

A COMPENDIUM OF SPY WRITING

EDITED BY
MICHAEL SMITH

Biteback Publishing

First published in Great Britain in 2014 by
Biteback Publishing Ltd
Westminster Tower
3 Albert Embankment
London SE1 7SP

ISBN 978-1-84954-740-6

10 9 8 7 6 5 4 3 2 1

A CIP catalogue record for this book is available from the British Library.

Set in Bulmer
Printed and bound in Great Britain by
CPI Group (UK) Ltd, Croydon CR0 4YY

CONTENTS

INTRODUCTION

MICHAEL SMITH

F EW BRITISH GOVERNMENT institutions can have employed
as many successful writers as the Secret Intelligence Service,
the organisation now commonly known as MI6. The links
between Britain's spies and the writing profession go back to the six-
teenth century when the playwright Christopher Marlowe spied in
France and the Netherlands on behalf of the government of Queen
Elizabeth I, and was almost certainly murdered on behalf of his former employers. Marlowe reflected his experiences of the intelligence
world in his play *The Massacre in Paris*, where the 'English Agent'
is called to the deathbed of King Henry III of France, who has just
been stabbed by a Catholic friar. Henry tells the English Agent to
send word to his mistress the Queen of England 'whom God has
blessed for hating papistry' to let her know of the Catholic assassination attempt. Some have interpreted the English Agent as being
Marlowe, although Sir Francis Walsingham, the head of Elizabeth's
secret service, who was in Paris at the time, is a more likely candidate.

Walter Christmas, one of the first agents of the Secret Service
Bureau, set up ahead of the First World War, was probably the first

member of the modern intelligence services to write an espionage novel, in 1911, when he was still a very active agent of the British secret service. The enemy agents in *Sven Spies* were Germans, as they were for Christmas in real life. Many members of MI6 followed suit, with Somerset Maugham, Compton Mackenzie, Graham Greene and John le Carré only the most famous in literary terms.

Christmas's own life was the stuff of fiction. He was a Danish naval officer who travelled frequently into Germany to collect intelligence, and also provided Mansfield Cumming, the first 'Chief' of the Secret Intelligence Service, with reports on German shipping movements from the Danish Navy's coast-watching service. The 48-year-old Christmas insisted that the courier who collected his intelligence should always be a pretty, young woman who was to meet him in a hotel in Skagen in northern Denmark. A succession of prostitutes were procured to collect his reports and deliver not just his pay but an additional, more traditional exchange between the world's two oldest professions. When the Germans became suspicious of Christmas and he had to be exfiltrated to London, he was lodged in the notorious Shepherd Market area of Mayfair, where there were plenty of pretty young women, all pursuing the same business as the go-betweens who had collected his intelligence from the Skagen hotel.

When it came to their experiences in the British secret service, Maugham, Greene and le Carré stuck to fiction, although Maugham's *Ashenden* short stories, published in 1928, sailed very close to the wind, barely disguising accounts of his genuine exploits in Switzerland and Russia during the First World War. Compton Mackenzie did something similar in *Extremes Meet*, basing the activities of Roger Waterlow, Chief of British Intelligence in a small Balkan country during the First World War, on his own time in First World War Greece, but he followed it up with a series of memoirs which culminated in one that went too far for his former employers. The original version of *Greek Memories* was banned, and remains banned, although it appears here in its original form.

It wasn't just MI6. The other branches of British intelligence produced more than their own share of successful authors. William Le Queux, whose 'invasion novels' provoked the spy scares of the early 1900s, did so with the assistance of War Office intelligence, in a classic 'agent of influence' role. Ian Fleming, Charles Morgan and Angus Wilson all worked for Naval Intelligence during the Second World War. Denis Wheatley and Peter Fleming worked on deception operations in association with MI5 and MI6. John Bingham, apparently le Carré's inspiration for Smiley, was actually in MI5, as was his daughter Charlotte. Evelyn Waugh, Samuel Beckett, Peter Churchill and Paddy Leigh Fermor worked with the Special Operations Executive.

It is scarcely surprising that people accustomed to writing intelligence reports should be good story-tellers. As a relatively minor cog in the army's Cold War intelligence machine, I still remember the pride I felt at my own elevation to what seemed at the time to be a small elite of intelligence reporters. The civilian intelligence officer who kept our military prejudices in check told me at the outset that a good intelligence report should be constructed in much the same way as you would tell a joke. It seemed so at odds with the importance of our work that I inevitably questioned it, but he said it was simple. We were writing reports for people very few of whom would have the same degree of knowledge of the subject area as us. It was important that we made sure that everything was in the right place and as straightforward as possible to understand, just as you would when telling a joke. Only then would our reports have the impact they needed to make. It is probably no coincidence that on my first shift on the *Sunday Times* foreign desk, one of the newspaper's senior editors told me exactly the same thing about writing a news story.

Intelligence officers have to be able to tell a very good story, whether it is in an intelligence report or in the 'legend' they adopt for an undercover operation. It is not for nothing that this is known as the cover story and the measure of how good it has to be is that for the author it may well mean the difference between life and death. So it is hardly surprising that, over the years, authors and journalists have made good intelligence officers, and a relatively large number of intelligence officers have gone on to become successful writers.

This is a selection of some of their very best work, a mixture of extracts from great espionage novels, of factual accounts by former intelligence officers of real life operations, and a number of actual intelligence reports or instructions and memos on intelligence issues. Apart from Joseph Conrad – whose brilliant *The Secret Agent* inspires the title of this book – all of the writers featured here served in some role with British intelligence, from Le Queux's dubious claims about German spies rampaging across Britain to John le Carré (who worked for both MI5 and MI6) introducing us to George Smiley, the man widely seen as the ideal spy. Put simply, these are intelligence professionals writing about the world of espionage. Ian Fleming is represented not by a passage from a James Bond novel but by his defence of MI6 from his boss, the Director of Naval Intelligence, Admiral John Godfrey, who wanted to replace it with his own naval secret service. Fleming saved MI6 from that fate, ensuring a home for the world's most famous spy, the fictional hero with the licence to kill who did more for the service's reputation than even the very best of its real-life officers and agents.

Fleming is often dismissed as someone who never served in MI6 and therefore knew nothing about it. In fact, he was the chief liaison officer between MI6 and Naval Intelligence. His books are littered with elements of authentic detail garnered during his service in the Second World War, when guns actually were widely used by MI6 and 'liquidating' people was a real option. M's memos to Bond are written in the same green ink on the same blue paper as those sent out by C, and even on occasion typed on a typewriter with an unusually large type which the real wartime equivalent of Miss Moneypenny did sometimes use. Indeed so realistic were the Bond books deemed to be by some at the time they were published, that the Egyptian secret service ordered its London representative to buy a complete set for use by its training organisation.

There are plenty of other spies who have written about the world of espionage, either as fiction or in memoirs, and so could have appeared on these pages, A. E. W. Mason, Anthony Cavendish, Monty Woodhouse and Malcolm Muggeridge to name just a few, but those included here are among the very best and the story is brought right up to date with two very recent novels covering contemporary themes, *Slingshot* by Matthew Dunn, 'a former deep-cover officer' in MI6, and *Uncommon Enemy* by Alan Judd, who is described coyly in the author biography which appears in his books as a 'former soldier and diplomat'.

Michael Smith
September 2014

HISTORICAL NOTE

The British Secret Intelligence Service (SIS) has had a number of names over the years since its creation in 1909 as the Foreign Section of the Secret Service Bureau. Its founder was Commander Mansfield Cumming RN, who was known for reasons of secrecy as 'C' from the initial of his surname. The secret service swiftly became known as 'the C Organisation'; 'C's Organisation,' or even 'C's Show'.

In early 1916, when the War Office introduced a Military Intelligence Directorate, the War Office liaison section with the secret service was designated MI1c and this title became an alternative title for 'C's Organisation'. By the end of the First World War, Cumming's official title was CSS, Chief of the Secret Service, although 'C' was still far more commonly used, not by then as Cumming's initial but as an abbreviation for 'Chief'.

The current official title of Secret Intelligence Service was first used in 1919. When Cumming died in 1923, still in harness, and was replaced by Admiral Hugh Sinclair, the title of 'C' and Cumming's practice of writing in green ink (a naval tradition) were retained and are still in use to this day, as is the formal title of CSS. It was not until a reorganisation of military intelligence in 1940, when the title of the War Office section liaising with the Secret Intelligence Service was changed from MI1c to MI6, that the name by which the British secret service is now most commonly known was first used.

THE SECRET AGENT

JOSEPH CONRAD

This first extract from one of the earliest and greatest of all spy novels is the only one included in this book that is written by someone who did not – so far as is known – work for or collaborate with the British intelligence services. But Conrad's novel does provide the inspiration, as it has for so many other spy writers, and is therefore an appropriate way to open this collection. This particular passage is a worthwhile reminder that in the world of espionage some things never change. Conrad's protagonist Adolf Verloc is called to the embassy of the country for which he works – the reader is given the clear impression it is Tsarist Russia, though this is never stated as fact. There Verloc is softened up by the Head of Chancellery Wurmt before being castigated by the mysterious Mr Vladimir, the new spymaster. Although both the narrator and Vladimir paint Verloc as indolent, we discover that he has in fact produced the designs of the latest French guns, a substantial coup in the late nineteenth century, when the story is set. But this achievement is dismissed by Vladimir whose impatient demands bear a striking resemblance to those made more recently by British and American politicians. It is immediately clear that this will not end well.

I T WAS SO early that the porter of the Embassy issued hurriedly out of his lodge still struggling with the left sleeve of his livery coat. His waistcoat was red, and he wore knee-breeches, but his aspect was flustered. Mr Verloc, aware of the rush on his flank, drove it off by simply holding out an envelope stamped with the arms of the Embassy, and passed on. He produced the same talisman also to the footman who opened the door, and stood back to let him enter the hall.

A clear fire burned in a tall fireplace, and an elderly man standing with his back to it, in evening dress and with a chain round his neck, glanced up from the newspaper he was holding spread out in both hands before his calm and severe face. He didn't move; but another lackey, in brown trousers and clawhammer coat edged with thin yellow cord, approaching Mr Verloc listened to the murmur of his name, and turning round on his heel in silence, began to walk, without looking back once. Mr Verloc, thus led along a ground-floor passage to the left of the great carpeted staircase, was suddenly motioned to enter a quite small room furnished with a heavy writing-table and a few chairs. The servant shut the door, and Mr Verloc remained alone. He did not take a seat. With his hat and stick held in one hand he glanced about, passing his other podgy hand over his uncovered sleek head.

Another door opened noiselessly, and Mr Verloc immobilising his glance in that direction saw at first only black clothes, the bald top of a head, and a drooping dark grey whisker on each side of a pair of wrinkled hands. The person who had entered was holding a batch of papers before his eyes and walked up to the table with a rather mincing step, turning the papers over the while. Privy Councillor Wurmt, *Chancelier d'Ambassade*, was rather shortsighted. This meritorious official, laying the papers on the table, disclosed a face of pasty complexion and of melancholy ugliness surrounded by a lot of fine, long dark grey hairs, barred heavily by thick and bushy eyebrows. He put

2

on a black-framed pince-nez upon a blunt and shapeless nose, and seemed struck by Mr Verloc's appearance. Under the enormous eyebrows his weak eyes blinked pathetically through the glasses.

He made no sign of greeting; neither did Mr Verloc who certainly knew his place; but a subtle change about the general outlines of his shoulders and back suggested a slight bending of Mr Verloc's spine under the vast surface of his overcoat. The effect was of unobtrusive deference.

'I have here some of your reports,' said the bureaucrat in an unexpectedly soft and weary voice, and pressing the tip of his forefinger on the papers with force. He paused; and Mr Verloc, who had recognised his own handwriting very well, waited in an almost breathless silence. 'We are not very satisfied with the attitude of the police here,' the other continued, with every appearance of mental fatigue.

The shoulders of Mr Verloc, without actually moving, suggested a shrug. And for the first time since he left his home that morning his lips opened.

'Every country has its police,' he said, philosophically. But as the official of the Embassy went on blinking at him steadily he felt constrained to add: 'Allow me to observe that I have no means of action upon the police here.'

'What is desired,' said the man of papers, 'is the occurrence of something definite which should stimulate their vigilance. That is within your province – is it not so?'

Mr Verloc made no answer except by a sigh, which escaped him involuntarily, for instantly he tried to give his face a cheerful expression. The official blinked doubtfully, as if affected by the dim light of the room. He repeated vaguely:

'The vigilance of the police – and the severity of the magistrates. The general leniency of the judicial procedure here, and the utter absence of all repressive measures, are a scandal to Europe. What is wished for just now is the accentuation of the unrest – of the fermentation which undoubtedly exists…'

'Undoubtedly, undoubtedly,' broke in Mr Verloc in a deep, deferential bass of an oratorical quality, so utterly different from the tone in which he had spoken before that his interlocutor remained profoundly surprised. 'It exists to a dangerous degree. My reports for the last twelve months make it sufficiently clear.'

'Your reports for the last twelve months,' State Councillor Wurmt began in his gentle and dispassionate tone, 'have been read by me. I failed to discover why you wrote them at all.'

A sad silence reigned for a time. Mr Verloc seemed to have swallowed his tongue, and the other gazed at the papers on the table fixedly. At last he gave them a slight push.

'The state of affairs you expose there is assumed to exist as the first condition of your employment. What is required at present is not writing, but the bringing to light of a distinct, significant fact – I would almost say of an alarming fact.'

'I need not say that all my endeavours shall be directed to that end,' Mr Verloc said, with convinced modulations in his conversational husky tone. But the sense of being blinked at watchfully behind the blind glitter of these eyeglasses on the other side of the table disconcerted him. He stopped short with a gesture of absolute devotion. The useful hard-working, if obscure member of the Embassy had an air of being impressed by some newly-born thought.

'You are very corpulent,' he said.

This observation, really of a psychological nature, and advanced with the modest hesitation of an office-man more familiar with ink and paper than with the requirements of active life, stung Mr Verloc in the manner of a rude personal remark. He stepped back a pace.

'Eh? What were you pleased to say?' he exclaimed, with husky resentment.

4

The *Chancelier d'Ambassade*, entrusted with the conduct of this interview, seemed to find it too much for him.

'I think,' he said, 'that you had better see Mr Vladimir. Yes, decidedly I think you ought to see Mr Vladimir. Be good enough to wait here,' he added, and went out with mincing steps.

At once Mr Verloc passed his hand over his hair. A slight perspiration had broken out on his forehead. He let the air escape from his pursed-up lips like a man blowing at a spoonful of hot soup. But when the servant in brown appeared at the door silently, Mr Verloc had not moved an inch from the place he had occupied throughout the interview. He had remained motionless, as if feeling himself surrounded by pitfalls.

He walked along a passage lighted by a lonely gas-jet, then up a flight of winding stairs, and through a glazed and cheerful corridor on the first floor. The footman threw open a door, and stood aside. The feet of Mr Verloc felt a thick carpet. The room was large, with three windows; and a young man with a shaven, big face, sitting in a roomy armchair before a vast mahogany writing-table, said in French to the *Chancelier d'Ambassade*, who was going out with the papers in his hand:

'You are quite right, *mon cher*. He's fat – the animal.'

Mr Vladimir, First Secretary, had a drawing-room reputation as an agreeable and entertaining man. He was something of a favourite in society. His wit consisted in discovering droll connections between incongruous ideas; and when talking in that strain he sat well forward on his seat, with his left hand raised, as if exhibiting his funny demonstrations between the thumb and forefinger, while his round and clean-shaven face wore an expression of merry perplexity.

But there was no trace of merriment or perplexity in the way he looked at Mr Verloc. Lying far back in the deep armchair, with squarely spread elbows, and throwing one leg over a thick knee, he had with his smooth and rosy countenance the air of a preter-naturally thriving baby that will not stand nonsense from anybody.

'You understand French, I suppose?' he said.

Mr Verloc stated huskily that he did. His whole vast bulk had a forward inclination. He stood on the carpet in the middle of the room, clutching his hat and stick in one hand; the other hung life-lessly by his side. He muttered unobtrusively somewhere deep down in his throat something about having done his military ser-vice in the French artillery. At once, with contemptuous perversity, Mr Vladimir changed the language, and began to speak idiomatic English without the slightest trace of a foreign accent.

'Ah! Yes. Of course. Let's see. How much did you get for obtain-ing the design of the improved breech-block of their new field-gun?'

'Five years' rigorous confinement in a fortress,' Mr Verloc answered, unexpectedly, but without any sign of feeling.

'You got off easily,' was Mr Vladimir's comment. 'And, anyhow, it served you right for letting yourself get caught. What made you go in for that sort of thing – eh?'

Mr Verloc's husky conversational voice was heard speaking of youth, of a fatal infatuation for an unworthy...

'Aha! *Cherchez la femme,*' Mr Vladimir deigned to interrupt, unbending, but without affability; there was, on the contrary, a touch of grimness in his condescension. 'How long have you been employed by the Embassy here?' he asked.

'Ever since the time of the late Baron Stott-Wartenheim,' Mr Verloc answered in subdued tones, and protruding his lips sadly, in sign of sorrow for the deceased diplomat. The First Secretary observed this play of physiognomy steadily.

'Ah! ever since ... Well! What have you got to say for yourself?' he asked, sharply.

Mr Verloc answered with some surprise that he was not aware of having anything special to say. He had been summoned by a letter – and he plunged his hand busily into the side pocket of his overcoat, but before the mocking, cynical watchfulness of Mr Vladimir, concluded to leave it there.

'Bah!' said the latter. 'What do you mean by getting out of condition like this? You haven't got even the physique of your profession. You – a member of a starving proletariat – never! You – a desperate socialist or anarchist – which is it?'

'Anarchist,' stated Mr Verloc in a deadened tone.

'Bosh!' went on Mr Vladimir, without raising his voice. 'You startled old Wurmt himself. You wouldn't deceive an idiot. They all are that by-the-by, but you seem to me simply impossible. So you began your connection with us by stealing the French gun designs. And you got yourself caught. That must have been very disagreeable to our government. You don't seem to be very smart.'

Mr Verloc tried to exculpate himself huskily.

'As I've had occasion to observe before, a fatal infatuation for an unworthy…'

Mr Vladimir raised a large, white, plump hand.

'Ah, yes. The unlucky attachment – of your youth. She got hold of the money, and then sold you to the police – eh?'

The doleful change in Mr Verloc's physiognomy, the momentary drooping of his whole person, confessed that such was the regrettable case. Mr Vladimir's hand clasped the ankle reposing on his knee. The sock was of dark blue silk.

'You see, that was not very clever of you. Perhaps you are too susceptible.'

Mr Verloc intimated in a throaty, veiled murmur that he was no longer young.

'Oh! That's a failing which age does not cure,' Mr Vladimir remarked, with sinister familiarity. 'But no! You are too fat for that.

You could not have come to look like this if you had been at all susceptible. I'll tell you what I think is the matter: you are a lazy fellow. How long have you been drawing pay from this Embassy?'

'Eleven years,' was the answer, after a moment of sulky hesitation. 'I've been charged with several missions to London while His Excellency Baron Stott-Wartenheim was still ambassador in Paris. Then by his Excellency's instructions I settled down in London. I am English.'

'You are! Are you? Eh?'

'A natural-born British subject,' Mr Verloc said, stolidly. 'But my father was French, and so...'

'Never mind explaining,' interrupted the other. 'I daresay you could have been legally a Marshal of France and a Member of Parliament in England – and then, indeed, you would have been of some use to our Embassy.'

This flight of fancy provoked something like a faint smile on Mr Verloc's face. Mr Vladimir retained an imperturbable gravity.

'But, as I've said, you are a lazy fellow; you don't use your opportunities. In the time of Baron Stott-Wartenheim we had a lot of soft-headed people running this Embassy. They caused fellows of your sort to form a false conception of the nature of a secret service fund. It is my business to correct this misapprehension by telling you what the secret service is not. It is not a philanthropic institution. I've had you called here on purpose to tell you this.'

Mr Vladimir observed the forced expression of bewilderment on Verloc's face, and smiled sarcastically.

'I see that you understand me perfectly. I daresay you are intelligent enough for your work. What we want now is activity – activity.'

On repeating this last word Mr Vladimir laid a long white forefinger on the edge of the desk. Every trace of huskiness disappeared from Verloc's voice. The nape of his gross neck became crimson above the velvet collar of his overcoat. His lips quivered before they came widely open.

'If you'll only be good enough to look up my record,' he boomed out in his great, clear, oratorical bass, 'you'll see I gave a warning only three months ago on the occasion of the Grand Duke Romuald's visit to Paris, which was telegraphed from here to the French police, and…'

'Tut, tut!' broke out Mr Vladimir, with a frowning grimace. 'The French police had no use for your warning. Don't roar like this. What the devil do you mean?'

With a note of proud humility Mr Verloc apologised for forgetting himself. His voice, famous for years at open-air meetings and at workmen's assemblies in large halls, had contributed, he said, to his reputation of a good and trustworthy comrade. It was, therefore, a part of his usefulness. It had inspired confidence in his principles. He was always put up to speak by the leaders at a critical moment, Mr Verloc declared, with obvious satisfaction. There was no uproar above which he could not make himself heard, he added; and suddenly he made a demonstration.

'Allow me,' he said. With lowered forehead, without looking up, swiftly and ponderously, he crossed the room to one of the French windows. As if giving way to an uncontrollable impulse, he opened it a little. Mr Vladimir, jumping up amazed from the depths of the armchair, looked over his shoulder; and below, across the courtyard of the Embassy, well beyond the open gate, could be seen the broad back of a policeman watching idly the gorgeous perambulator of a wealthy baby being wheeled in state across the Square.

'Constable!' said Mr Verloc, with no more effort than if he were whispering; and Mr Vladimir burst into a laugh on seeing the policeman spin round as if prodded by a sharp instrument. Mr Verloc shut the window quietly, and returned to the middle of the room.

'With a voice like that,' he said, putting on the husky conversational pedal, 'I was naturally trusted. And I knew what to say, too.'

Mr Vladimir, arranging his cravat, observed him in the glass over the mantelpiece.

'I daresay you have the social revolutionary jargon by heart well enough,' he said, contemptuously. '*Vox et* ... You haven't ever studied Latin, have you?'

'No,' growled Mr Verloc. 'You did not expect me to know it. I belong to the million. Who knows Latin? Only a few hundred imbeciles who aren't fit to take care of themselves.'

For some thirty seconds longer Mr Vladimir studied in the mirror the fleshy profile, the gross bulk, of the man behind him. And at the same time he had the advantage of seeing his own face, clean-shaved and round, rosy about the gills, and with the thin, sensitive lips formed exactly for the utterance of those delicate witticisms which had made him such a favourite in the very highest society. Then he turned, and advanced into the room with such determination that the very ends of his quaintly old-fashioned bow necktie seemed to bristle with unspeakable menaces. The movement was so swift and fierce that Mr Verloc, casting an oblique glance, quailed inwardly.

'Aha! You dare be impudent,' Mr Vladimir began, with an amazingly guttural intonation not only utterly un-English, but absolutely un-European, and startling even to Mr Verloc's experience of cosmopolitan slums. 'You dare! Well, I am going to speak plain English to you. Voice won't do. We have no use for your voice. We don't want a voice. We want facts – startling facts – damn you.'

Extracted from *The Secret Agent: A Simple Tale* by Joseph Conrad (first published by Methuen in 1907)

SPIES OF THE KAISER

WILLIAM LE QUEUX

The first decade of the twentieth century saw a series of books based on the threat of a war with Germany of which *Spies of the Kaiser* was one of the most influential. It resulted from extensive briefing of the author William Le Queux by his friend Colonel James Edmonds, the head of the War Office's Secret Service. Le Queux was what is known in the espionage world as an 'agent of influence', a role in which he was very effective. 'I think I can claim to be the first person to warn Great Britain that the Kaiser was plotting war against us,' Le Queux said. 'I discovered, as far back as 1905, a great network of espionage spread over the United Kingdom.'

The *Daily Mail* serialised Le Queux's novel, *The Invasion of 1910*, carefully rerouting the invading German troops through towns and villages where its circulation was at its highest. Le Queux's books sparked a series of spy scares, as Edmonds had hoped they would. The Prime Minister Herbert Asquith ordered an inquiry into 'the dangers from German espionage' at which Edmonds forced home his point but left a poor impression on some of those present.

He told them that a secret service's motto should be to 'trust no one' and quoted from Rudyard Kipling's Kim that one should 'trust a snake before a harlot and a harlot before a Pathan'. Despite being dismissed by one member of the inquiry as 'a silly witness' with 'espionage on the brain', his arguments won the day and led to the creation of a Secret Service Bureau with a Home Section to catch German spies coming to Britain and a Foreign Section to collect intelligence on Germany. The Home Section was run by an army officer Colonel Vernon Kell, codenamed K, and became what we now know as MI5. The Foreign Section, was run by a naval officer Commander Mansfield Cumming, codenamed C, and would eventually become MI6. Le Queux's dubious influence was therefore critical in the creation of today's British intelligence and security services.

<hr />

'WELL, THAT'S RATHER curious,' I remarked, closing the door of the old oak-panelled smoking-room at Metfield Park, and returning to where my friend Ray Raymond was seated.

'Was anyone outside the door?' he asked, quickly on the alert.

'Mrs Hill-Mason's German maid. You remember, Vera pointed her out yesterday.'

'Hm! And she was listening – after every one else has gone to bed!' he remarked. 'Yes, Jack, it's curious.'

It was past one o'clock in the morning. Two months had passed since the affair down at Portsmouth, but we had not been inactive. We were sitting before the great open fireplace where the logs were blazing, after the rest of the men had taken their candles and retired, and had been exchanging confidences in ignorance of the fact that the door remained ajar. I had, however, detected the frou-frou of a woman's skirt, and creeping across to the door had seen the maid of one of the guests disappearing down the stone passage which led to the great hall now in darkness.

Metfield Park, 3 miles from Melton Constable, in Norfolk, the seat of the Jocelyns, was a fine old Tudor place in the centre of a splendid park, where the pheasant shooting was always excellent. Harry Jocelyn, the heir, had been with us at Balliol, hence Ray and I usually received invitations to the shooting parties. On this occasion, however, Vera Vallance with her aunt, Mrs Mortimer, had been invited, much to Ray's satisfaction.

Among the party was a well-known naval officer, captain of a first-class cruiser, two military officers, and several smart women, for both Sir Herbert and Lady Jocelyn moved in a very smart set. Several of the ladies had joined us in the smoking-room for cigarettes, and the conversation around the fire had been mainly the usual society chatter, until at one o'clock everyone had left for bed except our two selves.

Over the great fireplace were the arms of the Jocelyns carved in stone, with the date 1573, and in the corner near the window was a stand of armour upon which the dancing flames glinted ever and anon. Through the long uncurtained window shone the bright moon from over the park, and just as I reseated myself the stable clock chimed the half-hour.

We had been there four days, and the sport had been excellent. On the previous day Ray had excused himself on account of the bad weather, and had spent the hours mostly with Vera.

It was of how he had employed his time that he had been telling me when I had discovered the eavesdropper.

'I wonder why our conversation should prove so interesting to that maid?' he remarked thoughtfully, gazing into the fire. 'She's rather good-looking for a German, isn't she?'

'Yes,' I said. 'But who is this Mrs Hill-Mason? She seems a rather loud and buxom person, fond of the display of jewellery, dark, somewhat oleaginous, and devoted to bridge.'

'Harry says his mother met her in Cairo last winter. She's one of the Somerset Masons – half-sister to the Countess of Thanet.'

'Oh, she is known, then?'

'Of course. But we must get Vera to make some inquiry tomorrow as to where she obtained her maid,' declared Ray. 'The woman is interested in us, and we must discover the cause.'

'Yes, I somehow mistrust her,' I said. 'I met her crossing the hall just before dinner, and I detected a curious look in her eyes as she glanced at me.'

'Merely your fancy, Jack, old chap – because she's German,' he laughed, stretching his long legs.

'Well, what you were telling me about Vera and her discovery has alarmed me,' I said, tossing away the end of my cigar.

'Yes, she only returned last week from Emden, where she's been visiting her old German governess, who, it seems, is now married to an official in the construction department of the German Admiralty. From her friend she was able to learn a lot, which will, no doubt, cause our Lords of the Admiralty a bad quarter of an hour. What would the British public think if they were told the truth – that Germany is rapidly building a secret fleet?' I said.

'Why, my dear fellow, the public would simply say you were a liar,' he laughed. 'Every Englishman fancies himself top-dog, even though British diplomacy – apart from that of our excellent King – is the laughing-stock of the Powers. No,' he added, 'the truth is out. All yesterday I spent with Vera, preparing the information which she forwarded to the Admiralty to-night. I registered the letter for her at the village post office. The authorities owe her a very deep debt for succeeding in obtaining the information which our secret service has always failed to get. She, an admiral's daughter, is now able to furnish actual details of the ships now building in secret and where they are being constructed.'

'A matter which will, no doubt, be considered very seriously by the government,' I said.

'Oh, I suppose they treat the whole thing lightly, as they always do. We invite invasion,' he sighed as he rose, adding: 'Let's turn in now. Tomorrow we'll keep an eye upon that unusually inquisitive maid.'

That night the eyes of the German maid haunted me. I could not rid myself of their recollection. Was it that this hunting down of German spies was getting on my nerves?

Next day we were shooting Starlings Wood, about 5 miles distant, but Ray having cried off one day, could not do so again. Therefore, at his suggestion, I made an excuse and remained at home with the ladies.

The morning I spent walking through the park with Vera, a smart, sweet-faced little figure in her short tweed skirt and furs, with her bright and vivacious chatter. From her I learnt some further details concerning her visit to Emden.

'Ray is most excited about it, Mr Jacox,' she was saying. 'Of course, I had to make my inquiries with great caution and discretion, but I managed to find out what I wanted, and I sent all the details to the Admiralty yesterday.'

Then as we went along the wide beech avenue I told her of the curious incident in the smoking-room on the previous evening.

'Ray was telling me about it just before breakfast,' she said, turning her splendid eyes to mine. 'I have already made some inquiries of Mrs Hill-Mason, and it appears that the maid Erna Stolberg was recommended to her by a friend when she was in Dresden last year. She's a most exemplary person, and has a number of friends in England. She was previously with a French *baronne*.'

'Mrs Hill-Mason often moves in a military set, doesn't she?' I remarked. 'Somebody last night stated that she's the widow of a general, and is well known down at Aldershot.'

'I believe so.'

'If Mrs Hill-Mason visits at the houses of military officers, as it seems she does, then this inquisitive maid would be afforded many opportunities for gathering information. I intend to watch her,' I said.

'And so will I, Mr Jacox,' replied the admiral's daughter, drawing her Astrakhan collar tighter about her throat.

Half an hour later, we drove in the wagonette out to the shooting-party in the woods, where a merry luncheon was served in a marquee. I, however, returned to the house before the rest of the party and haunted the servants' hall. With Williams the butler I was on friendly terms, and finding him in the great hall, began to make inquiries regarding the guests' servants.

'You've got a German woman among them, haven't you?' I remarked.

'Yes, sir,' was his reply. 'A rather funny one she is, I fancy. She goes out alone for walks after she's dressed her mistress for dinner, and is out sometimes till quite late. What she does wandering about in the dark nobody knows. But it ain't for me to say a word, sir; she's a visitor's maid.'

I held my own counsel, but resolved to watch.

Tea in the great hall, over which Lady Jocelyn presided, proved the usual irresponsible function, but when I went to my room to dress for dinner I became convinced that certain papers in my suitcase had been turned over and investigated.

That night I did not go in to dinner. I heard the gong sound, and when the company had gone in, I put on thick boots, overcoat, and cap, and passed through the back way along the old wing of the house, through the smoking-room, and out upon the drive.

Behind some holly bushes where I could see any one leave by the great paved courtyard where the servants' entrance was situated, I concealed myself and waited in patience. The night was dark and overcast.

The stable chimes had rung out half past eight, but I still remained until, about twenty minutes later, footfalls sounded, and from out the arched entrance to the courtyard came a female figure in a close-fitting hat and long dark Ulster.

She passed close by me, under the light of the lamp, and I saw it was the fair-haired woman for whom I was waiting.

Instead of walking straight down the avenue to the lodge-gates, she struck along a footpath which led for a mile across the park, first skirting the lake – the fishpond of the monks who lived there before the Dissolution; then, passing under the dark shadow of a spinney, led to a stile by which the high park wall could be negotiated and the main road to East Dereham reached.

As she went forward so I followed. I knew the path well. I watched her ascend the stile and cross the wall into the road. Then I crept up and peered over into the darkness. She had turned to the right, and I could discern her waiting at the roadside about 30 yards away.

From my place of concealment I could hear her slow footsteps as she idled up and down in the darkness, evidently waiting for someone.

I think about ten minutes passed when I heard the whir of a motor-car approaching, its big glaring headlamps shedding a stream of white brilliance over the muddy road. As it approached her it slowed down and stopped. Then I distinguished it to be a big limousine, the occupant of which opened the door, and she entered with a word of greeting.

I stood peering into the darkness, in surprise and disappointment at not catching sight of the person with whom she was keeping these nightly appointments. As soon as the door had banged the driver drove across the road, backed, and turning, sped away in the direction he had come.

But while he was turning I had gained the road, advancing

beneath the hedgerow in an endeavour to see the number of the car. But I was baffled. It was covered with mud.

Afterwards, much disappointed, and certainly hungry, I made my way back across the park to the Hall, where, after managing to get a snack from Williams, I joined the party at bridge.

That night the woman Stolberg returned at five minutes to eleven, and later, when Ray went upstairs with me, I described what I had seen.

Next night, instead of following her out, I waited at the spot at half past ten, when, sure enough, the car returned ten minutes later and deposited her. The number plates, however, were obliterated by the mud both front and back – purposely it seemed to me. The man within shook her hand as she alighted, but I could not see his face. Was he some secret lover? Apparently she went no great distance each evening, going and coming from the direction of Holt.

On the following day I took several opportunities of watching the woman at close quarters. Her eyes were peculiarly set, very close together, her lips were thin, and her cheek-bones rather high. Otherwise she was not bad-looking. Mrs Hill-Mason had, of course, no idea of her maid's nocturnal motor-rides.

Whether the woman had any suspicion that she was being watched I know not; but on the next night when Ray took a turn at keeping an eye upon her, she did not go out, but on the next she went, and Ray followed her to the park wall, but saw nothing more than I had done.

All this time, of course, Vera was greatly interested in the result of our observations. Through her own maid, Batson, she discovered the room occupied by the German, and to this I made my way, at considerable risk, one morning while the maid was busy attending upon her mistress. I had a good look through her belongings, finding in her trunk a small, flat tin box, japanned dark green, strong, and secured by a lock of well-known make. What, I wondered, did it contain?

Could I have but seen the number of the mysterious car I could have discovered the identity of her nocturnal visitor.

The same day that I discovered the tin box in her trunk, Mrs Hill-Mason, however, returned to London, taking with her the mysterious *Fräulein*.

Extracted from *Spies of the Kaiser: Plotting the Downfall of England* by William Le Queux (first published by Hurst and Blackett in 1909)

THE RIDDLE OF
THE SANDS

ERSKINE CHILDERS

The Riddle of the Sands, the story of how Charles Carruthers and his friend
Arthur Davies uncover German preparations for an invasion of Britain
while sailing in northern Germany, inspired a whole generation of young
men to dream of spying on the Hun, and led in 1910 to the first major
spy scandal to be suffered by the organisation we now know as MI6.
Two young naval officers, Captain Bernard Trench and Lieutenant Vivian
Brandon, were sent to northern Germany to collect intelligence on German coastal defences. They were swiftly spotted, arrested and put on trial.
Reporting on the case, the German press managed to make the *Daily
Mail*'s attitude to enemy spies look almost liberal. A German spy recently
arrested in Portsmouth was merely collecting information he could 'have
learned more cheaply and with less trouble by buying picture postcards',
but Brandon and Trench were 'very dangerous men' who should have
medical treatment to erase their memories.

By comparison, the trial was a relatively sedate affair. The general mood
back home was that Trench and Brandon were innocent officers and gentlemen fitted up by the Germans. The evidence demonstrated beyond a

shadow of a doubt that they were guilty as charged. Nevertheless, they were treated not as criminals but as officers simply doing their job. The atmosphere in the court room was remarkably relaxed. At one point, their barrister held up a copy of *The Riddle of the Sands* and asked them in turn if they were familiar with it. Trench simply said that he knew of it. Brandon confirmed that he had read it and then said, to raucous laughter from the court, that he liked it so much that he had read it three times.

Childers had not served in intelligence before he wrote *The Riddle of the Sands*, but he went on to work for Cumming running agents into Turkish-occupied territory in the Near East. His was a far better book than anything Le Queux could have produced, but he also included the obligatory mysterious *Fräulein*, the *femme fatale* for whom Arthur Davies has already fallen when the novel begins.

T HE INCONGRUITY OF the whole business was striking me. Why should anyone want to kill Davies, and why should Davies, the soul of modesty and simplicity, imagine that anyone wanted to kill him? He must have cogent reasons, for he was the last man to give way to a morbid fancy.

'Go on,' I said. 'What was his motive? A German finds an Englishman exploring a bit of German coast, determines to stop him, and even to get rid of him. It looks so far as if you were thought to be the spy.'

Davies winced. 'But he's not a German,' he said, hotly. 'He's an Englishman.'

'An Englishman?'

'Yes, I'm sure of it. Not that I've much to go on. He professed to know very little English, and never spoke it, except a word or two now and then to help me out of a sentence; and as to his German, he seemed to me to speak it like a native; but, of course, I'm no judge.' Davies sighed. 'That's where I wanted someone like you. You would have spotted him at once, if he wasn't German. I go more by a … What do you call it? A…?'

'General impression,' I suggested.

'Yes, that's what I mean. It was something in his looks and manner; you know how different we are from foreigners. And it wasn't only himself, it was the way he talked – I mean about cruising and the sea, especially. It's true he let me do most of the talking; but, all the same – how can I explain it? I felt we understood one another, in a way that two foreigners wouldn't.

'He pretended to think me a bit crazy for coming so far in a small boat, but I could swear he knew as much about the game as I did; for lots of little questions he asked had the right ring in them. Mind you, all this is an afterthought. I should never have bothered about it – I'm not cut out for a Sherlock Holmes – if it hadn't been for what followed.'

'It's rather vague,' I said. 'Have you no more definite reason for thinking him English?'

'There were one or two things rather more definite,' said Davies, slowly. 'You know when he hove to and hailed me, proposing the short cut, I told you roughly what he said. I forget the exact words, but "*abschneiden*" came in – "*durch Watten*" and "*abschneiden*'"(they call the banks Watts, you know); they were simple words, and he shouted them loud, so as to carry through the wind. I understood what he meant, but, as I told you, I hesitated before consenting. I suppose he thought I didn't understand, for just as he was drawing ahead again he pointed to the suth'ard, and then shouted through his hands as a trumpet "*Verstehen Sie*? Short-cut through sands; follow me!" the last two sentences in downright English. I can hear those words now, and I'll swear they were in his native tongue. Of course I thought nothing of it at the time. I was quite aware that he knew a few English words, though he had always mispronounced them; an easy trick when your hearer suspects nothing. But I needn't say that just then I was observant of trifles. I don't pretend to be able to unravel a plot and steer a small boat before a heavy sea at the same moment.'

'And if he was piloting you into the next world he could afford to commit himself before you parted! Was there anything else? By the way, how did the daughter strike you? Did she look English too?'

Two men cannot discuss a woman freely without a deep foundation of intimacy, and, until this day, the subject had never arisen between us in any form. It was the last that was likely to, for I could have divined that Davies would have met it with an armour of reserve. He was busy putting on this armour now; yet I could not help feeling a little brutal as I saw how badly he jointed his clumsy suit of mail. Our ages were the same, but I laugh now to think how old and blasé I felt as the flush warmed his brown skin, and he slowly propounded the verdict, 'Yes, I think she did.'

'She talked nothing but German, I suppose?'

'Oh, of course.'

'Did you see much of her?'

'A good deal.'

'Was she…?' (How to frame it?) 'Did she want you to sail to the Elbe with them?'

'She seemed to,' admitted Davies, reluctantly, clutching at his ally, the match-box. 'But, hang it, don't dream that she knew what was coming,' he added, with sudden fire.

I pondered and wondered, shrinking from further inquisition, easy as it would have been with so truthful a victim, and banishing all thought of ill-timed chaff. There was a cross-current in this strange affair, whose depth and strength I was beginning to gauge with increasing seriousness. I did not know my man yet, and I did not know myself. A conviction that events in the near future would force us into complete mutual confidence withheld me from pressing him too far. I returned to the main question; who was Dollmann, and what was his motive? Davies struggled out of his armour.

'I'm convinced,' he said, 'that he's an Englishman in German service. He must be in German service, for he had evidently been in those waters a long time, and knew every inch of them; of course, it's a very lonely part of the world, but he has a house on Norderney Island; and he, and all about him, must be well known to a certain number of people. One of his friends I happened to meet; what do you think he was? A naval officer. It was on the afternoon of the third day, and we were having coffee on the deck of the *Medusa*, and talking about next day's trip, when a little launch came buzzing up from seaward, drew alongside, and this chap I'm speaking of came on board, shook hands with Dollmann, and stared hard at me. Dollmann introduced us, calling him Commander von Brüning, in command of the torpedo gunboat *Blitz*. He pointed towards Norderney, and I saw her – a low, grey rat of a vessel – anchored in the Roads about 2 miles away. It turned out that she was doing the work of fishery guardship on that part of the coast.

'I must say I took to him at once. He looked a real good sort, and a splendid officer, too – just the sort of chap I should have liked to be. You know I always wanted – but that's an old story, and can wait. I had some talk with him, and we got on capitally as far as we went, but that wasn't far, for I left pretty soon, guessing that they wanted to be alone.'

'Were they alone then?' I asked, innocently.

'Oh, *Fräulein* Dollmann was there, of course,' explained Davies, feeling for his armour again.

'Did he seem to know them well?' I pursued, inconsequently.

'Oh, yes, very well.'

Scenting a faint clue, I felt the need of feminine weapons for my sensitive antagonist. But the opportunity passed.

'That was the last I saw of him,' he said. 'We sailed, as I told you, at daybreak next morning. Now, have you got any idea what I'm driving at?'

'A rough idea,' I answered. 'Go ahead.'

Davies sat up to the table, unrolled the chart with a vigorous sweep of his two hands, and took up his parable with new zest.

'I start with two certainties,' he said. 'One is that I was "moved on" from that coast, because I was too inquisitive. The other is that Dollmann is at some devil's work there which is worth finding out. Now' – he paused in a gasping effort to be logical and articulate. 'Now – well, look at the chart. No, better still, look first at this map of Germany. It's on a small scale, and you can see the whole thing.' He snatched down a pocket-map from the shelf and unfolded it.

'Here's this huge empire, stretching half over central Europe – an empire growing like wildfire, I believe, in people, and wealth, and everything. They've licked the French, and the Austrians, and are the greatest military power in Europe. I wish I knew more about all that, but what I'm concerned with is their sea-power. It's a new thing with them, but it's going strong, and that Emperor of theirs is running it for all it's worth. He's a splendid chap, and anyone can see he's right.

They've got no colonies to speak of, and must have them, like us. They can't get them and keep them, and they can't protect their huge commerce without naval strength. The command of the sea is the thing nowadays, isn't it? I say, don't think these are my ideas,' he added, naively. 'It's all out of Mahan and those fellows. Well, the Germans have got a small fleet at present, but it's a thundering good one, and they're building hard. There's the ... And the...' He broke off into a digression on armaments and speeds in which I could not follow him. He seemed to know every ship by heart.

I had to recall him to the point. 'Well, think of Germany as a new sea-power,' he resumed. 'The next thing is, what is her coast-line? It's a very queer one, as you know, split clean in two by Denmark, most of it lying east of that and looking on the Baltic, which is practically an inland sea, with its entrance blocked by Danish islands. It was to evade that block that William built the ship canal from Kiel to the Elbe, but that could be easily smashed in wartime. Far the most important bit of coast-line is that which lies west of Denmark and looks on the North Sea. It's there that Germany gets her head out into the open, so to speak. It's there that she fronts us and France, the two great sea-powers of Western Europe, and it's there that her greatest ports are and her richest commerce.

'Now it must strike you at once that it's ridiculously short compared with the huge country behind it. From Borkum to the Elbe, as the crow flies, is only 70 miles. Add to that the west coast of Schleswig, say 120 miles. Total, say, 200. Compare that with the seaboard of France and England. Doesn't it stand to reason that every inch of it is important? Now what sort of coast is it? Even on this small map you can see at once, by all those wavy lines, shoals and sand everywhere, blocking nine-tenths of the land altogether, and doing their best to block the other tenth where the great rivers run in. Now let's take it bit by bit. You see it divides itself into three. Beginning from the west the first piece is from Borkum to Wangeroog – 50-odd miles. What's that like? A string of sandy islands backed by sand; the Ems river at the western end, on the Dutch border, leading to Emden – not much of a place. Otherwise, no coast towns at all. Second piece: a deep sort of bay consisting of the three great estuaries – the Jade, the Weser, and the Elbe – leading to Wilhelmshaven (their North Sea naval base), Bremen, and Hamburg. Total breadth of bay 20-odd miles only; sandbanks littered about all through it. Third piece: the Schleswig coast, hopelessly fenced in behind a 6- to 8-mile fringe of sand. No big towns; one moderate river, the Eider. Let's leave that third piece aside. I may be wrong, but, in thinking this business out, I've pegged away chiefly at the other two, the 70-mile stretch from Borkum to the Elbe – half of it estuaries, and half islands. It was there that I found the *Medusa*, and it's that stretch that, thanks to him, I missed exploring.'

I made an obvious conjecture. 'I suppose there are forts and coast defences? Perhaps he thought you would see too much. By the way, he saw your naval books, of course?'

'Exactly. Of course that was my first idea; but it can't be that. It doesn't explain things in the least. To begin with, there are no forts and can be none in that first division, where the islands are. There might be something on Borkum to defend the Ems; but it's very unlikely, and, anyway, I had passed Borkum and was at Norderney. There's nothing else to defend. Of course it's different in the second division, where the big rivers are. There are probably hosts of forts and mines round Wilhelmshaven and Bremerhaven, and at Cuxhaven just at the mouth of the Elbe. Not that I should ever dream of bothering about them; every steamer that goes in would see as much as me. Personally, I much prefer to stay on board, and don't often go on shore. And, good Heavens!' (Davies leant back and laughed joyously) 'do I look like that kind of spy?'

I figured to myself one of those romantic gentlemen that one reads of in sixpenny magazines, with a Kodak in his tie-pin, a sketch-book in the lining of his coat, and a selection of disguises in his hand luggage. Little disposed for merriment as I was, I could not help smiling.

Extracted from *The Riddle of the Sands: A Record of Secret Service* by Erskine Childers (first published by Smith, Elder & Co. in 1903)

TRACKING GERMAN SPIES IN THE FIRST WORLD WAR

BASIL THOMSON

Basil Thomson was appointed as head of the Criminal Investigation Department of the Metropolitan Police in June 1913 and as such was responsible
for arresting and interrogating any spies tracked down by the intelligence
services. In *Queer People*, his memoirs of this period, he recalled the lunacy
of the spy scares provoked by Edmonds, via Le Queux and the *Daily Mail*.
Lord Roberts, the former armed forces commander-in-chief and popular
hero of both the Indian Rebellion and the Second Anglo-Afghan War, went
so far as to claim in Parliament that there were some 80,000 Germans
working in Britain's railway stations and hotels just waiting to reinforce
the invasion army. The *Daily Mail* instructed its readers that they should
'refuse to be served by a German waiter', adding as an afterthought: 'If
your waiter says he is Swiss, demand to see his passport.'

I BEGAN TO think in those days that war hysteria was a pathological condition to which persons of mature age and generally normal intelligence were peculiarly susceptible. War work was evidently not a predisposing cause, for the readiest victims were those who were doing nothing in particular. In ante-bellum days there were a few mild cases. The sufferers would tell you gravely that at a public dinner they had turned suddenly to their German waiter and asked him what post he had orders to join when the German invaders arrived, and that he, taken off his guard, had clicked his heels and replied, 'Portsmouth'; or they would whisper of secret visits of German aircraft to South Wales by night and mysterious rides undertaken by stiff guttural persons with square heads who would hire horses in the Eastern Counties and display an unhealthy curiosity about the stable accommodation in every farm that they passed. But in August 1914, the malady assumed a virulent epidemic form accompanied by delusions which defied treatment. It attacked all classes indiscriminately, and seemed even to find its most fruitful soil in sober, stolid, and otherwise truthful people. The second phase of the malady attached itself to pigeons. London is full of pigeons – wood pigeons in the parks, blue rocks about the churches and public buildings – and a number of amiable people take pleasure in feeding them. In September 1914, when this phase was at its height, it was positively dangerous to be seen in conversation with a pigeon; it was not always safe to be seen in its vicinity. A foreigner walking in one of the parks was actually arrested and sentenced to imprisonment because a pigeon was seen to fly from the place where he was standing and it was supposed that he had liberated it.

The delusion about illicit wireless ran the pigeons very hard. The pronouncement of a thoughtless expert that an aerial might be hidden in a chimney, and that messages could be received through an open window even on an iron bedstead, gave a great impetus to this form of delusion. The high scientific authority of the popular play, *The Man who Stayed at Home*, where a complete installation was concealed behind a fireplace, spread the delusion far and wide. It was idle to assure the sufferers that a Marconi transmitter needed a four-horse-power engine to generate the wave, that skilled operators were listening day and night for the pulsations of unauthorised messages, that the intermittent tickings they heard from the flat above them were probably the efforts of an amateur typist: the sufferers knew better. At this period the disease attacked even naval and military officers and special constables. If a telegraphist was sent on a motor-cycle to examine and test the telegraph poles, another cyclist was certain to be sent by some authority in pursuit. On one occasion the authorities dispatched to the Eastern Counties a car equipped with a Marconi apparatus and two skilled operators to intercept any illicit messages that might be passing over the North Sea. They left London at noon; at 3 they were under lock and key in Essex. After an exchange of telegrams they were set free, but at 7 p.m. they telegraphed from the police cells in another part of the county, imploring help. When again liberated they refused to move without the escort of a Territorial officer in uniform, but on the following morning the police of another county had got hold of them and telegraphed, 'Three German spies arrested with car and complete wireless installation, one in uniform of British officer.'

Next in order was the German governess, also perhaps the product of *The Man who Stayed at Home*. There were several variants of this story, but a classic version was that the governess was missing from the midday meal, and that when the family came to open her trunks they discovered under a false bottom a store of high explosive bombs. Everyone who told this story knew the woman's employer; some had even seen the governess herself in happier

31

days – 'Such a nice quiet person, so fond of the children; but now one comes to think of it, there was a something in her face, impossible to describe, but a something.'

The next delusion was that of the grateful German and the Tubes. The commonest form of the story was that an English nurse had brought a German officer back from the door of death, and that in a burst of gratitude he said at parting, 'I must not tell you more, but beware of the Tubes in April.' As time wore on the date was shifted forward month by month, to September, when it died of expectation deferred. We took the trouble to trace this story from mouth to mouth until we reached the second mistress in a London Board School. She declared that she had had it from the charwoman who cleaned the school, but that lady stoutly denied that she had ever told so ridiculous a story.

A near kin to this was the tale that a German officer of rank had been seen in the Haymarket by an English friend; that he returned the salute involuntarily but then changed colour and jumped into a passing taxi, leaving his friend gaping on the pavement. A good many notable Prussians, from von Bissing, the Governor of Belgium downwards, figured in this story; a good many places, from Piccadilly to the Army and Navy Stores, have been the scene. The best attested version is that of the English girl who came suddenly upon her fiancé, an officer in the Prussian Guards, who shook hands with her, but as soon as he recovered from his surprise the callous ruffian froze her with a look and jumped into a passing omnibus. Another version was that on recognising her German fiancé the girl looked appealingly into his countenance and said, 'Oh, Fritz!' whereupon he gave one startled look and jumped into the nearest vehicle. This, it may be remarked, might have happened to any Englishman, for who would not, when accosted by a charming stranger under the name of 'Fritz', have jumped into anything that happened to be passing?

A new phase of the malady was provoked by the suggestion that advertisements in the agony columns of newspapers were being used by spies to communicate information to Germany. It is uncertain who first called public attention to this danger, but since refugees did make use of the agony columns for communicating with their friends abroad, there was nothing inherently improbable in the idea. In order to allay public alarm it was necessary to check the insertion of apparently cryptic advertisements. Later in the war a gentleman who had acquired a considerable reputation as a code expert, and was himself the author of commercial codes, began to read into these advertisements messages from German submarines to their base, and vice versa. This he did with the aid of a Dutch-English dictionary on a principle of his own. As we had satisfied ourselves about the authors of the advertisements we treated his communications rather lightly. In most cases the movements he foretold failed to take place, but unfortunately once, by an accident, there did happen to be an air-raid on the night foretold by him. We then inserted an advertisement of our own. It was something like this: 'Will the lady with the fur boa who entered No. 14 bus at Hyde Park Corner yesterday communicate with Box 29.' Upon this down came our expert hot-foot with the information that six submarines were under orders to attack the defences at Dover that very night. When we explained that we were the authors of the advertisement, all he said was that, by some extraordinary coincidence, we had hit upon the German code and that by inserting the advertisement we had betrayed a military secret. It required a committee to dispose of this delusion.

The longest-lived of the delusions was that of the night-signalling, for whenever the scare showed signs of dying down a Zeppelin raid was sure to give it a fresh start. As far as fixed lights were concerned, it was the best-founded of all the delusions, because the Germans might well have inaugurated a system of fixed lights to guide Zeppelins to their objective, but the sufferers went a great deal farther than a belief in fixed lights. Morse-signalling from a window in Bayswater, which could be seen only from a window on the opposite side of the street, was believed in some way to be conveyed to the commanders of German submarines in the North Sea, to whom one had to suppose news from Bayswater was of paramount importance. Sometimes the watcher – generally a lady – would call in a friend, a noted Morse expert, who in one case made out the letters 'P. K.' among a number of others that he could not distinguish. This phase of the malady was the most obstinate of all. It was useless to point out that a more sure and private method of conveying information across a street would be to go personally or send a note.

The self-appointed watcher was very apt to develop the delusion of persecution. She would notice a man in the opposite house whose habits seemed to be secretive, and decide in her own mind that he was an enemy spy. A few days later he would chance to leave his house immediately after she had left hers. Looking round, she would recognise him and jump to the conclusion that he was following her. Then she would come down to New Scotland Yard, generally with some officer friend who would assure me that she was a most unemotional person. One had to listen quite patiently to all she said, and she could only be cured by a promise that the police would follow her themselves and detain any other follower if they encountered one.

On one occasion a very staid couple came down to denounce a waiter in one of the large hotels, and brought documentary evidence with them. It was a menu with a rough sketch plan in pencil made upon the back. They believed it to be a plan of Kensington Gardens with the Palace buildings roughly delineated by an oblong figure. They had seen the waiter in the act of drawing the plan at an unoccupied table. I sent for him and found before me a spruce little Swiss with his hair cut *en brosse*, and a general air of extreme surprise. He gave me a frank account of all his movements, and then I produced the plan. He gazed at it a moment, and then burst out laughing.

'So that is where my plan went! Yes, monsieur, I made it, and then I lost it. You see, I am new to the hotel and, in order to satisfy the head waiter, I made for myself privately a plan of the tables, and marked a cross against those I had to look after.'

⬦⬦

Extracted from *Queer People* by Basil Thomson (first published by Hodder & Stoughton in 1922 and due to be republished by Biteback in 2015 as *Odd People: Hunting Spies in the First World War*)

MY ADVENTURES
AS A SPY

ROBERT BADEN-POWELL

Robert Baden-Powell created the Boy Scouts almost inadvertently as a result of his 1908 book *Scouting for Boys*, which led to the creation of Boy Scout troops across the country. Baden-Powell had served as a military scout during the Fourth Anglo-Ashanti War in what is now Ghana, during the Second Matabele War in South Africa, and as an intelligence officer in the Mediterranean. He also distinguished himself in the Boer War as the garrison commander during the Siege of Mafeking (1899 to 1900), which made him a national hero. There have been suggestions that his service as a spy during the First World War was a myth but here he describes spying on Turkish fortifications ahead of the war in what appears to be an authentic account, although he gives no indication of precisely when the mission took place.

A BIG NEW Turkish fort had been recently built, and my business was to get some idea of its plan and construction. From my inn in the town I sauntered out early one morning before sunrise, hoping to find no sentries awake, so that I could take the necessary angles and pace the desired bases in order to plot in a fairly accurate plan of it.

To some extent I had succeeded when I noticed among the sandhills another fellow looking about, and, it seemed to me, trying to dodge me. This was rather ominous, and I spent some of my time trying to evade this 'dodger', imagining that he was necessarily one of the guard attempting my capture.

In evading him, unfortunately, I exposed myself rather more than usual to view from the fort, and presently was challenged by one of the sentries. I did not understand his language, but I could understand his gesture well enough when he presented his rifle and took deliberate aim at me. This induced me to take cover as quickly as might be behind a sandhill, where I sat down and waited for a considerable time to allow the excitement to cool down.

Presently, who should I see creeping round the corner of a neighbouring sandhill but my friend the 'dodger'! It was too late to avoid him, and the moment he saw me he appeared to wish to go away rather than to arrest me. We then recognised that we were mutually afraid of each other, and therefore came together with a certain amount of diffidence on both sides.

However, we got into conversation, in French, and I very soon found that, although representatives of different nationalities, we were both at the same game of making a plan of the fort. We therefore joined forces, and behind a sandhill we compared notes as to what information we had already gained, and then devised a little plan by which to complete the whole scheme.

My friend took his place in a prominent position with his back to the fort and commenced to smoke, with every appearance of indifference to the defence work behind him. This was meant to catch the sentry's eye and attract his attention while I did some creeping and crawling and got round the other side of the work, where I was able to complete our survey in all its details.

It was late that night when we met in the dodger's bedroom, and we made complete tracings and finished drawings, each of us taking his own copy for his own headquarters. A day or two later we took steamer together for Malta, where we were to part on our respective homeward journeys – he on his way back to Italy.

As we both had a day or two to wait at Malta, I acted as host to him during his stay. As we entered the harbour I pointed out to him the big 110-ton guns which at that time protected the entrance, and were visible to anybody with two eyes in his head. I pointed out various other interesting batteries to him which were equally obvious, but I omitted to mention other parts which would have been of greater interest to him.

He came away from Malta, however, with the idea that, on the whole, he had done a good stroke of business for his government by going there, and convinced of his luck in getting hold of a fairly simple thing in the shape of myself to show him around.

It was my good fortune to meet him a few years later, when perhaps unwittingly he returned the compliment which I had done him in Malta. He was then in charge of a large arsenal in one of the colonies of his country. This was situated in a citadel perched on a high ridge with a rapid river flowing around the base.

My orders at that time were to try and ascertain whether any organisation existed in this colony for mobilising the natives as a reserve, should the regular troops be called away for action elsewhere. Also whether there was any means arranged for arming these natives; if so, in what way and in what numbers.

Knowing that my friend was quartered in the place, I called upon him as the first step, without any definite plan in my mind as to how I was to set about getting the information. He was kind enough to take me for a tour of inspection round the town, down to the river, and up in the citadel.

By a lucky chance I got on to the idea that the citadel ought to be lit with electric light since the water power produced by the torrent below could work a dynamo at very low cost if properly engineered. This was so much in my thoughts that as we went through the barracks and buildings in the fort, I kept pointing out how easily and inexpensively places might be wired and lit. And I gradually persuaded him that it was a matter that he should take up and suggest to his superior.

Finally, when he had seen almost everything, my friend remarked: 'I don't suppose you would care to see inside the arsenal, it is so much like many others you must have seen before.' But I assured him that it would interest me very much; in fact, it was rather essential to forming any approximate estimate for the lighting; and so he took me in.

There was gallery after gallery filled with racks of arms, all beautifully kept, and over the door of each room was the name of the tribe and the number of men who could be mobilised in the event of their being required, and the number of arms and the amount of ammunition that was available for each.

After taking me through two or three rooms, he said: 'There are many more like this, but you have probably seen enough.' But I eagerly exclaimed that I must see the others in order to judge of this electric lighting scheme. If there were many more rooms it might necessitate an extra sized dynamo, therefore a greater expense, but I hoped that by due economy in the number of lamps to be able to keep down to the original estimate which I had thought of.

So we went steadily through all the rooms, looking at the places where lamps might be most economically established, and I made calculations with pencil and paper, which I showed him, while I jotted on my shirt cuff the names of the tribes and the other information required by my superiors at home – which I did not show him.

The armament of native auxiliaries and their organisation and numbers were thus comparatively easily found out – thanks to that little stroke of luck which I repeat so often comes in to give success whether in scouting or spying.

But a more difficult job was to ascertain the practical fighting value of such people.

Reports had got about that some wonderful new guns had been installed in one of the forts on the Bosphorus and that a great deal of secrecy was observed in their being put up. It became my duty to go and find out any particulars about them.

My first day in Constantinople was spent under the guidance of an American lady in seeing the sights of the city, and when we had visited almost all the usual resorts for tourists she asked whether there was anything else that I wanted to see, and to a certain extent I let her into my confidence when I told her that I would give anything to see the inside of one of these forts, if it were possible.

She at once said she would be delighted to take me to see her old friend Hamid Pasha, who was quartered in one of them and was always willing to give her and her friends a cup of tea.

When we arrived at the gate of the fort the sentry and the officer in charge would on no account allow us to pass until the lady said that she was a friend of the Pasha, when we were at once admitted and passed to his quarters.

He was a charming host, and received us with the greatest kindness, and after showing us his own quarters and the many curiosities he had collected he took us all round the fort and pointed out its ancient and modern devices for defence, and finally showed us its guns. Two of these, in a somewhat prominent position where they could easily be seen from outside, were covered with canvas covers.

My excitement naturally grew intense when I saw these, and I secretly begged the lady to persuade him to allow us to look at them, and he at once acquiesced, thinking I was an American, and, grinning all over his face, said, 'These are our very latest development.'

I almost trembled as the covers were drawn off, and then I recognised guns, truly of a modern make but not very new nor powerful, and then he gave away the whole secret by saying: 'Of course, we are trying to impress a certain power with the idea that we are re-arming our forts, and therefore we are letting it be known that we are keeping these guns a dead secret and covered from view of any spies.'

On another occasion it fell to my lot to inspect some of the defences of the Dardanelles, and I found it could best be done from the seaward. This involved my taking passage in an old grain steamer running between Odessa and Liverpool, and my voyage in her was one of the most charming and original that it has been my lot to take.

A tramp steamer loaded down with grain until its cargo is almost running out of the ventilators is – contrary to all expectations – quite a comfortable boat for cruising in. The captain and his wife lived in comfortable cabins amidships under the bridge; the after deck was stocked with pigs and chickens, which fed liberally on the cargo. The captain's good lady was a Scotch woman, and therefore an excellent cook.

Everything was most clean and comfortable, and the captain most thoroughly entered into my various schemes for observing and examining the defences of the coast as we went along.

He allowed me practically to take command of the ship as regards her course and anchoring. From side to side of the Dardanelles we wandered, and when we came abreast of one of the forts that needed study we anchored ship.

Our erratic procedure naturally invited investigation, and when a government pilot boat put off to enquire our reason for anchoring in a certain bay he came to the conclusion that our steering gear was not in very good order and that we had stopped to repair it.

While the ship was at anchor a boat was lowered and I whiled away the time, nominally in fishing, but really in cruising about close to the forts and fishing for information rather than for fish by observing the different types of the guns employed and sketching their position and the radius of fire allowed to take them by the splay of their embrasures; also we took soundings where necessary and made sketch maps of possible landing places for attacking or other purposes.

Extracted from *My Adventures as a Spy* by Lieutenant-General Sir Robert Baden-Powell KCB (first published by C. Arthur Pearson in 1915)

The 1894 arrests by Chief Inspector William Melville of the anarchists Theodule Meunier and John Ricken as depicted in the Illustrated London News. *According to the* Dublin County Telegraph, *as Meunier was arrested, he cried out: 'To fall into your hands Melville! You, the only man I feared, and whose description was engraved on my mind!'*

THE MAN WHO WAS M
WILLIAM MELVILLE

Superintendent William Melville, the head of the Special Branch, retired in 1903 and was immediately recruited by the War Office to take over as its main secret service agent-runner. Melville was an expert on anarchists and Irish terrorists. Born at Sneem in County Kerry, Melville was one of a long line of Irishmen recruited to watch their own. He was very keen on disguises, his favourite being that of a sanitary inspector, but his methods were sometimes dubious. Edward Henry, the Metropolitan Police Commissioner, asked by the War Office to comment on Melville's suitability for the post of 'intermediary for the employment of secret service agents', replied: 'He is shrewd, resourceful and although he has a tendency towards adventuring, he can keep this in check when it suits his interest to do so. For the purpose for which he is needed, to be an intermediary, no better person could be secured – probably no one nearly so good for the money.'

Melville had become a popular hero for the Victorian press, which took delight in chronicling the activities of 'the ever-watching Chief Inspector' in his fight against anarchists and Fenians. The most famous of his exploits, depicted opposite in a print from the *Illustrated London News*, was the April 1894 arrest of the Paris bomber Theodule Meunier and his fellow anarchist John Ricken.

I TOOK UP duty with the War Office on the late December, 1903. I started work in two rooms at Victoria Street, London, SW, with the name of 'W. MORGAN, General Agent' on the door. I chose the offices specially for the reason that while the public entrance in Victoria Street showed almost innumerable offices in the building, immediately round the comer was another entrance. Thus in case of necessity, I used either door – a great asset.

My duties were rather vague, but were generally to enquire into suspicious cases which might be given to me; to report all cases of suspicious Germans which might come to my notice; the same as to Frenchmen and foreigners generally; to obtain suitable men to go abroad to obtain information; to be in touch with competent operators to keep observation on suspected persons when necessary.

Thus there was ample work. I had to travel to all parts of the country to make enquiries re suspected persons. In these duties I found the police, whether in London or the provinces – absolutely useless. Their invariable estimate of a suspect was his apparent respectability and position. Just as though only blackguards would be chosen for espionage. But the fact was the police could not understand such matters. The idea was foreign to them.

I may perhaps give the following as a concrete example: There was at one time a strong suspicion that Germans intended to blow up railway tunnels leading to London in case of war. In this connection, we learned that a German photographer had resided at Merstham, where there is a very long tunnel. I went there, but found the German had already disappeared. It must be remembered that in those days, I was absolutely forbidden to mention the word 'Spy'. All sorts of pretexts had therefore to be resorted to, even with the police, William Le Queux's book *Invasion of London* in 1915 had a good deal to do with waking up the public. In the present case, I found that a constable of the Surrey police was living in the same street as the German suspect, in fact, opposite to him. I called on this officer and told him who I was. He knew of me well and became most willing to assist. In reply to my questions, he said he knew the German well, yes, he was a splendid photographer he did not care for taking photographs of people, he went in for landscapes. He had shown many photos to the constable, and the latter said they were marvellously good. I then spoke to the officer for some time on the fact that the times were strange, and that we all should take stock of those foreigners and have our suspicions of them, etc., etc. 'Yes Sir,' he said, 'I am sure you are right; I believe these fellows are the authors of nearly all the burglaries we have around the country.' Thus my eloquence was absolutely thrown away. As a fact, I learned that this German had made a photographic survey of the whole of the country around Merstham and Surrey generally. Also, I found that the man he lodged with was a general sort of handyman at Merstham railway station. In carrying out his duties, he had to travel through and examine the tunnel twice a week at least. In those walks he was frequently accompanied by his lodger, the German photographer, who, of course, went out of 'mere curiosity', so the handyman thought. It will thus be seen that altogether this German was clever at his work.

The favourite callings of German agents in vogue in those days were:

Poultry farming;

Teaching of foreign languages;

Learning agriculture;

Commercial travellers;

Selling marine lamps in various shipping centres;

Hotel waiters;

and many other callings. Besides, there were the rich, independent Germans who bought land and houses; and the well-to-do

German shopkeeper, all as it were looked up to in their respective localities, and, of course, beyond suspicion.

To get behind these people was a difficult matter, necessitating weary months of enquiry and almost indefinite patience. And this at a time when the Post Office was sealed against us and, as stated already, the police were useless.

As with the latter, so also with the public, not to one in a thousand did the idea occur that Germans might be here on espionage.

Russian spies and police agents also came in for considerable attention.

The notorious German, Gustav Steinhauer, came to this country several times with other police officers, supposedly for the protection of the Kaiser when visiting England. The Kaiser himself asked me one day at Windsor whether I knew Steinhauer, and on my answering in the affirmative, he told me with gusto, and a wealth of detail, how a captain in the German Army had sold secrets to the French and seconded to Brussels. Steinhauer was sent to the latter place, where he remained for six months, succeeded in becoming fast friends with the captain, and finally by a trick succeeded in luring him to Herbestal, the frontier town, where he was arrested and was ultimately sentenced to thirty years' penal servitude. 'Yes,' said the Kaiser, 'Steinhauer is a splendid fellow.' The latter, having been many years in America, spoke English fluently. He was in correspondence with many German spies in this country. He also travelled England as a Commercial man and visited his agents. On one occasion he had an exceedingly narrow escape of arrest in London. He did not venture to come here again.

In the summer of 1907, three Germans were engaged at West Hartlepool for three months in photographing the coast at high and low water; the railway stations along the coast; the railway viaducts – in height and perspective. Also farmhouses within as far as

3 miles of the coast; railway junctions, coal sidings, etc. They got the pictures developed by a chemist named Walburn in business in West Hartlepool.

Walburn did much of this sort of business and took no notice whatever of the pictures or their nature. He informed me that after three months a fourth German arrived. He at once paid £15 to Walburn, being cash owing by the other Germans for developing.

This man was much looked up to by the others, and was evidently their chief. He went over all the pictures taken by the others, in some cases finding fault, in others having them done again. The Germans for an excuse told Mr Walburn that they were on holidays, and were sending to their friends in Germany the pictures, to let them see what a nice country they were staying in.

One day, however, the four Germans had quite a row in the chemist's shop. While it was going on, a stranger came into the shop and taking apparently no notice of the Germans and looking at various articles in the shop. He then left and soon after the Germans leaving, the stranger returned and said to Mr Walburn, 'I am a complete stranger in this town, in fact I am an Irishman, but I have lived for some years in Germany and thoroughly understand the German language. Those four Germans were wrangling in the shop are spies. The row was because they had not photographed a gun which is down by some lighthouse close by. It was one of those disappearing guns. The German newcomer was the aggressor. He called them "lazy dogs" etc. In reply, the other Germans said they had been at all hours on the spot, but the gun was always "down" and it was impossible to photograph it.'

As a fact, the gun was where the stranger described it. I visited the spot, and if the gun was 'up' it could easily be photographed from the steps leading up to the lighthouse, which is only about thirty yards from the gun emplacement. On receiving this information, the chemist informed the local correspondent of the *Standard* and it was through the latter that the matter came to the knowledge of the War Office.

Those Germans had left Hartlepool long previous to this and said they were going along the coast to Bridlington.

Early in 1909 two Germans were at Trearder Bay, just south of Holyhead, taking soundings. They put up at the Roberts Hotel, Trearder Bay, and had a small yacht from there for their excursion to sea, and along by Holyhead mountains. They said they were doing the soundings to take the various temperatures of the sea at different depths. They carried their own paraphernalia with them. But information was given to the Chief Boatman, Holyhead Coastguard Station. He, putting on full uniform, went to Trearder Bay, and arrived there just as the Germans were coming to land. He went on board the yacht and asked them their business. They replied something about scientific soundings as to temperature of various waters and left the yacht at once. They then went direct to their hotel, had their dinner, brought their own luggage down stairs, and took a carriage at once for Holyhead. I saw the boatman afterwards. He informed me that when out in the yacht they were very hesitating as to where they wished to go. They were sounding all the time, but he took no notice of this. They wished to take out the yacht on their own, but the boatman declined this. He said they were much frightened when coming ashore and seeing the naval officer on the jetty, as described above. They wished him not to land there, to turn round and put them ashore anywhere along the coast; or sail to Holyhead. But the boatman replied that this was impossible. They were very angry with him. They went even so far as to say that he (the boatman) was later to go back to the hotel and send their luggage on to Liverpool.

For the few evenings that those Germans were at the Roberts Hotel, their demeanour was typically German. They overshadowed everyone in the dining room. But on arrival there, after seeing the naval officer, there was a marked change in their conduct. The other visitors noticed it. They ate their dinner in silence and sneaked away like mice. Evidently they were in mortal terror of arrest. Their names were never taken at the hotel.

I have given the few foregoing details, thought of haphazard, as furnishing some idea of my general work prior to the establishment of MI5. To go into details on everyday work would be of little interest. It is always a question of using one's wits against someone else's. Infinite patience, of course, is necessary, and always tenacity of purpose. Resource and tact are powerful factors in making enquiries, and above all, the mysterious manner should be avoided. It only engenders distrust. A frank and apparently open style generally gains confidence; at all events, people as a rule, are not averse to seeing you again. One can joke and humbug much in a jovial manner, one can talk a great deal and say nothing. But after all it is impossible to lay down any particular lines to go upon. You must judge your subject and pay attention to his remarks.

On giving up active work in connection with MI5, extending over a period of fourteen years, I must say that notwithstanding 'ups and downs' inseparable from the work, I have had very pleasant times. In Colonel Kell, I had a remarkable chief, who was always enthusiastic for work, and ever encouraging. He quickly saw the necessity of doing things in a logical way. We were frequently at variance as to how certain matters should be dealt with, but after a friendly discussion – to which he was always open and indeed invited, the difficulties invariably melted away and we were of entire accord.

In leaving the Branch now, it is to me a very great personal satisfaction that I cannot remember a single enquiry or mission on which I have been engaged, which was not carried out in a satisfactory manner. Another source of satisfaction is that I have always felt I had the support and confidence of my Chiefs, and never had a wry word with any of them.

I wish the department all 'Good Luck'.

W. Melville
31 December 1917

<hr />

Extracted from the memoir of William Melville MVO MBE, ex-Superintendent of the Metropolitan Police and Kell's First Detective (held at the UK National Archives in file KV 1/8)

Courtesy of the Metropolitan Police Museum

William Melville, the former Special Branch Chief
Inspector who was the main agent-runner for the
War Office Secret Service and then for MI5.

GREENMANTLE

JOHN BUCHAN

John Buchan's *The Thirty-Nine Steps* is always lauded as the classic spy novel of the early twentieth century but if anything, the sequel *Greenmantle* is even better. Whereas in *The Thirty-Nine Steps*, the hero Richard Hannay found himself caught in a web of intrigue that he hadn't sought, in *Greenmantle* he is specifically recruited as a spy. Buchan had some experience as an intelligence officer himself, albeit mainly writing propaganda. He was commissioned into the Intelligence Corps and given access to classified documents to compile a magazine that charted the progress of the war. Both *The Thirty-Nine Steps* and *Greenmantle* demonstrate Buchan's suitability as a propagandist. The language used, with its jingoistic references to 'Brother Bosche' and talk of being 'a good chap' evoke an era when the British secret service recruited the right type of fellow from the upper classes because he could be trusted to do the decent thing by his country. The recruitment of the spy is always a key moment in any espionage novel and here, despite the fact that *Greenmantle* was published in the middle of the First World War, Hannay's mission to Constantinople targets a strikingly familiar threat.

I HAD JUST FINISHED breakfast and was filling my pipe when I got Bullivant's telegram. It was at Furling, the big country house in Hampshire where I had come to convalesce after Loos, and Sandy, who was in the same case, was hunting for the marmalade. I flung him the flimsy with the blue strip pasted down on it, and he whistled.

'Hullo, Dick, you've got the battalion. Or maybe it's a staff billet. You'll be a blighted brass-hat, coming it heavy over the hard-working regimental officer. And to think of the language you've wasted on brass-hats in your time!'

I sat and thought for a bit, for the name 'Bullivant' carried me back eighteen months to the hot summer before the war. I had not seen the man since, though I had read about him in the papers. For more than a year I had been a busy battalion officer, with no other thought than to hammer a lot of raw stuff into good soldiers. I had succeeded pretty well, and there was no prouder man on earth than Richard Hannay when he took his Lennox Highlanders over the parapets on that glorious and bloody twenty-fifth day of September. Loos was no picnic, and we had had some ugly bits of scrapping before that, but the worst bit of the campaign I had seen was a tea-party to the show I had been in with Bullivant before the war started. [Major Hannay's narrative of this affair has been published under the title of *The Thirty-Nine Steps*.]

The sight of his name on a telegram form seemed to change all my outlook on life. I had been hoping for the command of the battalion, and looking forward to being in at the finish with Brother Boche. But this message jerked my thoughts on to a new road. There might be other things in the war than straightforward fighting. Why on earth should the Foreign Office want to see an obscure Major of the New Army, and want to see him in double-quick time?

'I'm going up to town by the ten train,' I announced; 'I'll be back in time for dinner.'

'Try my tailor,' said Sandy. 'He's got a very nice taste in red tabs. You can use my name.'

An idea struck me. 'You're pretty well all right now. If I wire for you, will you pack your own kit and mine and join me?'

'Right-o! I'll accept a job on your staff if they give you a corps. If so be as you come down tonight, be a good chap and bring a barrel of oysters from Sweeting's.'

I travelled up to London in a regular November drizzle, which cleared up about Wimbledon to watery sunshine. I never could stand London during the war. It seemed to have lost its bearings and broken out into all manner of badges and uniforms which did not fit in with my notion of it. One felt the war more in its streets than in the field, or rather one felt the confusion of war without feeling the purpose. I dare say it was all right; but since August 1914 I never spent a day in town without coming home depressed to my boots.

I took a taxi and drove straight to the Foreign Office. Sir Walter did not keep me waiting long. But when his secretary took me to his room I would not have recognised the man I had known eighteen months before. His big frame seemed to have dropped flesh and there was a stoop in the square shoulders. His face had lost its rosiness and was red in patches, like that of a man who gets too little fresh air. His hair was much greyer and very thin about the temples, and there were lines of overwork below the eyes. But the eyes were the same as before, keen and kindly and shrewd, and there was no change in the firm set of the jaw.

'We must on no account be disturbed for the next hour,' he told his secretary. When the young man had gone he went across to both doors and turned the keys in them.

'Well, Major Hannay,' he said, flinging himself into a chair beside the fire. 'How do you like soldiering?'

'Right enough,' I said, 'though this isn't just the kind of war I would have picked myself. It's a comfortless, bloody business. But we've got the measure of the old Boche now, and it's dogged as does it. I count on getting back to the front in a week or two.'

'Will you get the battalion?' he asked. He seemed to have followed my doings pretty closely.

'I believe I've a good chance. I'm not in this show for honour and glory, though. I want to do the best I can, but I wish to heaven it was over. All I think of is coming out of it with a whole skin.'

He laughed. 'You do yourself an injustice. What about the forward observation post at the Lone Tree? You forgot about the whole skin then.'

I felt myself getting red. 'That was all rot,' I said, 'and I can't think who told you about it. I hated the job, but I had to do it to prevent my subalterns going to glory. They were a lot of fire-eating young lunatics. If I had sent one of them he'd have gone on his knees to Providence and asked for trouble.'

Sir Walter was still grinning.

'I'm not questioning your caution. You have the rudiments of it, or our friends of the Black Stone would have gathered you in at our last merry meeting. I would question it as little as your courage. What exercises my mind is whether it is best employed in the trenches.'

'Is the War Office dissatisfied with me?' I asked sharply.

'They are profoundly satisfied. They propose to give you command of your battalion. Presently, if you escape a stray bullet, you will no doubt be a Brigadier. It is a wonderful war for youth and brains. But … I take it you are in this business to serve your country, Hannay?'

'I reckon I am,' I said. 'I am certainly not in it for my health.'

He looked at my leg, where the doctors had dug out the shrapnel fragments, and smiled quizzically.

'Pretty fit again?' he asked.

'Tough as a *sjambok*. I thrive on the racket and eat and sleep like a schoolboy.'

He got up and stood with his back to the fire, his eyes staring abstractedly out of the window at the wintry park.

'It is a great game, and you are the man for it, no doubt. But there are others who can play it, for soldiering today asks for the average rather than the exception in human nature. It is like a big machine where the parts are standardised. You are fighting, not because you are short of a job, but because you want to help England. How if you could help her better than by commanding a battalion – or a brigade – or, if it comes to that, a division? How if there is a thing which you alone can do? Not some *embusqué* business in an office, but a thing compared to which your fight at Loos was a Sunday-school picnic. You are not afraid of danger? Well, in this job you would not be fighting with an army around you, but alone. You are fond of tackling difficulties? Well, I can give you a task which will try all your powers. Have you anything to say?'

My heart was beginning to thump uncomfortably. Sir Walter was not the man to pitch a case too high.

'I am a soldier,' I said, 'and under orders.'

'True; but what I am about to propose does not come by any conceivable stretch within the scope of a soldier's duties. I shall perfectly understand if you decline. You will be acting as I should act myself – as any sane man would. I would not press you for worlds. If you wish it, I will not even make the proposal, but let you go here and now, and wish you good luck with your battalion. I do not wish to perplex a good soldier with impossible decisions.'

This piqued me and put me on my mettle.

'I am not going to run away before the guns fire. Let me hear what you propose.'

Sir Walter crossed to a cabinet, unlocked it with a key from his chain, and took a piece of paper from a drawer. It looked like an ordinary half-sheet of note-paper.

'I take it,' he said, 'that your travels have not extended to the East.'

'No,' I said, 'barring a shooting trip in East Africa.'

'Have you by any chance been following the present campaign there?'

'I've read the newspapers pretty regularly since I went to hospital. I've got some pals in the Mesopotamia show, and of course I'm keen to know what is going to happen at Gallipoli and Salonika. I gather that Egypt is pretty safe.'

'If you will give me your attention for ten minutes I will supplement your newspaper reading.'

Sir Walter lay back in an arm-chair and spoke to the ceiling. It was the best story, the clearest and the fullest, I had ever got of any bit of the war. He told me just how and why and when Turkey had left the rails. I heard about her grievances over our seizure of her ironclads, of the mischief the coming of the Goeben had wrought, of Enver and his precious committee and the way they had got a cinch on the old Turk. When he had spoken for a bit, he began to question me.

'You are an intelligent fellow, and you will ask how a Polish adventurer, meaning Enver, and a collection of Jews and gipsies should have got control of a proud race. The ordinary man will tell you that it was German organisation backed up with German money and German arms. You will inquire again how, since Turkey is primarily a religious power, Islam has played so small a part in it all. The Sheikh-ul-Islam is neglected, and though the Kaiser proclaims a Holy War and calls himself Hadji Mohammed Guilliamo, and says the Hohenzollerns are descended from the Prophet, that seems to have fallen pretty flat. The ordinary man again will answer that Islam in Turkey is becoming a back number, and that Krupp guns are the new gods. Yet, I don't know. I do not quite believe in Islam becoming a back number.'

'Look at it in another way,' he went on. 'If it were Enver and Germany alone dragging Turkey into a European war for purposes that no Turk cared a rush about, we might expect to find the regular army obedient, and Constantinople. But in the provinces, where Islam is strong, there would be trouble. Many of us counted on that. But we have been disappointed. The Syrian army is as fanatical as the hordes of the Mahdi. The Senussi have taken a hand in the game. The Persian Moslems are threatening trouble. There is a dry wind blowing through the East, and the parched grasses wait the spark. And that wind is blowing towards the Indian border. Whence comes that wind, think you?'

Sir Walter had lowered his voice and was speaking very slow and distinct. I could hear the rain dripping from the eaves of the window, and far off the hoot of taxis in Whitehall.

'Have you an explanation, Hannay?' he asked again.

'It looks as if Islam had a bigger hand in the thing than we thought,' I said. 'I fancy religion is the only thing to knit up such a scattered empire.'

'You are right,' he said. 'You must be right. We have laughed at the Holy War, the *Jihad* that old Von der Goltz prophesied. But I believe that stupid old man with the big spectacles was right. There is a *Jihad* preparing. The question is, How?'

'I'm hanged if I know,' I said; 'but I'll bet it won't be done by a pack of stout German officers in *Pickelhaubes*. I fancy you can't manufacture Holy Wars out of Krupp guns alone and a few staff officers and a battle-cruiser with her boilers burst.'

'Agreed. They are not fools, however much we try to persuade ourselves of the contrary. But supposing they had got some tremendous sacred sanction – some holy thing, some book or gospel or some new prophet from the desert, something which would cast over the whole ugly mechanism of German war the glamour of the old torrential raids which crumpled the Byzantine Empire and shook the walls of Vienna? Islam is a fighting creed, and the mullah still stands in the pulpit with the Koran in one hand and a drawn sword in the other. Supposing there is some Ark of the Covenant which will madden the remotest Moslem peasant with dreams of Paradise? What then, my friend?'

'Then there will be hell let loose in those parts pretty soon.'

Extracted from *Greenmantle* by John Buchan (first published by Hodder & Stoughton in 1916)

STRANGE INTELLIGENCE

H. C. BYWATER & H. C. FERRABY

Hector Bywater was one of Mansfield Cumming's best agents operating in Germany before the war. Although British, he was working at the time as a journalist for the *New York Herald*. He later wrote for the *Daily Telegraph*. Cumming gave Bywater the designation H2O, in what was a rather obvious play on his name. He was tasked to collect intelligence on naval installations in northern Germany ahead of the First World War. During the war he operated against German saboteurs on the US East Coast. His experiences were written up originally in a series of articles in the *Daily Telegraph* in 1930 and a year later in a book co-authored with the *Daily Express* journalist H. C. Ferraby. The identities of all of the British spies carrying out the missions in *Strange Intelligence* are disguised but most of them are Bywater himself, including the Mr Brown whose sole foray into purely military intelligence is documented below. Although Brown is supposedly working for the 'naval secret service', Bywater worked throughout for Cumming.

IN THE LATE summer of 1913, an agent of our naval secret service, whom we will call Brown, was in Hanover, where he had several German acquaintances. He had, of course, perfectly good reasons for his visit to that city, since a legitimate occupation which served as a 'cover', not only for his residence in Germany, but also for the almost constant travelling which his real work entailed, was as essential to the Intelligence agent as the pursuit of cricket was to 'Raffles'.

Amongst Brown's friends in Hanover was an Army reserve officer, who was inordinately proud of the privilege of wearing the Kaiser's uniform on certain occasions. That night Brown's friend, Herr Schultz, was attending a reserve officers' reunion dinner, more properly termed a *Bierabend*, and he was kind enough to invite Brown to accompany him as his guest, these occasions being very informal and *gemütlich*. Brown accepted with alacrity, knowing by experience how expansive and communicative the sternest Prussian often became under the mellowing influence of plentiful beer.

Good fellowship and camaraderie were the order of the evening. Among the other guests were eight or nine regular officers of the Hanover garrison who were relatives or close friends of their hosts.

The simple meal over, beer mugs were refilled, cigars were lighted, and the company 'proceeded to harmony.' Old favourites such as the *'Gaudeamus'* were succeeded by the more classical melodies of Schubert and Schumann. After these came tuneful *Volkslieder*, and the stirring patriotic ballads of which German music has so rich a store.

A lull in the conversation, and then the strains of the 'Song of the Sword', with its almost mystical, staccato verses which the Saxon poet Körner penned only a few hours before he fell at the Battle of the Nations at Leipzig in 1812, steal through the room.

A murmur of astonishment runs round the table, for the singer

is the English guest, yet he is singing this essentially German martial song with all the impassioned fervour of one of Körner's own
countrymen.

The song is greeted with rapturous applause, which is, perhaps,
less of a tribute to the quality of the rendering than to the singer
himself for entering so heartily into the spirit of the thing.

After this, the singer was hailed as good comrade and brother.
His health was drunk with acclamation, and he was not sorry when
the enthusiasm died down and he was left in peace to listen to the
general conversation. It had turned, as was but natural, on the pros-
pects of war, for in 1913 thunderclouds were already lowering on the
political horizon of Europe. Ordinarily the presence of a stranger
would have enjoined reticence, but the beer had circulated merrily,
the atmosphere was convivial, and Mr Brown's vocal efforts had
made him free of the fold.

That war was not only inevitable, but near at hand, was the
unanimous opinion, openly expressed. But despite their martial
ardour, one and all were alive to the dangers of a war on two fronts.
Supremely confident of their ability to crush either France or Russia
single-handed, they were less positive as to the issue if both Powers had to be fought simultaneously. They attached little value to
the military co-operation of their Austrian allies, and some of those
present deplored the tendency of the German Foreign Office to
give unquestioning support to the devious policy which Austria-
Hungary was then, as always, pursuing in the Balkans – the European powder magazine that the Fates had timed to explode only
twelve months later.

'Of course we shall have to fight on both fronts,' declared an
Infantry Major. 'The only question is, where shall we mass our
main strength and deal the heaviest blows? My view is that we
ought to keep strictly on the defensive in the East and concentrate

on a tremendous drive into France. We must smash right through them' – emphasising his point with a vigorous sweep of the arm – 'hammering our way to Paris, and beyond if necessary, until all the fight is beaten out of them.'

'All very well,' said another officer; 'but don't forget we cannot burst into France until her frontier forts are in our hands. It is not a question of merely containing them while our main army marches past. They are so placed that we cannot deploy until their guns are silenced.'

The Major stared coolly at his colleague.

'What forts are those? Do you imagine that we are going to break our heads against Belfort, Toul, and Verdun? No, there's a better way than that, and everybody knows we are going to take it. Yes, everybody,' he repeated, banging his fist on the table. 'For what else have we built those colossal railway stations at Eupen and Malmedy? It's an understood thing that we shall be over the Luxemburg and Belgian border almost from the word "go", There's no secret about it at all!'

'But that means a breach of neutrality,' objected one of his hearers. 'And suppose Belgium resisted? Her army may not amount to much, but we couldn't take Liege and Namur in our stride. They are said to be as strong as any of the French forts, and we should have to begin a regular siege, and what about Antwerp, which may prove a still tougher nut? But it would have to be cracked, unless we were content to leave it, with perhaps the whole Belgian army and some French divisions inside, as a perpetual menace to our right flank and line of communications?'

The young engineer officer, hitherto shy and silent in the presence of so many seniors, now joined in.

'Liege is certainly very strong. I spent a month in Belgium last summer, and made as close an inspection as possible of Liege and

Namur. The big-gun cupolas at Liege are said to be armoured with 9-inch plating, and the ferro-concrete shelters are given in our textbooks as 4 feet thick. If that be so, they could probably defy our 12-inch howitzers.'

'Ah,' said the Major; 'we're not relying on those. My brother Ulrich, who's in the War Ministry, told me something the other day that would give our neighbours across the border a pretty shock. We've got something much heavier than the 12-inch, so much heavier as to be almost unbelievable. *Ganz geheim*, of course, but they're all ready at Essen. The shells are colossal; in fact, they weigh about…'

The speaker did not finish his sentence, for the Colonel of artillery, who had been chatting with a friend, and only at that moment appeared to become aware of the conversation further down the table, suddenly rapped with his knuckles on the board and exclaimed: '*Achtung!*'

There was an embarrassed silence, and the garrulous Major slowly reddened beneath his tan. Then the Colonel rose, and beckoned to the Major, who, with a muttered '*Zu Befehl, Herr Oberst*' joined him in a corner of the room. It was very obvious that the gallant Infantryman was receiving a lecture for having talked 'shop' rather too freely.

'*Ach, Quatsch,*' exclaimed another officer in low tones. 'What's the old man fussing about? We're all friends here.'

He shot a glance at Mr Brown, who, apparently unaware of the slightly strained atmosphere, was discussing with his neighbour the respective merits of light and dark beer.

Two days later Mr Brown's business took him to Wiesbaden, or so he told his Hanoverian friends. But apparently he got into the wrong train, for that same evening found him at Düsseldorf, which attractive city lies within easy distance of Essen. It is unnecessary to go into his subsequent activities in any detail. He spent most of the time at Essen, returning to Düsseldorf every night and sending a number of business telegrams to Brussels – whence, strange to say, they were instantly relayed to London.

On the evening of the fifth day Brown was seated in a little *estaminet* at Roermond, a tiny Dutch hamlet within sight of the German frontier. A west-bound train drew up at the station and several passengers descended, among them a man wearing the unmistakable ill-made but respectable Sunday garments of a German artisan. He glanced about him rather furtively, and remained on the platform until the rest of the passengers had dispersed. Then, having made inquiry of a porter, he set off towards the *estaminet* where Brown awaited him.

The two men took not the slightest notice of each other. Brown continued to read his paper and sip his beer, while at another table the German artisan stolidly munched sandwiches between copious draughts from the largest Stein the little inn could boast. Presently, Brown paid his score and left, taking the long straight road that runs parallel with the railway until he reached a side path bordered with stunted poplars. He turned into this and followed it for a few hundred yards, then sat down and lighted his pipe. It was a radiant autumn afternoon. The flat Dutch landscape, over which the eye could range for miles, seemed deserted, but Brown, keeping well under cover of the poplars, waited patiently, his gaze fixed on the dusty highway whence he had come.

In twenty minutes, he saw a figure approaching from the direction of Roermond. It came slowly on until it reached the poplar-bordered lane, halted there for a moment, then plodded down the lane. Brown rose to his feet as the man advanced.

The latter, in spite of his outward stolidity, was somewhat excited.

'I'm sure there was an Essen policeman on the train,' he said nervously. 'But he didn't get out at Roermond, so I suppose it's all right.'

'You certainly haven't been followed from there,' Brown reassured him. 'I've been watching the road for the past half-hour, and no one has passed save yourself. Where are the papers?' he held out his hand.

'Not so fast, *mein Herr*,' said the other. 'How do I know you have got what you promised me?'

Brown took from his wallet a fat roll of German bank-notes and counted them before the man's eyes, which glistened at the sight. He in his turn opened his coat, produced a pocket-knife, and ripped open the stitches in the lining, out of which he took several sheets of paper.

These he proffered to Brown, who took them, while still retaining the wad of bank-notes.

'One moment,' he said, as the German, suspicious and growing angry, demanded the money. 'I must look through these first to make sure that you have delivered the goods. Sit down and smoke this excellent cigar. I shall not keep you many minutes.'

Still grumbling, his companion complied, while Brown, having run swiftly through the papers, settled down to a more careful scrutiny.

'I do not see the blueprint you promised,' he remarked.

The other hastily explained:

'It was impossible to obtain, *mein Herr*. Schmidt got cold feet at the last moment, and said he would have nothing to do with the business. I told him the Ehrhardt people at Düsseldorf only wanted the plans for business purposes, but I think he smelt a rat. He said that the typed descriptive notes didn't matter, because half a dozen of his colleagues might have supplied them; but if a blueprint were missed he would at once come under suspicion. But there is a rough drawing, which he told me gave all the important details.'

Brown did not answer, but continued to study the papers. Finally he appeared to be satisfied, placed them in his pocket, and handed over the money without further parley. He watched amusedly as the German hurriedly sewed the notes into the lining of his coat with a needle and thread which he had produced from a capacious purse.

'Your idea of a hiding-place is rather primitive, my friend,' he said at length. 'If I were searching you I should begin by ripping open your coat.'

The man was obviously taken aback.

'It's the best place I could think of,' he grumbled. 'Anyway, in spite of seeing that policeman, I'm sure nobody suspects anything. Friedrich Müller is known at Essen as a respectable man who has been at the works for twenty years, and never had a black mark against him. Besides, what harm, after all, is there in handing over a few trade secrets to a rival firm at Düsseldorf? The big people might kick up a fuss if they knew, but it's not really a crime, if you look at it reasonably.'

Mr Brown listened to this rather clumsy attempt to allay the prickings of a conscience which even the goodly plaster of bank-notes had not wholly soothed.

'Quite so,' he observed drily. 'I have no doubt that Herr Friedrich Müller is a perfectly respectable member of society, though I have not had the pleasure of meeting him.'

His companion started violently and turned pale.

'But, *mein Herr*, I am Friedrich Müller, as you very well know.'

'Indeed,' said Brown, lighting a cigar; 'I rather fancied you were Otto Behncke, residing at 42, Brückestrasse, third étage. Come, come,' he continued, raising his hand as the other began to bluster a denial, 'I naturally took the trouble to check your identity when our little transaction was first broached. But, believe me, there's no harm done, and you have nothing to fear. You may have opportunities of earning much more money in future, with just as little risk, if you care to do so.'

Three days later, Behncke's typescript and drawings were in the hands of the Intelligence Department in London, by whom, no doubt, they were promptly transmitted to the War Office. They gave a fairly complete description of the German 16.5-inch howitzers, mountings, and ammunition, and of the method of transporting them. There is reason to believe that the authenticity of the documents was doubted at first, though later they were passed as genuine, as indeed they were. But while Mr Brown's divergence from his purely naval Intelligence duties in pursuit of an important but purely military secret had proved entirely successful, the official appreciation of his achievement was not warm enough to encourage him to step outside his own particular field again. Nor did his partiality for German *Volkslieder* produce any other noteworthy results in connection with his work, though it was undoubtedly valuable as a passport into circles where information was to be gleaned.

Extracted from *Strange Intelligence: Memoirs of Naval Secret Service* by H. C. Bywater & H. C. Ferraby (first published by Constable in 1931)

The portrait of Mansfield Cumming,
the original C, which still hangs in
the current C's office.

MATA HARI AND OTHER FEMALE AGENTS

BASIL THOMSON

Thomson's misogynist attitude to the suitability of women as spies, demonstrated here in his dismissal of the effectiveness of Mata Hari, was widely shared at the time, despite the fact that their success in the field is now not only widely accepted but the subject of numerous positive stories both in fiction and reality. Vernon Kell, the first head of MI5, agreed with Thomson. 'The difficulty with the female agent is her lack of technical knowledge of naval and military matters,' he said. 'The beautiful vamp, who removes secret treaties from the pockets of ambassadors after a couple of cocktails, has I fear no counterpart in real life.' In fact it was a woman who was to bring about Thomson's own downfall after he upset one too many people in his post-First World War role as Home Office Director of Intelligence. In what has all the hallmarks of a sting operation, he was forced to resign after being arrested for indecency in Hyde Park with prostitute Thelma de Lava.

I T IS NO disparagement of the sex to say that women do not make good spies. Generally they are lacking in technical knowledge, and therefore are apt to send misleading reports through misunderstanding what they hear. Their apologists have urged that one of their most amiable qualities, compunction, often steps in at the moment when they are in a position to be most useful: just when they have won the intimacy of a man who can really tell them something important they cannot bring themselves to betray his confidence.

Throughout the War, though women spies were convicted, no woman was executed in England. In France, there were one or two executions apart from any that may have taken place near the Front, where espionage was highly dangerous. The case of Margaret Gertrud Zeller, better known as Mata Hari ('Eye of the Morning'), has overshadowed all the other cases. Her father was a Dutchman who, while in the Dutch East Indies, married a Javanese woman. He brought her home to Holland, and there the daughter became known as an exponent of a form of voluptuous oriental dancing that was new to Europe at that time. She was tall and sinuous, with glowing black eyes and a dusky complexion, vivacious in manner, intelligent and quick in repartee. She was, besides, a linguist. When she was about twenty she married a Dutch naval officer of Scottish extraction named Macleod, who divorced her.

She was well known in Paris, and until the outbreak of war she was believed to be earning considerable sums of money by her professional engagements. She had a reputation in Holland, where people were proud of her success and, so cynics said, of her graceful carriage, which was rare in that country.

In July 1915, she was fulfilling a dancing engagement in Madrid, when information reached England that she was consorting with members of the German secret service, and might be expected before long to be on her way back to Germany via Holland. This actually happened early in 1916. The ship put into Falmouth, and she was brought ashore, together with her very large professional wardrobe, and escorted to London. I expected to see a lady who would bring the whole battery of her charms to bear upon the officers who were to question her. There walked into the room a severely practical person who was prepared to answer any question with a kind of reserved courtesy, who felt so sure of herself and of her innocence that all that remained in her was a desire to help her interrogators. The only thing graceful about her was her walk and the carriage of her head. She made no gestures and, to say truth, time had a little dimmed the charms of which we had heard so much, for at this time the lady must have been at least forty.

I have said she was openness itself. She was ready with an answer to every question, and of all the people that I examined during the course of the War she was the 'quickest in the uptake'. If I quoted to her the name of some person in Spain with whom it was compromising to be seen in conversation she was astounded. He a suspect? Surely we must be mistaken.

'I see how it is,' she said at last, 'you suspect me. Can I speak to you alone?' The room was cleared of all but one officer and myself. She looked at him interrogatively.

'I said alone.'

'Yes,' I replied, 'this gentleman and I may be regarded as one person.'

'Very well,' she said, 'then I am going to make a confession to you. I am a spy, but not, as you think, for the Germans, but for one of your allies – the French.'

I do not know to this moment whether she thought we would believe her, but she plunged then into a sea of reminiscence, telling us of the adventures she had undergone in pursuit of the objects of her employers. I wondered how many of them were true.

We had altogether two long interviews with Mata Hari, and I am sure that she thought she had had the best of it. We were convinced now that she was acting for the Germans, and that she was then on her way to Germany with information which she had committed to memory. On the other hand, she had no intention of landing on British soil or of committing any act of espionage in British jurisdiction, and with nothing to support our view we could not very well detain her in England; so at the end of the second interview I said to her, 'Madame, we are going to send you back to Spain, and if you will take the advice of someone nearly twice your age, give up what you have been doing.' She said, 'Sir, I thank you from my heart. I shall not forget your advice. What I have been doing I will do no more. You may trust me implicitly,' and within a month of her return to Spain she was at it again.

This time she was captured on the French side of the frontier and, as I heard at the time, with compromising documents upon her. I should have thought that so astute a lady would have avoided documents at all hazards. They carried her to Paris, put her on her trial, and on 25 July 1916 condemned her to death, but there was, as there is usually in such cases, an interminable delay, and it was not until 15 October that she was taken from Saint Lazare Prison to Vincennes for execution. A French officer who was present described to me what happened. She was awakened at five o'clock in the morning, and she dressed herself in a dark dress trimmed with fur, with a large felt hat and lavender kid gloves. With an escort of two soldiers, her counsel and a padre, she was driven to Vincennes. When she came into sight of the troops she gently put aside the ministrations of the padre and waved a salute to the soldiers. She refused to be blindfolded, and she was in the act of smiling and greeting the firing-party when the volley sent her pagan spirit on its journey.

∞∞

Extracted from *Queer People* by Basil Thomson (first published by Hodder & Stoughton in 1922 and due to be republished by Biteback in 2015 as *Odd People: Hunting Spies in the First World War*)

BOMBING TARGETS
IN BRUGES

PIERRE-MARIE CAVROIS O'CAFFREY

The First World War saw the first major involvement of air power in
war and Cumming, who was himself a trained pilot and one of the pio-
neers of flying, set up a highly successful air section run by a French Jesuit
priest. Pierre-Marie Cavrois O'Caffrey, who was working as a missionary
in Ceylon when war broke out, was one of Cumming's best and most
enthusiastic agent-handlers. His family on his father's side were descend-
ants of an Irishman called O'Caffrey who had settled in France – 'Cavrois'
being the French rendition of the Irish name. Pierre-Marie Cavrois added
the Irish version to his name in order to get into the British armed forces
and arrived, unannounced, at a Royal Naval Air Service airfield in Dunkirk
on the outbreak of war. O'Caffrey, who had been born and brought up in
Dunkirk, immediately volunteered to travel through the German lines to
Lille to gather intelligence. His first major agent network consisted of a
group of young French boys, each given a bicycle and paid a Franc a day
to collect intelligence. O'Caffrey recruited agents with remarkable ease,
not merely because of his fluency in French but as a direct result of a per-
sonable and sympathetic character which persuaded his agents they could

trust him. (Developing a 'relationship of trust' remains the aim of every SIS case officer when dealing with an agent.) O'Caffrey soon moved to London as head of Cumming's air section and was based at Park Mansions, which overlooked Vauxhall Park and was just a stone's throw from the Service's current headquarters at Vauxhall Cross. His reports were models of good intelligence reporting and were usually accompanied by detailed plans of airfields and key locations that would have made a professional draughts-man proud. Sadly the maps sent with this report on bombing targets in Bruges have long since disappeared, but it is notable for the standard O'Caffrey care and attention and for its recognition of the need to avoid civilian casualties, long before the risk of collateral damage became a mat-ter of concern when planning aerial bombardments.

⌇⌇⌇

25.5.15
NASF 110
AIRCRAFT
Bomb Targets
Bruges

A large building in the centre of the town between the *Grand Place* and the *Place du Bourg*, the seat of the provincial government in peace-time and now the Headquarters of Admiral von Schröder, the German Governor of the occupied province. When any high German official passes through Bruges he generally stays at the '*Gouvernment Provincial*'. It must be pointed out that this build-ing is of great architectural value and rather difficult to hit without touching at the same time the adjoining buildings of the Town Hall where about 100 Belgian clerks are employed daily.

Two big motor lorries containing the wireless apparatus. They are stationed on a piece of land between the Nieuwport and the

Torhout roads on the site where a new church was about to be built. [See Belgium 1:40,000, sheet 13, C, between 16c and 22a 8/10]

The old arsenal of Western Flanders where workshops have been installed for the repair of war material and of motor cars especially (*vide* NASF81).

Railway shed now used as a petrol depot.

An important petrol depot, easily recognisable as it is almost surrounded by the hot houses of the Sanders Nursery. Notices with the word *Tankstelle* and an arrow point the direction are seen everywhere in the town directing to the depot the numerous cars which come there daily to renew their supply of petrol.

The depot of the Petroleum Co. in which there were at the beginning of March 100,000 litres of paraffin oil.

Next to the Brauer Printing Works there is a building in bricks with a red roof used as an office by the Krupp employees. It should noticed that in the adjoining building, the Brauer Printing Works, a number of workmen are employed.

A shed about 300 yards long and only 15 feet in height, built of wood with a red tile roof, used as a cavalry depot, in which there is a supply of straw and hay. There are other small sheds and important timber yards close by.

The electric power station of La Brugeoise Iron Works which provides the current for all German installations. It has been reported before (*vide* NASF 98) that a cable was being laid for this section to Zeebrugge in case the power station happened to fail there.

There are five [sic] defensive positions against air raids in Bruges

7. Machine guns near the Brugeoise Works

10. Machine guns on top of the Market Tower (*Tour des Halles*)

11. Guns in the quadrangle of the Pormorel Barracks

13. Machine guns near the wireless installations

25.5.15
NASF110
The Port of Bruges

Several tents represented by red squares. At the end of the Railway Line, just opposite the first red square, the Germans have built an underground cavity in which they store wagons of ammunition and explosives.

Three electric cranes on rails capable of lifting 25 tons. They are used for unloading and lifting heavy pieces of all descriptions.

An electric central station supplying the current for the harbour installations generally; the lighting in the hangers, charging accumulators for submarines etc.

Revolving railway bridge. Under the bridge is the Northern gate of the lock which commands the entrance to the harbour and the passage from the Ghent-Bruges canal into the Zeebrugge canal. Though not so important as the *Port de Damme*, though which all shipping from the Ghent-Bruges canal to either Ostend or Zeebrugge has to pass, this lock has however become more important since the establishment by the Germans of a weir (see N5 on the map) which tends to show that the Zeebrugge route is the one used for their submarines.

Railway bridge over the Bruges-Ostend canal. On the 15 March the Germans commenced to build a weir at the western end of the Outer Post and at the entrance of the Bruges-Ostend canal. To do so they bricked up part of the narrow viaduct which existed a few yards east of the bridge. Sluice gates were let into this weir by means of which the depth of water in the Bruges-Ostend canal could be reduced to about 4 feet. This is possible as the Bruges-Ostend canal is fed by the Ghent-Bruges canal. The construction of the weir has two main objects.

To draw the water from the Nieuwport Plasschendale canal from the Yser and the Moerdyk River into the Ostend canal, thus raising the level of the water in it and drying up the flooded area in the Yser region.

To raise the water level in the Ghent-Bruges Canal where navigation was specially difficult, this water being very shallow in parts of that waterway. This tends to show that submarines got from Bruges to Zeebrugge and not to Ostend.

Hanger No. 2 built in yellow bricks with corrugated iron roof, used as a depot for ammunition and stores and also as a workshop for repairs. A great number of German civilian workmen are employed there.

Two wooden sheds, black with bright red tiles roof, which used to be the coal stores, now used as a depot for various kinds of goods. These sheds were partly destroyed about two months ago by air bombardment.

A shed, brown in colour, with tarpaulin roof, used as a stables.

Guns concealed under pine wood stacks.

House where Krupp's men are quartered.

A large shed where ammunition is packed, dispatched and even, it is said, manufactured.

The *Porte de Damme* lock already mentioned in the report on submarines in Belgium, NASF, April 1915, which commands the only practicable waterway from Bruges to the sea, either towards Ostend or Zeebrugge.

A bridge between the *Bassin de Commerce* and the Outer Port, the fall of which into the canal would temporarily stop all shipping from passing into either the Zeebrugge or Ostend Canals.

Place where five motor boats used to convey the submarines along the canals are usually stationed.

There are three other bomb targets in the neighbourhood of

Bruges which are beyond the area covered by the accompanying plans.

A new house of refuge a block of buildings in yellow bricks with turrets and slate roofs in the middle of gardens right out in the country almost due west of the town. [Belgium 1:40,000, sheet 13 G 15c 2/9] This building has been used as barracks by the Germans and was full of troops at the end of April. The troops have now left, but the place remains ready to receive them at any moment.

A wooden shed, greyish colour, tarpaulin roof, about 50 yards long and 30 feet high, used as a garage and repair workshop for motor cars. [Belgium 1:40,000, sheet 13 G 21 4/2]

A very important underground petrol depot in a wood near the drill ground. [Belgium 1:40,000, sheet 13 M 14 a 5/8]

This information has been compiled from various sources and confirmed by a very reliable informant who lived in Bruges from 12 February to 23 April and maintains that he never saw an airship and twice a German aeroplane. On the contrary the Allied aeroplanes were often seen over the town.

Up to the 23 April not a single civilian living in Bruges had been either killed or wounded by any of the bombs dropped by Allied aeroplanes and no Allied machine had ever up to that date been brought down by the Germans in the neighbourhood of Bruges.

PMC O'C

This and other reports by O'Caffrey are held at the UK National Archives in file AIR 1/562/16/15/64

SPREADING
THE SPY NET

HENRY LANDAU

Henry Landau was a young South African serving with the British Army when he was recruited into what was now known as MIIc by Cumming who was anxious to find someone who spoke Dutch to set up and run train-watching networks in Belgium. Talent-spotted by one of Cumming's secretaries, Landau was ordered to report to Cumming's deputy chief, Colonel Freddie Browning, at the MIIc headquarters in Whitehall Court.

He informed me that I had been transferred to the Intelligence Corps, and that as I had been attached for special duty to the secret service, he would take me up to the chief immediately. Up several flights of stairs I went, until I reached the very top of the building. Here, in a room which resembled the stateroom of a ship, I was confronted with a kindly man who immediately put me at my ease. It was the chief, Captain C. He swung round in a swivel chair to look at me – a grey-haired man of about sixty, in naval uniform, short in stature, with a certain stiffness of movement which I later discovered to be due to an artificial leg. After a few preliminary remarks, he suddenly came to the point: 'You are just the man we want. Our train-watching service has

broken down completely in Belgium and north-eastern France – we are getting absolutely nothing through. It is up to you to reorganise the service. I
can't tell you how it is to be done – that is your job.'

Landau went on to run *La Dame Blanche*, a group of more than a thousand
Belgian and French agents who monitored the movement of German troop
trains to and from the Western Front. Named after a mythical White Lady
whose appearance was supposed to presage the downfall of the Hohenzollerns, it was arguably the most effective intelligence operation of the
First World War and according to Cumming produced seventy per cent
of Allied intelligence on the German forces.

After the war, Landau was sent to Berlin but soon became bored. He
left the Service and during the '30s wrote a series of books about his
time as a spy, all of which were published in the US to avoid prosecution
under the Official Secrets Act. This passage is a deliberately disguised
account of the work of the best MI1c agent inside Germany, Karl Krüger,
not in fact a Dane, but a German naval engineer. Krüger, known variously
as TR16, H16, or as here, R16, was recruited by Landau's boss, the head
of MI1c's Rotterdam bureau, Richard Tinsley, who was a less than scrupulous ex-merchant seaman. One colleague described him as 'a very rough
looking character, rather like the cartoon pictures of convicts.' Tinsley
ran an immensely successful operation with agents across occupied Belgium and France and a number inside Germany itself, of whom Krüger
was only the most important.

I KNEW HIM as the Dane. What his name was, or where he
came from, I do not know, although I met him several times.
Slight of build, fair, with blue eyes, he looked the reserved,
well-bred Scandinavian of cultured and professional interests. He
certainly did not look the arch-spy that he was. When I came to

know him better, however, I realised why he was so successful. He was a marine engineer of exceptional quality; he was a man without nerves, always cool and collected; nothing escaped his austerely competent eye; and he was possessed of an astounding memory for the minutest detail of marine construction.

I read his reports from time to time and marvelled at them. In my opinion, he was undoubtedly by far the most valuable agent the Allies ever had working in Germany. To the chief in England belonged the credit of finding him; at least, I believe so. He became the solitary agent in Germany that our naval section in Holland possessed, but he was all they needed. He covered every ship-building yard and every Zeppelin shed in Germany. I can only give a very general survey of his activities, as his reports dealt chiefly with naval matters which were handled by the naval section. But he rendered such outstanding services to our military section as well as his own, and his reports were so brilliant, that I am sure the reader will be interested in the meagre details I can offer.

The key to his success was that he made the Germans believe that he was working for them against us. As a representative of a Danish shipbuilding yard, which was supplying the Germans from time to time with tug boats and marine equipment, he was allowed to travel freely to Kiel, Wilhelmshaven, Hamburg, Bremen, Emden, Lübeck, Flensburg, and other shipbuilding centres. His capable and affable management of company affairs caused such a sea of orders that they were unable to meet the demands. His popularity with German clients and their trust in his apparently candid nature were unbounded. When in due time he applied for a pass to proceed through Germany to Holland it was readily granted, especially in view of his suggestion to the German authorities that he could buy much needed raw material there, and also tug boats and other small craft, which could be purchased as if by his Danish

company, but in reality for supply to Germany. He was so successful with his purchases in Holland that regularly, once every three
weeks, he was permitted to make the trip.

Little did the Germans know that it was we who were largely
responsible for the Dane's success. Tinsley, because of his shipping connections, was able to give him valuable information as
to where he could purchase material, and secure an odd tug boat
now and then; and since in the natural course of affairs the British authorities would have protested or prevented such purchases
as he made, our lack of action enabled him to return to Germany
and ingratiate himself by boasting how successful he had been in
covering up his purchases from the British. In this way, he became
persona grata with the German authorities, and by bringing back
small presents in the way of clothing, food-stuffs, and luxuries
which were then unobtainable in Germany, he was able to ingratiate himself with the heads of the shipbuilding yards, and with
other German officials.

With his extraordinary memory, he was able to sit down, when
in Holland, and write out page after page of reports, giving an exact
description of the ships which were under construction or repair,
and supplying us with the invaluable naval information on which
the admiralty relied absolutely. Every battleship and cruiser has
a distinctive silhouette which is as individual as that of a human
being. The silhouettes of all the pre-war German warships were
known to us, and in these the Dane was so thoroughly drilled that
at a distance of several miles he rarely made a mistake in identifying the larger of them.

From him we got full engineering details of the submarines which
the Germans were turning out as fast as they could in order to put
over their unrestricted submarine warfare campaign. We learned
of the number under construction, the repairs which were being

made, and, what was very important, the number which were missing. In the Allied defence against submarines, with the use of depth bombs, mines and gunfire, it was often difficult to tell whether these enemy craft had been sunk or had submerged of their own accord.

Long before the *Deutschland*, the German merchant submarine, was ready for its trip to America, we had received a full description of it from the Dane. From him we also knew of the commerce raiders, which were then being fitted out. He reported the successful return of the *Möwe* when we thought it was still at large. Through him the British Admiralty got exact details of the German losses at Jutland, and also a minute account of the damage done to some of the ships which returned. In a battle of this description, fought during periods of fog and darkness, it was impossible to make an accurate estimate of losses from direct observation during the action.

A check was kept on all Zeppelin hangars, and here again an account was given of damage done to the ships during their raids on England.

His most sensational report was a detailed description of the big high angle fire guns, weighing several hundred thousand pounds, which several months later fired their three hundred pound shells at Paris from the forest of St Gobain, a distance of 75 miles. Full particulars of the trials which were carried out with these guns firing out to sea from the coast of Helgoland were given by the Dane. The actual damage done by these guns on Paris was relatively insignificant, considering the expense incurred. I believe the total casualties were only about two hundred. The guns were expected to be chiefly effective as a cause of shock and alarm, the mystery of their position and operation being kept up as long as possible. On the mind of the general public the almost magic quality of the great new guns' power did produce something like panic, but once again the secret service had destroyed for GHQ the element of surprise planned by the Germans. I have often wondered whether the High Command had placed any faith at first in this particular report of the Dane, the facts seemed at the time so incredible.

In addition to these technical details which he brought us, he was able to give us valuable information about political and economic conditions in Germany. Because he was in contact with high officials and officers in Germany, he brought us back the point of view of the men who really knew what was going on, not the opinion of the man in the street, who was told what the German High Command wanted him to believe.

The greatest danger that the Dane ran was in his contact with us, as he never carried any incriminating materials whatever – notes, lists, letters, even special papers or inks – when he was in Germany. With him we employed the same methods that I used in meeting all our agents working in enemy territory. We kept several houses in Rotterdam and in The Hague, which we were continually changing. To reach these places from the office we employed every trick conceivable, such as never going there on foot from the office, never driving up to the door, doubling back on our tracks, and sliding into a doorway to see if we were being followed. As far as possible, we always met these agents at night, not only to avoid recognition, but to prevent the taking of photographs, in which the Germans were expert. A photograph of a man going into a house owned by us was sufficient evidence in the eyes of the Germans for his immediate execution, if they caught him in Germany or the occupied territory.

As soon as the Dane arrived in Holland, he called us by telephone, announcing his arrival under an assumed name known to us. Then we fixed a time of meeting at one of our houses, A, B, C, D, the addresses of which, corresponding to these alphabetical letters, were known to him. In this way all danger arising from a possible overheard telephone message was removed. One of the girls at the telephone exchange might have been in German pay, or the Germans might have tapped our wire, as we once successfully did with theirs until a Dutch telephone linesman discovered it.

On his arrival in the house, the Dane immediately got down to the writing of his report, which he did in German, and this occupied sometimes three or four hours. One by one the German shipbuilding yards, such as Blohm and Voss at Hamburg, the Vulkan Yard at Bredow near Stettin, the Schichau Works at Elbing and Danzig, the Weser Company at Bremen, the *Germania Werft*, and the *Danziger Werft* were gone over, and a description was given of the ships on every single slip in these yards, until every shipbuilding yard in Germany was covered.

When I first saw him write out his reports without any notes, in a calm and matter-of-fact manner, I felt convinced he was faking some of them, but I soon learned to respect his statements, when time after time, later on, we received verification of details which he had reported. As soon as his reports were completed, they were rushed to our office on the Boompje for translating, coding, and cabling to London. The Dane generally remained over in Holland for two or three days, sufficient time for the Admiralty to cable back any questions on his reports which they wished answered, or to acquaint him with details of information which they wanted him to secure on his return to Germany.

The Dane continued his work to the very date of the Armistice. He was paid huge sums, far in excess of any of our other agents; and as he was the father of a family, and apparently of high moral character, I am sure he saved his money, which was amply sufficient for him to retire on. In his villa in Denmark today, none of his neighbours suspect, I am sure, the great role this reserved and observant gentleman played during the war. But it was those very characteristics, with a memory truly phenomenal, that made him undoubtedly the master spy.

Extracted from *Spreading the Spy Net: The Story of a British Spy Director* by Henry Landau (first published by Jarrolds in 1938 and due to be republished by Biteback in 2015)

Whitehall Court, the First World War headquarters of MI6. Cumming's office was in the round tower on the right.

THE GERMAN LOSSES IN THE BATTLE OF JUTLAND

AGENT R16 (KARL KRÜGER)

The Battle of Jutland, which took place from 31 May to 1 June 1916, led to an urgent request to all of MIIc's agents operating in Germany for information on the German losses. The long-awaited clash of the Royal Navy's Grand Fleet with the German High Seas Fleet was initially portrayed by many as a defeat for the British, with the Kaiser claiming that his navy had 'torn down the nimbus of invincibility of British sea power'.

There had been unrealistic expectations in Britain of another Trafalgar, a war-winning blow of the kind that seemed impossible in the stalemate on the Western Front, and there was a palpable shock that the British losses in men and ships were much greater than those of their German opponents – more than 6,000 dead, compared to the 2,500 Germans killed, and fourteen Royal Navy ships sunk, while the Germans claimed initially they had lost only seven, although the real figure was in fact eleven. The heavier British losses were in large part a result of the Admiralty's failure to take note of Cumming's pre-war reports on the superior German naval shells and it badly needed to show that Britannia still ruled the waves.

After three weeks spent touring the northern German ports, Krüger arrived in Rotterdam in late June and, over the next two days, he sat in one of Tinsley's safe houses compiling two reports on the damage to the High Seas Fleet.

What followed was an extraordinarily detailed report obtained, as ever, from his own observations and from conversations with naval officers and dockyard officials who believed Krüger to be a loyal German citizen, one of their own. He occasionally got the precise point where a ship was hit wrong, but he was accurate on the extent of the damage to all the various ships under repair. He also located all of them to the correct shipyards, as well as accurately identifying German problems with torpedo nets, later removed, as being an indirect cause of the loss of the battle cruiser *Lützow*, one of the two largest and most powerful German warships, and of the removal from the battle of the other, the *Derflinger*. The following day, Krüger wrote a shorter, less detailed report, which pointed out that the *Hindenberg*, which the British had claimed to have sunk, had not even been launched at the time but, in much more reassuring news for the Admiralty, he added: 'Having spoken to some naval officers about the action in the North Sea, they said that the German Fleet had only been saved from annihilation by the failing light and the mist. The impression in the Fleet is that this experiment will not be repeated.'

This confirmed the Admiralty view that in relative and perhaps more importantly psychological terms, the German losses had been more damaging. The British Grand Fleet remained much larger than the High Seas Fleet, which would never again attempt to take on its British counterpart.

Krüger's reporting was deemed so accurate by Admiral Reginald 'Blinker' Hall, the Director of Naval Intelligence, that alongside his signature he noted: '100 per cent'.

SECRET
NAVAL INTELLIGENCE
ROTTERDAM, 27.6.16
Recd. 28.6.16
Ref: Your telegram 2.6.16 reading: 'Reliable information urgently required regarding German losses in North Sea action yesterday.'

Following report from 'R.16':

In accordance with instructions received from you on 2 June I went at once to BREMEN, travelling from there to DANZIG, KIEL, ROSTOCK, GEESTEMÜNDE, EMDEN and to SANDE near WILHELMSHAVEN, in order to ascertain the exact German losses in the North Sea action of 31 May.

Following is the result of my investigations:

On 3 June I learned that the 'PILLAU' was coming to BREMEN and the 'MÜNCHEN' was going to VEGESACK.

The 'PILLAU' arrived at the *Weser Werft* at 6 a.m. on 4 June, and I learned from people of this ship, that the 'LÜTZOW', 'ROSTOCK' and 'SEYDLITZ' had also been lost, although this loss was not acknowledged by the German Admiralty. The 'SEYDLITZ' had been in tow of the 'PILLAU' but in the outer Weser, the cables had to be cut as the ship was sinking rapidly. I have learned afterwards from men of the 'SEYDLITZ' that the ship has been salved since with the help of the big floating crane of WILHELMSHAVEN, and is now in dock (floating dock) at this latter port.

When the 'DANZIG', which was still in dock, had come out the 'PILLAU' took her place. She was hit once under the waterline near the stern and her funnels and superstructure were damaged. She left the dock on 13 June, and on 25 June she was still lying near the yard to repair the damage on deck. She has also damage to the furnace of one of her boilers through the feed pumps getting out of order. She will probably be seaworthy again by the end of the month. The 'DANZIG' will not be ready before August.

The 'MÜNCHEN' which is under repairs at the Bremer Vulkan at VEGESACK, has only some damage on deck, except for a shot in the stokehold, which damaged a feed pump, and is probably at the present moment ready again for service.

On 5 June I went to SANDE near WILHELMSHAVEN, as this latter place is closed to all traffic. Here I met men of the 'LÜTZOW' and learned that part of her torpedo nets had got entangled in the propellers, which was the cause of reducing her speed, and eventually of her loss.

On 6 June I proceeded to EMDEN. In both the docks of the *Nordseewerke* were destroyers of the latest type, whilst three more destroyers were lying near the docks. All had been hit under the waterline, but they were still seaworthy.

On 7 June I was in Geestemünde. In the dock of the *Tecklemborg Werft* was a merchant vessel, whilst in both docks of the *Seelbeck Werft* were auxiliary cruisers.

I proceeded the same day to HAMBURG. No ships had arrived here yet, with the exception of the 'STETTIN' lying at the *Reiherstieg Werft* with light damage on deck and in the engine-room. She will be ready end of next month.

On 8 June I arrived in KIEL. Here the 'FRANKFURT' was in dock at the *Kaiserliche Werft (KW)*. She has been hit once under the waterline near the stern, and was ready again for service on 24 June. The 'BAYERN' was also lying at KIEL. This ship did not take part in the action, but was guarding the SUND during this time.

From 9 June till 12 June I was at DANZIG. In the docks of the *Kaiserliche Werft* were one destroyer of the newest type with three funnels, and one small cruiser with two funnels, one of which was partly shot away. Near the *Schichau Werft* were lying seven destroyers, but I was unable to ascertain their damage.

On 13 June I was in ROSTOCK on the *Neptun Werft*, but there were no men-of-war there.

When I arrived in KIEL again on 14 June, following ships were there:

BAYERN (undamaged)

DEUTSCHLAND (undamaged)

BRAUNSCHWEIG (undamaged)

SCHLESIEN (light damage, under repairs in the Outfitting Harbour of the *KW*)

SCHLEBWIG-HOLSTEIN (ditto)

HANNOVER (ditto)

KÖNIG (lying at the *Howaldt Werft* with some severe damage in engine-room and on deck and will have very long repairs)

STRALSUND (light damage)

On 15 June I was again at HAMBURG, where in the meantime following ships had arrived:

At Blohm & Voss:

MOLTKE – was in dock (when I went again to Hamburg on 21 June the damage under the waterline had been repaired and the damaged part had already had a coat of paint).

MARKGRAF – this ship must have been severely damaged and has been hidden between the floating dock and the giant steamer of the HAL.

At the *Vulkan Werft*:

GROSSER KURFÜRST – is in dock and has received very severe damage under the waterline from a torpedo. Engines also damaged.

On 16 June I returned to SANDE near WILHELMSHAVEN

and learned that the following ships are under repairs at WILHELMSHAVEN:

KAISER (in dry dock)

KAISERIN (in dry dock)

NASSAU (in dry dock)

OSTERIESLAND (in dry dock)

THÜRINGEN (in dry dock)

SEYDLITZ (floating dock)

All with damage under the waterline. On 25 June three of them, the KAISERIN, OSTFRIESLAND and SEYDLITZ were still in dock.

Besides the above ships, there were also in WILHELMSHAVEN: the VON DER TANN, DERFLINGER, OLDENBURG, HEL-GOLAND, RHEINLAND, WESTFALEN, REGENSBURG, KÖNIG ALBERT (This latter ship was not in the action). Of those ships the VON DER TANN has all her turrets out of action and some severe damage on deck. The DERFLINGER has also received severe damage (*vide* KIEL later on).

When I arrived back in BREMEN on 16 June, the 'PILLAU' had left the dock, and the 'MÜNCHEN' was still lying at VEGESACK.

On 19 June I was at GEESTEMÜNDE and EINSWARDEN, but did not see any damaged ships.

At HAMBURG, where I was on 20 June, there were still the same ships I saw on my previous visit.

I then proceeded again to KIEL, where had arrived the: HESSEN: light damage being repaired at the *Kaiserliche Werft (KW)*.

DERFLINGER: has been hit once under the waterline, forward, and three times above the waterline. Her forefunnel has also been hit, the guns have been taken out of all her turrets and the latter are covered with tarpaulins.

On account of the damage sustained following ships will not be

ready for service within the next three months:
KAISERIN – SEYDLITZ
MARKGRAF – DERFLINGER
KÖNIG – VON DER TARN
GROSSER KURFÜRST – OSTFRIESLAND
And probably the THÜRINGEN

Copies to:

MI1 (2)
DID (7)
Alexandria (1)
Rome (1)
Whalley (2)
Petrograd (1)
29.6.16

The above report is held at the UK National Archives in file ADM 223/637

Krüger continued to report from Germany after the war, providing detailed information on the build-up of German forces under the Nazis. He fell under suspicion shortly before the Second World War and the Service put one of its Dutch agents on his tail to make sure he wasn't being followed.

Unfortunately, the Dutchman was a double agent who confirmed to the Gestapo that Krüger was a British spy. It is unclear whether the Germans ever discovered the extent of his work for British intelligence but, shortly after the start of the Second World War, they announced that he had been beheaded. There is, however, some evidence that this was propaganda and that he had pre-empted them, avoiding execution by committing suicide.

ASHENDEN

W. SOMERSET MAUGHAM

The author and playwright Somerset Maugham was employed by both MIIc and John Wallinger of Indian political intelligence, who sent him to Geneva in part to monitor the activity of Indian seditionists operating in Switzerland. Maugham subsequently recreated his experiences as a spy in the *Ashenden* short stories, an authentically downbeat depiction of the life of a typical intelligence officer. The stories were presented as fiction – Maugham apparently wanted to publish his memoirs of secret service and consulted Winston Churchill who cautioned against it – but they were anchored heavily in reality. When Ashenden was sent to Moscow to monitor the situation ahead of the Bolshevik Revolution he was merely repeating Maugham's own experience, although Ashenden's reporting was a good deal more prescient than that of his creator, who had given the Bolsheviks no chance of success. In this passage, Maugham immortalises a genuine agent, his courier, 'the old butter woman' who would travel from France to sell her butter, eggs and vegetables, carrying messages from Wallinger, and go home with Maugham's reports hidden between her 'voluminous breasts'. The scene in the hotel, with a collection of different spies, all crowded into the restaurant suspiciously eyeing each other and wondering for which country each of the others is working, is

also genuine and very typical of the major neutral cities of Europe during both world wars.

<hr />

ASHENDEN, LYING COMFORTABLY in his bath, was glad to
think that in all probability he would be able to finish his
play in peace. The police had drawn a blank and though
they might watch him from now on with some care it was unlikely
that they would take a further step until he had at least roughed
out his third act. It behoved him to be prudent (only a fortnight
ago his colleague at Lausanne had been sentenced to a term of
imprisonment), but it would be foolish to be alarmed: his predecessor in Geneva, seeing himself, with an exaggerated sense of his
own importance, shadowed from morning till night, had been so
affected by the nervous strain that it had been found necessary to
withdraw him. Twice a week, Ashenden had to go to the market
to receive instructions that were brought to him by an old peasant
woman from French Savoy who sold butter and eggs. She came
in with the other market-women and the search at the frontier was
perfunctory. It was barely dawn when they crossed and the officials
were only too glad to have done quickly with these chattering noisy
women and get back to their warm fires and their cigars. Indeed this
old lady looked so bland and innocent, with her corpulence, her fat
red face, and her smiling good-natured mouth, it would have been
a very astute detective who could imagine that if he took the trouble to put his hand deep down between those voluminous breasts
of hers, he would find a little piece of paper that would land in the
dock an honest old woman (who kept her son out of the trenches
by taking this risk) and an English writer approaching middle-age.
Ashenden went to the market about nine when the housewives of
Geneva for the most part had done their provisioning, stopped in

front of the basket by the side of which, rain or wind, hot or cold, sat that indomitable creature and bought half a pound of butter. She slipped the note into his hand when he was given change for ten francs and he sauntered away. His only moment of risk was when he walked back to his hotel with the paper in his pocket, and after this scare he made up his mind to shorten as much as possible the period during which it could be found on him.

Ashenden sighed, for the water was no longer quite so hot; he could not reach the tap with his hand nor could he turn it with his toes (as every properly regulated tap should turn) and if he got up enough to add more hot water he might just as well get out altogether. On the other hand he could not pull out the plug with his foot in order to empty the bath and so force himself to get out, nor could he find in himself the will-power to step out of it like a man. He had often heard people tell him that he possessed character and he reflected that people judge hastily in the affairs of life because they judge on insufficient evidence: they had never seen him in a hot, but diminishingly hot, bath. His mind, however, wandered back to his play, and telling himself jokes and repartees that he knew by bitter experience would never look so neat on paper nor sound so well on the stage as they did then, he abstracted his mind from the fact that his bath was growing almost tepid, when he heard a knock at the door. Since he did not want anyone to enter, he had the presence of mind not to say 'come in' but the knocking was repeated.

'Who is it?' he cried irascibly.

'A letter.'

'Come in then. Wait a minute.'

Ashenden heard his bedroom-door open and getting out of the bath flung a towel round him and went in. A page-boy was waiting with a note. It needed only a verbal answer. It was from a lady staying in the hotel asking him to play bridge after dinner and was signed in the continental fashion Baronne de Higgins. Ashenden, longing for a cosy meal in his own room, in slippers and with a book leaned up against a reading-lamp, was about to refuse when it occurred to him that under the circumstances it might be discreet to show himself in the dining-room that night. It was absurd to suppose that in that hotel the news would not have spread that he had been visited by the police and it would be as well to prove to his fellow-guests that he was not disconcerted. It had passed through his mind that it might be someone in the hotel who had denounced him and indeed the name of the sprightly baroness had not failed to suggest itself to him. If it was she who had given him away there would be a certain humour in playing bridge with her. He gave the boy a message that he would be pleased to come and proceeded slowly to don his evening clothes.

The Baroness von Higgins was an Austrian, who on settling in Geneva during the first winter of the war, had found it convenient to make her name look as French as possible. She spoke English and French perfectly. Her surname, so far from Teutonic, she owed to her grandfather, a Yorkshire stable-boy, who had been taken over to Austria by a Prince Blankenstein early in the nineteenth century. He had had a charming and romantic career; a very good-looking young man, he attracted the attention of one of the arch-duchesses and then made such good use of his opportunities that he ended his life as a baron and minister plenipotentiary to an Italian court. The baroness, his only descendant, after an unhappy marriage, the particulars of which she was fond of relating to her acquaintance, had resumed her maiden name. She mentioned not infrequently the fact that her grandfather had been an ambassador, but never that he had been a stable-boy and Ashenden had learned this interesting detail from Vienna; for as he grew friendly with her he had thought it necessary to get a few particulars about her past, and he knew among other things that her private income did not permit her to live on the somewhat lavish scale on which she was living in Geneva. Since she had so many advantages for espionage, it was fairly safe to suppose that an alert secret service had enlisted her services and Ashenden took it for granted that she was engaged somehow on the same kind of work as himself. It increased if anything the cordiality of his relations with her.

When he went into the dining-room it was already full. He sat down at his table and feeling jaunty after his adventure ordered himself (at the expense of the British government) a bottle of champagne. The baroness gave him a flashing, brilliant smile. She was a woman of more than forty, but in a hard and glittering manner extremely beautiful. She was a high-coloured blonde with golden hair of a metallic lustre, lovely no doubt but not attractive, and Ashenden had from the first reflected that it was not the sort of hair you would like to find in your soup. She had fine features, blue eyes, a straight nose, and a pink and white skin, but her skin was stretched over her bones a trifle tightly; she was generously *décolletée* and her white and ample bosom had the quality of marble. There was nothing in her appearance to suggest the yielding tenderness that the susceptible find so alluring. She was magnificently gowned, but scantily bejewelled, so that Ashenden, who knew something of these matters, concluded that the superior authority had given her carte blanche at a dressmaker's but had not thought it prudent or necessary to provide her with rings or pearls. She was notwithstanding so showy that but for R's[1] story of the minister, Ashenden would have thought the sight of her alone must have aroused in anyone on whom she desired to exercise her wiles, the sense of prudence.

---

1   R was the codename of Maugham's immediate boss, Major Rhys Samson, who controlled MI1c operations in the Middle East and Switzerland.

While he waited for his dinner to be served, Ashenden cast his eyes over the company. Most of the persons gathered were old friends by sight. At that time Geneva was a hot-bed of intrigue and its home was the hotel at which Ashenden was staying. There were Frenchmen there, Italians and Russians, Turks, Rumanians, Greeks and Egyptians. Some had fled their country, some doubtless represented it. There was a Bulgarian, an agent of Ashenden's, whom for greater safety he had never even spoken to in Geneva; he was dining that night with two fellow-countrymen and in a day or so, if he was not killed in the interval, might have a very interesting communication to make. Then there was a little German prostitute, with china-blue eyes and a doll-like face, who made frequent journeys along the lake and up to Berne, and in the exercise of her profession got little titbits of information over which doubtless they pondered with deliberation in Berlin. She was of course of a different class from the baroness and hunted much easier game. But Ashenden was surprised to catch sight of Count von Holzminden and wondered what on earth he was doing there. This was the German agent in Vevey and he came over to Geneva only on occasion. Once Ashenden had seen him in the old quarter of the city, with its silent houses and deserted streets, talking at a corner to a man whose appearance very much suggested the spy and he would have given a great deal to hear what they said to one another. It had amused him to come across the Count, for in London before the war he had known him fairly well. He was of great family and indeed related to the Hohenzollerns. He was fond of England; he danced well, rode well and shot well; people said he was more English than the English. He was a tall, thin fellow, in well-cut clothes, with a close-cropped Prussian head, and that peculiar bend of the body as though he were just about to bow to a royalty that you feel, rather than see, in those who have spent their lives about a court.

He had charming manners and was much interested in the Fine Arts. But now Ashenden and he pretended they had never seen one another before. Each of course knew on what work the other was engaged and Ashenden had had a mind to chaff him about it – it seemed absurd when he had dined with a man off and on for years and played cards with him, to act as though he did not know him from Adam – but refrained in case the German looked upon his behaviour as further proof of the British frivolity in face of war. Ashenden was perplexed. Holzminden had never set foot in that hotel before and it was unlikely that he had done so now without good reason.

Extracted from *Ashenden: or the British Agent* by W. Somerset Maugham (first published by Heinemann in 1928 and later by Vintage Classics, with whose permission this has been reproduced)

The in-house MI6 cartoon of Richard Tinsley,
the chief of the MI1c Rotterdam bureau who
recruited Karl Krüger and is believed to have
written the instructions for agents going into
Germany during the First World War.

INSTRUCTIONS
FOR AGENTS GOING
TO GERMANY

MIIc ran a considerable number of operations inside Germany during the First World War, including a sabotage ring known as 'Nemesis'. The agents were sent in from Holland, Denmark and Switzerland. These instructions, used by MIIc officer Redmond Cafferata when he was running agents into Germany from Switzerland, are believed to have been written by Richard Tinsley, who trained Cafferata in the art of agent-running. Cafferata was commissioned as a lieutenant in the Royal Naval Volunteer Reserve (RNVR) and sent to set up a new base at Pontarlier, in the French Alps, the closest French town to Lausanne. His headquarters was known as 'the Nunnery', although whether it was based in the town's real convent is not clear. Cafferata not only looked for potential spies to go into Germany from among the refugees crossing the border, but also liaised with the French *Commissariat Special de Police* to prevent German spies getting through the net into Allied-occupied France.

E VERY AGENT PROCEEDING to Germany should be made to realise the importance of the mission he sets out to accomplish. It is absolutely vital to have, behind the enemy's lines, agents who are willing and capable of furnishing particulars of the movements of troops, concentrations, defences, new measures of offense and the hundred and one details, which are impossible to obtain by 'contact' information at the Front.

By means of listening posts, examination of prisoners, patrols, aerial observation etc. at the Front, our headquarters is fully acquainted with the actual enemy forces opposing it, on each sector. But it is impossible by these methods to establish what troops are being transported behind the lines and what direction and therefore without the aid of reliable information received through our agents in the enemy country, it is impossible for our headquarters to determine with any degree of accuracy and in sufficient time where a concentration of enemy troops is taking place, where the enemy is weakening his line by the withdrawal of effective etc. etc. The value of such information is very great for it is only when in possession of all particulars regarding the disposition of enemy troops both at the Front and in reserve that our headquarters can decide on the possibilities of future operations.

At times when the enemy is carrying out some exceptionally large concentration at a certain part of our Front information received from our agents on such a subject is of incalculable importance and has often been a means of carrying out a successful operation or saving a serious defeat and the lives of many of our soldiers.

The chief qualifications necessary to make a successful agent – intelligence of a high order, absolute discretion, patience, perseverance and constant attention to duty – are too well known to need our passing mention. Stress should be laid however on care in the receiving and expenditure of money.

More agents come under the suspicion of the authorities through reckless expenditure of money (especially where no real source of income is apparent) than by any other means.

The work of our agents can be divided broadly into two classes, the first of which is by far the more important:

1. Movement of troops and their identification
2. Information dealing with:
   a) Aviation
   b) Depots and new formations
   c) Munitions and factories
   d) New inventions
   e) Economic, industrial and political information

Special stress should be laid on the fact that an agent in his report should only give us the details of his observations – what he has actually seen himself – we do not want him to draw his own conclusions from what he sees for the obvious reason that it is only possible to draw accurate conclusions from certain facts by having a full knowledge of all other information from every source on that particular subject.

It is impossible to be correctly informed of the changes in the disposition of the enemy forces without having an organised system of train watchers who are installed *á post fixe* at regular intervals along all the principal railway lines.

In addition to receiving reports on the movements of large masses of troops on the railways it is also necessary wherever possible to obtain particulars of the identity of the troops moving.

Such information will give us value to the information on the movements of the troops.

The following example will explain the importance of identifying the troop movements. As already pointed out, our headquarters by means of contact information keeps itself acquainted with the various regiments and divisions which form the German front lines. We will assume that one of our agents is able to identify a certain regiment believed by our GHQ to be at the Front, en route at say 60 or 70 kilometres from the Front. As will be shewn later it is seldom that an isolated regiment is removed so far from the Front, without the entire division, of which it forms a part, leaving the line.

Our agent's information in this case would therefore be of the utmost value to our headquarters advising them as it does that the enemy has withdrawn probably an entire division from the front or reserve lines. Our headquarters will then ascertain by means of raiding parties, if the gap caused by the withdrawal of the notified regiment has been filled by extending the remaining units or if a new formation has been introduced. In the former case an attack on the weakened line might bear excellent results. If our agent has been unable to identify the regiment the value of his information would have been largely discounted, as the sector of the Front which had thereby been weakened would have been unknown.

It is often extremely difficult or impossible for train watchers to obtain identification of the troops being moved. It then becomes necessary to appoint a mobile agent, who has the entry to the nearest stopping station or refreshment halt. There he is able to mix with the troops or at any rate to get sufficiently near to identify one or two of the units. This agent may or may not act in conjunction with the train watcher, on that sector of the line, but in any case the reports from these two agents will be confirmatory one of the other.

The question of agents' cover should be carefully discussed and the utmost care should be given to make this as sound as possible. Especially at the beginning of an agent's visit to G he should devote a considerable amount of time every day to the building up of his business connections. Especially in the case of a neutral, certain suspicion is attached to every arrival in a German town, and it is essential that for some time at least an agent should occupy himself entirely with his cover business, by calls, correspondence, note books etc.

This would apply to a man who is going to G under the cover as representative or traveller of a neutral House. The agents who takes up a fixed post in a German firm which will tie him to definite office hours, can obviously be of little or no use to us, whilst so employed, but this may be a means for him to get into G and after some time he could find an excuse to leave his employment and launch out for himself.

Students in art, music, medicine etc. find good cover for train watching, as also do professionals such as doctors, dentists, architects, and those whose profession or business enable them to dispose of their time as they will and to establish themselves as they wish in localities of their own choice.

Bear in mind:

The trains crossing or passing the train in which one is sitting. Only give your attention to movements involving a series of trains. Note exactly the date and itinerary followed, even if nothing is encountered, this precise information has its value.

The series of trains passing through the locality in which the agent is, or stopping for entrainments (only trains with constituted units).

Interruptions of traffic remarked or announced.

The addresses of the soldier relatives of the families that are visited. Repeat carefully all conversations on this subject.

The dates and where soldier relatives of the families visited have been killed, etc.

Places not far removed from the Front where there are factories engaged on war materials.

The numbers above 381[2] – try and ascertain if these formations are in the place where you are.

New formations – ascertain whether any are in cantonments in the surroundings. They are recognised by their unusual numbers. Do not confuse them with *Landsturm* formations, which wear their number in the form of a fraction, the numerator being that of the region.

The classes – try and ascertain from proclamations, conversations etc. whether the 1918 class has been called-up.

The Depots – try and find out in what manner they are filled. Each regiment forms an *ersatz* battalion (or division)

Notice whether the standard is as important as formerly whether the units are composed of young men.

The numbers of Zeppelins observed.

DESTRUCTIONS

It is well for agents who show themselves to be resolute, to be instructed in the use of explosives on railways (choice of point, installation of charge). They should be advised to use these only during large movements executed by the enemy by rail, at a time when an important engagement is certain to take place.

GENERAL ADVICE

The greatest possible prudence is required from agents in the service.

---

2   German units were numbered in sequence so the use of 381 indicates that the identities of all units up to that figure were known.

Never confide in women. Before being sure of anyone act as if he were a German agent.

Never give your photo to anyone, especially a female.

Never write to anyone in your own handwriting.

When you telegraph, disguise your hand; better still print the letters. Remember that the originals of all telegrams are kept. Always employ public telephones when you telephone.

Do not keep letters in your room, even inoffensive ones, it is better to destroy them, for in the case of your arrest the people who have written to you will be molested.

Never give or accept papers or letters from your agents in cafés or public places.

When you have to receive an agent in a public place never whisper in his ear, etc., this only arouses suspicion. Change your rendezvous often.

Counter-espionage agents should know everybody possible, it may help one day. Do not telephone important things; your conversation is always intercepted.

Try to know the greatest possible number of suspects personally.

Cultivate the impression that you are an ass, and have no brains; it is the greatest possible compliment to hear that you have the reputation of being an imbecile.

Never get drunk; when you drink you do not know what you say. If you are obliged to drink heavily on occasions, take two large spoonfuls of olive oil beforehand; you will not get drunk but can pretend to be so. If dealing with a suspect, make him drink as much as possible; he will probably tell you something interesting.

When drinking in a café always pay at once for your drinks; you can thus clear out, if necessary.

Never recognise your chiefs in a café or public place, unless they approach you first.

HOW TO DEFEND YOURSELF IF ARRESTED

Confess nothing. Never write in your own hand. Never have anything on your person, or at home, which could give you away. Have good cover. Give a certain amount of time to your supposed occupation. Never leave incriminating documents in the hands of anybody. Never denounce anybody; you will only aggravate your own case. Never admit having received money; this would tell heavily against you.

NEVER ADMIT ANYTHING.
NEVER MAKE A CONFESSION.

Extracted from *Six: The Real James Bonds 1909–1939* by Michael Smith (published by Biteback in 2011)

MY FIRST
MEETING WITH C

COMPTON MACKENZIE

The original version of Compton Mackenzie's memoir *Greek Memories*, which dealt with his work for Cumming in Greece during 1916, was published in 1932 and immediately banned. The publishers Cassell were advised politely that they should withdraw it. It was an offer they could not refuse and, while a few review copies had been issued, from one of which this passage derives, contemporaneous court reports state that it was withdrawn on the morning of publication and not a single copy went on sale.

Greek Memories named Cumming as 'C', the wartime chief of the British secret service. He had been dead for nine years by the time the book was published but revealing his name was still regarded as a heinous crime. Mackenzie reproduced parts of various secret documents in the text, named a number of other MI6 officers who were still serving, some of them in this particular passage, and described the cover they used in foreign capitals. This was a red line for the authorities who declared: 'There is scarcely a page of *Greek Memories* which does not damage the foundation of secrecy upon which the secret service is built.'

They hauled Mackenzie up before the courts where he was in fact dealt with quite lightly. He was fined £100 with a further £100 costs. He took his revenge with the satirical novel *Water on the Brain*, ridiculing the secret service MQ9(e) and its mysterious 'Chief', Colonel Nutting, known only as 'N', whose offices at Pomona Lodge were not yet 'officially' a lunatic asylum, but would eventually become one, full of typists 'feverishly' typing out reports 'that will never be read even in eternity'.

A re-written version of *Greek Memories* with all the offending passages removed was published in 1939. Biteback has now republished the original unexpurgated version, but officially it remains banned. You should not be reading this!

<hr />

AS SOON AS I reached London I left my bag at the Foreign Office, and then drove straight to a hatter's to buy myself a cap.

'It's just a leetle bit tight, the one you're wearing, sir,' observed the assistant. 'It's left a regular mark on your forehead.'

'I wonder it hasn't cracked my skull,' I said.

I gave the assistant the address of the kind Captain of Marines who had lent me his cap, and told him to have it sent back by post to Taranto at once. Then I drove to Bury Street, where my wife had taken a service flat. My light khaki uniform was cold in the autumnal weather of London, and I lost no time in getting equipped at my tailor's with one of those enviable blue uniforms of the Royal Marines. Braced by the prospect of new clothes, I felt better able to face the ordeal of my first meeting with C.

In those days taxis were hard to find. So when I reached 2 Whitehall Court I told the driver to wait, for I fancied that ten minutes would probably be the extreme limit of the interview, judging by the tone of the voice at the other end of the telephone which had

informed me that the Chief would see me at half past five that afternoon. I inquired for the whereabouts of Captain Spencer's flat[3] and
was directed up the familiar staircase which led to the Authors'
Club. I debated for a moment when I reached the first floor whether
I would turn aside into the Club and have a strong brandy before
climbing to the top of the building where C's headquarters were;
but, on reflecting that I might need one even more acutely ten minutes later, I resisted the temptation.

It is always possible to tell by the attitude of subordinates what
is likely to be the attitude of the head man in any show, and my
reception upstairs by various young lieutenants of the RNVR was
ambiguous. There was that air of nervous anticipation with which
schoolboys watch the attitude of a victim who has been sent for
by the Head. Even pink-faced lady secretaries came fluttering one
after another on some excuse into the room where I was waiting,
presumably to take a quick glance at the man who had ventured
to defy C for nine months. After about ten minutes of this embarrassed waiting a young man came in and announced that the Chief
wished to see Captain Mackenzie immediately. I followed him into
C's private room, tucked away under the roof, crowded with fil-
ing cupboards and shelves, and with the rest of the space almost
entirely filled by C's big table. The dormer windows looked out
across the plane-trees of the Embankment Gardens to the Thames,
over which twilight was creeping. I saw on the other side of the
table a pale clean-shaven man, the most striking features of whose
face was a Punch-like chin, a small and beautifully fine bow of a
mouth, and a pair of very bright eyes. He was dressed in the uniform of a naval captain.

---

3   Right up to the Second World War, the name Captain Spencer was used as a covername for the Chief of MI1c, the Secret Intelligence Service.

C paid no attention when I came in, but remained bent over the table, perusing through a pair of dark horn-rimmed spectacles some document. I stood watching the blue dusk and the tarnished silver of the Thames until presently C took off the glasses, leant back in his chair, and stared hard at me for a long minute without speaking.

'Well?' he said finally.

'Mackenzie, sir,' I replied. 'Reporting to you from Athens.'

'And what have you to say for yourself?' he asked, putting in an eyeglass and staring at me harder than ever.

Somehow I suppose I must have embarked on my tale in such a way as to win his attention, for after a few minutes he murmured in those faintly-slurred, immensely attractive accents of his:

'There's no need to tell me all this standing up. There's a chair beside you.'

So I sat down and went on talking until about a quarter to seven, when a pink-faced secretary with a bundle of papers put her head round the door. She conveyed an impression that she had been deputed as the least likely person to have her head bitten off if she was interrupting a conversation. C held out his hand for the papers and signed his name on them one after another in the bright green ink he always used. Presently we were left alone again.

At half past seven he said:

'Well, you'd better stop and have some dinner with us.'

'Thank you very much, sir,' I said. 'Would you mind if I went downstairs and sent away my taxi?'

'Have you been keeping a taxi waiting two hours?'

'Yes, sir, I thought you would probably be finished with me in a few minutes.'

'My God,' C exclaimed. 'No wonder you're always asking for another thousand pounds every month!'

I went down to pay off the taxi, and when I came back the offices were empty. C took me into the dining-room where I was introduced to Mrs Cumming as the man who had given him more trouble than anybody else in his service.

After dinner, C showed me various books he had been buying. They were mostly sets in bright leather bindings.

'These ought to be in your line,' he said. 'You're a writing fellow, aren't you?'

Those books and the large oil-painting of a young officer in the uniform of the Seaforth Highlanders were the chief features of the room. I remembered the tale of how C had cut off his leg with a penknife in order to reach his dying son and put an overcoat over him, and the little room filled with that large portrait expressed how large a place the original must have held in his heart.

It must have been after eleven o'clock when I got up to leave. C came along with me to the door of the flat.

'Well, you'd better look in every day while you're in London,' he told me. 'I thought this would happen.'

'You thought what would happen, sir?'

'Why, I intended to make myself extremely unpleasant to you; but I said that when I saw you I should probably find you a man after my own heart and fall on your neck. We'll have dinner at the Savoy one night soon.'

I felt, as I walked down the marble stairs of Whitehall Court, that we should get a real move on in Athens presently.

In the middle of October a telegram came from Athens to say that the French Admiral had demanded the surrender of the whole of the Greek Fleet; the disarmament of the forts dominating the Piræus and Salamis; French control of the Piræus and Larissa railway; French control of the Police; and French control of the port of Piræus. The Greek government had accepted all demands, and the crews had evacuated the warships immediately. I advised C that the only counter-offensive which could be taken was immediately to institute port control of the Peloponnese.

Remembering, too, de Roquefeuil's objection to our having a representative at Chalcis, I was anxious to test the cordiality of the Entente by demanding a representative there.

On 18 October I drafted a telegram for C which he sent to Plunkett in Athens:

Suggest sending immediately Kenneth Whittall[4] to Patras and Arthur Whittall to Kalamata as port officers. Ask Minister to endorse former's position with Consul. There must be no interference at present with Italian ships, but tell the Minister in confidence that we expect to control them shortly. Proposed agents for the Peloponnese and Missolonghi can now be got going gradually. Hugh Whittall must insist on maintaining a representative at Chalcis whatever the French say.

Following for Naval Attaché:

Please work hard to persuade de Roquefeuil to co-operate cordially in Patras with our new port officer there in preventing anybody's leaving Greece without Anglo-French control visa.

I had outlined to him my scheme for a check on contraband going northward from Greece to the enemy by establishing posts between Janina and Volo, and I had explained the importance of these outposts as a check to Royalist intrigue. This proposal of mine was to be brought up at an intelligence conference to be held shortly.

On the morning of the conference, a drenching October day, C said to me:

'Look here, Mackenzie, if you want the money for those places of yours with unpronounceable names, you'd better go out and buy

---

4   The Whittalls were British traders based in southern Turkey. Members of the family served in MI6 in both world wars and throughout the Cold War.

a half-crown map of Greece from Bartholomew's and mark each place with a cross before you start arguing what you want.'

So out I went out to secure my map, which I marked with crosses in red pencil. I had taken care not to buy too big a map, for I wanted the crosses to look as much like the Great Wall of China as possible.

The conference began, various generals and colonels being seated round a table in the War Office as I remember. Presently one of my sponsors said:

'Captain Mackenzie has a proposal to make, General, and he has brought a map to show exactly what he requires.'

There was a murmur of satisfaction when the generals and colonels heard that a map was available, and there was almost a buzz of excitement when they leant over and saw my red crosses presenting an apparently impenetrable barrier from sea to sea against the most intrepid and resourceful contrabandist.

'I see he's got it right across Greece,' said one general. 'That should be very effective. And how much do you think this scheme of yours will cost, Captain Mackenzie?'

My original request had been for something under six hundred pounds, but seeing the enthusiasm these crosses had aroused, like Harry Tate selling a car to what he fancies is a promising purchaser, I replied at once:

'I think I ought to be able to do it for twelve hundred pounds a month, sir.'

'That sounds very moderate,' said another general. 'Don't you think you'd want rather more than that?'

'Well,' I replied judiciously, 'no doubt with the gradual extension of our control it would be as well if I knew I could call on two thousand a month, though of course I do not anticipate that we should spend all that on this northern chain. I am hoping to make the Peloponnese completely secure also.'

In order to make the Peloponnese secure on paper I had drawn a red line right round it, and not even during the most favourable moments of the Lacedæmonian War can Sparta ever have looked so secure as it looked on that map of mine guarded by a pencilled ring.

C had promised me all the new officers he could get hold of in order to extend our scheme of port control wherever an opportunity of development occurred, and after meeting Edward Knoblock[5] at some party I suggested that he should come out to Athens. Knoblock at that time was working in a private capacity with the Indian Secret Intelligence, which was mysteriously housed somewhere near Sloane Street. I have an idea that W. S. Maugham was also engaged in that branch of secret activity.

Knoblock wanted a commission, and I thought I could promise him a lieutenancy in the RNVR. C agreed, but no sooner had Knoblock hurriedly set about procuring a naval uniform than it was discovered that he could not be a Lieutenant in the RNVR because he was an American subject.

'However,' said C, 'I believe we can get him a commission in the RNAS [Royal Naval Air Service].'

So Knoblock dashed out and bought a woollen bird to sew on his naval uniform. No sooner had he equipped himself as a naval airman than he was told he might have to be a Second-Lieutenant in General Service.

So Knoblock rushed out again from those wonderful Regency rooms of his in Albany and equipped himself with a khaki uniform and the green tabs of an intelligence officer.

As we were due to leave England on 3 November and as Knoblock's commission could not possibly be gazetted until long after that, we decided it would be safest to take all three uniforms

---

5   American-born playwright and novelist.

out to Greece, and possibly dispose out there of the superfluous equipment when it was settled which service he was to join. In his enthusiasm he even bought two swords, a naval and a military one.

The day before we left C presented me with the sword-stick he himself had always carried on spying expeditions in time of peace.

'That's when this business was really amusing,' he said. 'After the War is over we'll do some amusing secret service work together. It's capital sport.'

∞

Extracted from *Greek Memories* by Compton Mackenzie (first published by Cassell in 1932, but immediately banned, and republished by Biteback in 2011, although technically it remains banned)

THE SECRET AGENT'S
INSTRUCTIONS

Although Mackenzie's memoirs of his secret service work tended to over-play his own role, he was to be the architect of a system that was used by Cumming and his successors for the next three decades, both as a cover for their work abroad and a unique source of information. The Passport Control system involved checking passports and issuing visas to anyone wishing to travel to British-controlled territory, a useful cover for gathering intelligence and tracking enemy spies. The basis for this system was drawn up by Mackenzie in the early summer of 1916, purely to deal with the flow of refugees through Greece, and involved stationing a number of men, mainly operating under what had become the standard secret service cover of a junior RNVR officer, at various points around mainland Greece and the Greek islands to check the passports of anyone entering or leaving the country. These instructions are for an agent working for Arthur Whittall at Kalamata in southern mainland Greece, but were probably drawn up centrally by Mackenzie himself.

Patras, 18 March 1918

Sir,

Confirming our several interviews, I am now authorised to inform you that the offer of your services is accepted and you will act for us as a confidential agent in Kalamata. You must clearly understand however, that your duties must be kept extremely secret and that you must use the greatest discretion in obtaining information. Your value to us as an agent can only hold good so long as you are not suspected of being in our service, and it is only fair to warn you that should we hear from other sources that you are in our employ, your payment and employment will cease without notice.

Your salary will commence from the day you leave Patras and will be at the rate of five hundred francs per month.

Your duties will consist of keeping this office informed of everything concerning the following points:

All local suspects, enemy agents and their movements.

Information concerning submarines, signalling from the coast, possible landing of enemy agents, and communications with them. You will be careful in each case to give the approximate if not the exact time, the direction and all other details concerning same.

You will take note of all news and rumours which may be circulated by enemy propagandists with a view to creating dissension in the country and hamper the interests of both the Hellenic government and the Allies. You should endeavour to ascertain the source of creation of these rumours and keep an active, but unostentatious, surveillance over local suspects.

You will endeavour to obtain all information regarding the sentiments of the inhabitants, and at the same time obtain a correct

impression of what is likely to take place in the event of mobilisa-
tion taking place in your district. You should gather all information
concerning anti-Venizelists,[6] army officers and non-commissioned
officers, unfriendly to the present regime, who may be sowing
sedition amongst the soldiers.

All information concerning local politics and the situation from
a political point of view in your district is also of interest.

All coast information from Messina should be regularly
reported.

After studying local conditions for about a fortnight, you should
return to Patras and confer with me with a view to improving upon
the conditions of your work already lengthily discussed by us.

You should pay careful attention to all matters concerning
the emigration of men of military age, the sea passenger service
by steamers or *caiques*, whether the police enforce the passport
regulations conscientiously, centres of smuggling and anything
suspicious which you might hear of from the hinterland.

As soon as you have settled down in Kalamata you let me have
your correct address.

You will communicate with me in the manner already discussed
between us.

You should let me have a weekly report of your district. In
case of anything urgent and of importance you should not hesitate to let me know by confidential messenger or by coming to
Patras yourself.

You will bear in mind that your duties are essentially of such
a nature as to keep me correctly informed of all matters which
concern the interests of both the Hellenic government and of its

---

6   Opponents of the Greek Prime Minister Elefthérios Venizélos, who supported Britain
     and its Allies.

allies and you should not hesitate to report anything suspicious concerning the conduct of any government officials who do not appear to be acting correctly or loyally to the government.

Yours truly,

A. Whittall
Lieutenant, RNVR

P.S. You should in case of emergency immediately burn this letter and all documents in your possession.

You will endeavour to give every impression that your commercial vocation and occupations are entirely bona-fide.

∞∞

The above document is held in the Cafferata family archive

TALES OF
AEGEAN INTRIGUE

J. C. LAWSON

During the First World War, John Cuthbert 'Jack' Lawson, a Cambridge don whose knowledge of Greek and the Aegean owed more to his studies of Homer than any specialist training, was sent to Crete, from where he carried out a number of intelligence-gathering operations. He and Compton Mackenzie had little regard for each other. Mackenzie called Lawson 'priggish and consequential' and complained that a book recalling his exploits exaggerated his role, a true case of the pot calling the kettle black. Lawson was more subtly disparaging of Mackenzie describing all the intelligence officers he met in Greece as 'amateurs'. His contribution to intelligence history also included an attempt to answer a perennial question about the British secret service which still resonates today. Did the British 'secret agent' have what would later be called a 'licence to kill'? Lawson's response summed up in broad terms the situation that – despite the prim protests which emanate from Whitehall whenever the issue is raised – remains true to this day.

OUR POLITICIANS AND journalists assure us from time to time that the British secret service is the best in the world. I do not know whether that is true anymore than, I imagine, do they; but, if it is true, it must be the outcome of some natural genius in our people for such work, and not of training or organisation; for the secret-service work of the Aegean – a difficult enough area – was conducted by amateurs, and I for one never received one word of guidance.

Now it is hardly to be expected that international law should formulate the etiquette of espionage or of the methods permissible for countering it, more especially in a case where the two warring powers are using for their arena a neutral country. But, though the law be not such an ass as to bray enactments which could have no sanction, there still remain the principles of morality and of expediency; and these two, though commonly contrasted as antitheses, are in the domain of international policy so closely correlated that, even when due allowance is made for all the relaxations of moral standards which the state of war in itself implies, a code of conduct based on apparent expediency alone will still be not only morally wrong but politically inexpedient.

The reason of this is simple. On that delicate moral quality which we call 'honour' depends that solid political asset, prestige. Prestige may be buttressed by commerce and industry, by scientific invention and achievement, by naval and military might, but its foundation is character. If any one doubts it, let him ask any Greek, or anyone who has lived among Greeks in these latter years, what fact or event in the history of the war has most enhanced British prestige in those parts, and the answer will be, not our command of the sea, not our training and equipment of so many million troops, not our output of munitions nor the feeding and financing of our allies, nor yet any signal victory or feat of arms by land or sea, but the great fire of Salonica. And why? Because among all that medley of nations the British soldier did not loot. Of this I am persuaded, that in all the course of the war no British statesman or diplomat, admiral or general, has done so much to raise British prestige in the eyes of the Greek world as was done in that one day by the rank and file of our Salonica forces, who, happening to be at hand, refrained from looting and threw themselves into the work of rescue and salvage as heartily as if it had been their favourite sport.

Now the secret-service agent in the byways of war represents his country no less than the soldier in the open field; but just because he is more isolated his individual character is more prominent; and in proportion as the possibilities of his work are more complex, his personal opportunities for raising or lowering the prestige of his country are more frequent and varied. Of course his personal predilections in favour of keeping the Ten Commandments may be such that no act of his is likely to stain his country's good repute; but then an intransigent attitude towards moral standards in wartime will also impair his efficiency as an agent. 'Thou shalt not kill' does not veto the extermination of the enemy. 'Thou shalt not steal' does not prohibit the seizure of contraband. And possibly 'Thou shalt not bear false witness' has not interfered unduly with propaganda. The state of war automatically abrogates certain moral laws, or at least limits their application. The man who fails to recognise this fact, and makes a hobby of a rigid conscience to the detriment of his country, must prove a failure in secret-service work.

But the opposite type is worse than a failure: he constitutes a public danger. I have met more than one man engaged in intelligence duties who held that the state of war gave exemption from all moral restraints, and that secret-service work meant devilry unlimited, though of course, if possible, undetected. A man holding such views needs but sufficient foolhardiness to take the risk of detection, or sufficient self-conceit to think detection impossible, in order to commit the country which he represents to every form and degree of crime. He procures, let us say, the assassination of some eminent person in a neutral country whose political influence is tending to make that country privately or avowedly espouse the enemy's cause. The coup successfully effected promises to incline the scales in favour of his own country and her allies; and, if suspicion is aroused, he has funds enough to buy silence. It seems a small thing to him, if he gives it a thought, that the assassin whom he employs, and any others whose silence must be bought, write him down as lacking only the pluck to be a murderer himself, and as a fit subject therefore for blackmail. It would seem smaller still perhaps that in the esteem of a corrupt handful of assassins and blackmailers the character of the country which he represents should be an enlargement, as it were, of his own. And yet as surely as night follows day he has blackened his country's fair name. A whispered story to divert some wench, a hint to some journalist of sensations to seek, a version (incriminating in no way the teller) sold in political circles, a spasm of veracity induced by liquor – and naked truth, or bedizened rumour, is winged and abroad.

'Pshaw!' you say, good reader, 'a most sound homily, no doubt, but it is like sermons we have all heard, in which the preacher propounds some perversity of dogma or moral theory which no sane person ever entertained, and with complacent indignation turns his battery of texts upon it. The hypothesis is fantastic. No educated man, above all no Englishman, could be so mentally or morally depraved. We do not employ either fools or criminals in our public services.'

Good reader, in wartime, believe me, we employ all sorts: and, taking men haphazard, if they are to be sailors or soldiers, we give them a modicum of training and impose upon them known rules of conduct and of discipline; but, if they are to be secret-service agents, we leave them uninstructed to their own devices. Why so? In order that we may reap the benefit of their crimes until detection comes, and then save the honour of our country by disowning them? Is that the cynical principle which guides certain guardians of our national honour? Why, then, our public services lack not for fools or criminals even at their head – criminals by complicity in the staining of our honour, or fools to risk the wrecking of our prestige. And if that is 'unthinkable' (oh blessed word of our politicians' vocabulary!) what alternative explanation do you offer, good reader, of the fact that no instructions and guidance are given? Will you urge that the majority of our secret-service agents, if chosen haphazard, will belong to neither of the extreme types I have depicted? That they will neither be of the conscientious-objector breed, maintaining that the state of war cannot modify the universal application of any commandment, nor yet act as professional devils for whom all moral restraints are abrogated? Very true; but it is just that majority composed of men who wish to steer a middle course, to whom some instructions in navigation, some chart of the rocks and shoals, some opportunity to correct the compass of their own judgment, would be most welcome.

How be it in fact the principles of morality and of expediency by which the secret-service agent is to be guided are left to himself to formulate. What then shall they be? What restrictions shall he impose upon himself in respect of life, liberty, and property, and what relaxations of moral obligation shall he accept? And must he distinguish between the declared enemy and the neutral who is working in the enemy's service? Pretty points of ethical theory for debate, are they not? But involving ugly issues in practice.

Shall we rule out wilful and unprovoked assassination without more ado? Very good; I agree, though I have met men who do not. But what about assassination by way of reprisal?

Let me put a case. It came to my ears before I had been long in Crete that the German Consul in Canea had done me the honour to put a price of two thousand francs on my head. I do not know whether in fact he had done so, or had merely arranged that such a report should reach me in the hope of disturbing my equanimity. But, assuming for the moment that it was a firm offer, should I have been justified in retaliating, with insult added to injury, by pricing his head at two hundred? My own answer is 'No'. But carry it a stage further: suppose that the German Consul had not only made that offer but had had to pay up: would my successor have been justified in reprisals? Probably yes, if with his own hand, on the principle that, as in a duel, he would be facing the same risk as his opponent; probably no, if by means of a hired agent, but say that he adopts neither of these courses and decides that he will endeavour to capture the German Consul for trial before a competent court. He gets in touch with a couple of trusty men from the mountains (it is no great difficulty in Crete), men who have taken a hand in cattle-lifting and have no scruples against consul-lifting. He tells them that he wants the consul delivered to him alive and not unnecessarily damaged. In due time they reappear. 'Your Excellency,' they say, 'there was trouble; we meant to bring him alive as your Excellency desired, but he and his servants fired on us, and we more successfully on them; and when we saw that he was killed, we thought your Excellency would no longer desire him.' What judgment shall we pass on such a case?

Translated into the atmosphere of civil life, it would stand thus: A hired a couple of armed ruffians to kidnap an enemy B; B put up a fight, and they killed him; inasmuch as they were engaged in a felony and came armed to perpetrate it, the killing, even if not premeditated, ranks as murder, and A who incited them to the felony is some sort of accessory. But will the same reasoning hold in wartime? Decidedly no: the right verdict then is justifiable homi-cide, or, if you will, death by misadventure – some verdict in fact which imputes no blame.

So I at any rate should judge the case; and I may say that I have acted on my judgment to the extent of risking just such an occur-rence without qualms. There was an important enemy agent whom I wanted. A brigand-like but pro-British stalwart called on me and offered to shoot him for eight hundred francs. 'No,' said I, 'I don't buy corpses.' Very good; he would kidnap him if I preferred, and, as that would mean less risk of trouble afterwards with the *gendar-merie*, he would take four hundred. I accepted the offer; but in fact there were no developments, either happy or untoward. My brig-and failed of his enterprise, and I captured the said agent by other means. Yet obviously kidnapping, however stringent the terms of the bargain, is not a game which is usually played unarmed, or without risk to life; and, as I say, I authorised it without qualm.

What then is my conclusion? Roughly this, that the ethics of secret service in wartime do not permit the furtherance of schemes whose object is homicide, but neither do they prohibit enterprises from which the risk of incidental homicide cannot be excluded.

Extracted from *Tales of Aegean Intrigue* by J. C. Lawson (first published by E. P. Dutton in 1921)

A RATHER BAD MOMENT

NORMAN DEWHURST

Norman Dewhurst worked for SIS (referred to here as the C Organisation) intermittently from 1916 through to 1947 in a variety of roles. His memoire, privately published in Belgium in the '60s simply as *Norman Dewhurst MC*, provides interesting and often unique detail on SIS during this period. During the First World War, Dewhurst served in Greece running agents behind enemy lines. He was then in Latvia at a crucial moment in the first Cold War between Britain and Bolshevik Russia and subsequently worked for the 'Z' Organisation, which was set up by Claude Dansey, a senior SIS officer supposedly thrown out of the Service for fraud in what was in fact a cover to allow him to set up an alternative secret service collecting intelligence on Germany. This passage begins in August 1915 when, having been wounded at Gallipoli, Dewhurst was given his first intelligence post. After recuperating in Cairo, he was ordered to report to Major Stewart Newcombe, the explorer and adventurer, Dewhurst found himself working in the Arab Bureau alongside Newcombe's close friends the archaeologists Leonard Woolley, David Hogarth, who was also Keeper of the Ashmolean Museum, and T. E. Lawrence – now better known as Lawrence of Arabia. The Arab Bureau also included the Arabist and Middle-East explorer Gertrude Bell. Woolley, Bell and Hogarth, while subordinate to military intelligence, worked for Cumming. It has to be said that it is not clear that Bell ever understood the nature of this secret role. Sent to Iraq to compile a series of reports on the personalities and tribes of the region, she protested over the fact that they were never published, complaining that 'it is preposterous that I should take so much trouble to no end.'

~~~~~~

MAJOR NEWCOMBE TOLD me that I would be working as a cipher officer and introduced me to another Second Lieutenant T. E. Lawrence, who was in the map department, and told me that I would be working with him. Lawrence did not talk much and during those first days contented himself with giving me coded telegrams and accepting the answers. It soon became clear to me that Lawrence, although he only held a junior rank, was considered important – he was always in conference with the senior officers. For me, the atmosphere there was wonderful – for the first time since I had received my combatant commission from the ranks I was working with colleagues who were devoid of class distinction – being friendly and helpful, not snobbish and stand-offish. All the office staff, both civilian and service, were excellent linguists – among them were Miss Gertrude Bell, the noted Orientalist, Mr D. G. Hogarth and Mr L. Woolley.

From the contents of the telegrams I was decoding, I quickly realised that I was now a member of a cloak and dagger outfit. I got on well with Lawrence and found he had a delightful sense of humour – for on one occasion when I had trouble in deciphering a telegram he sent back to Prodrome, London (the War Office) for a repeat, when this came through and we were still unable to make sense of it, he sent another telegram to London with the message: 'Please cipher, don't understand puzzles.'

One day I found a *Sjambok* lying around in the cipher office. I asked Lawrence about it – and with a laugh he said I could keep it. Made of rhino hide – it tapered off, in its 24-inch length, from a thickness of 1 inch at the handle to a little over a quarter inch at the tip. A leather thong passed through the handle and I carried it by this means on my right wrist.

It came in very useful later on to intimidate Greek prisoners. I became very attached to this *Sjambok* and carried it in place of a cane on every possible occasion. When, in 1918, it cracked, I had the handle bound in polished copper, on which I had engraved the various episodes of my service career – India, Egypt, Gallipoli, Cairo, Salonica, Syra, Athens, Sofia, etc.

Meanwhile my popularity had grown, as my mechanical knowledge was in great demand. Lawrence had a baby two-stroke Triumph motor-cycle which I kept in good running order, and I frequently rode it when on duty. There was plenty of work to do all round but I found the work interesting and no one bothered you – yes, I considered myself lucky to have got the posting.

Lawrence gave me my first outside job in November. He briefed me on the new U-Code that he had devised and which was now to be distributed – it was to replace the old Coast Guard Code which, after being in use for twenty years, was seriously compromised.

My last briefing from Lawrence was to the effect that I was to purchase a Ford motor car and report to the Eastern Mediterranean Special Intelligence Bureau of the C Organisation in Salonica. I was stirred by the news as I was to be my own boss of a frontline outfit, getting agents in and out of enemy territory and operating a carrier pigeon service.

Salonica at that time was a hotbed of intrigue as it was the centre of the espionage services of all the warring nations. This situation was due to the fact that the Greeks were still neutral – one half of them supported King Constantine who was pro-German and the other half Elefthérios Venizélos the Prime Minister who supported the Allies.

So into this exciting atmosphere I went. The first person to greet me on behalf of the local C organisation was E. D. Macrae. He was a most interesting type – he had worked for many years in Turkey and knew that country well, he was an expert linguist, and this meeting was the beginning of an excellent partnership.

I drove to our local office where I found James Morgan the Consul, Commander Hugh Whittall (a member of the family so well known in Constantinople and the Levant), and my new OC Commander Harry Pirie-Gordon. I was received with great enthusiasm for the Ford represented their sole means of transport.

The local meeting place of the various agents was the Café Flocas. There, while you drank your morning coffee, allied French agents would be pointed out to you as well as these working for the Germans and Bulgars. As it was the only good cafe in town, I and the other members of the Organisation were regular customers.

For the rest of 1916, I was kept busy getting agents to, and from behind, the German and Bulgarian lines on the other side of the Macedonian Plain. I had a special carrier pigeon service as pigeons were then the only means of communication.

On 21 March I made my first trip to Serres which was about 70 miles from Salonica. Serres was at that time in the centre of a neutral strip of territory lying between the two front lines. This was our key point for putting agents through the Bulgarian lines. We kept pigeons there too for urgent messages back to Salonica. On my way back I picked up H. A. D. [Harold] Hoyland, British Consul at Drama. He later became a news item when he organised the kidnapping of the German Consul there, he sent him in an armoured car to Salonica thence by boat to Malta.

There was an air raid on Salonica on 27 March which caused a number of fires but I was still able the next day to get two Greek agents, one who was known as Takki and the other a Mr Doukas, up to Serres.

A few days later, I left Salonica in a new Wolseley car for Cavalla, a 150-mile drive on a rotten road. I had HM Consul [Geoffrey] Knox with me and after a rather rough day we reached our destination. The next morning when Knox opened his front door he found one of his agents cut to pieces in a sack which was hanging on the door handle. I had rather a bad moment when I realised that what I had just seen might become my lot.

A couple of weeks later, the Chief of Military Intelligence Lieutenant-Colonel Frederick Cunliffe-Owen asked us if we could get him to Verria. This was a rather special situation because he was very jealous of our organisation which was independent of his control. He took up arms regularly against us and the telegraph lines to London were frequently buzzing with the battle that went on between the Foreign Office and the War Office with regard to the liberty of action we enjoyed, and the fact that HQ could not keep a check on us. What infuriated him the most was that we got our reports to London quicker than he did. In fact, due to our excellent team of agents and the carrier pigeon service we got our reports in days before he did.

The next day I drove Hoyland, two Greek agents and a crate of carrier pigeons to Serres. I stayed overnight to collect a special report from a Bulgarian sergeant-major who had been recruited as an agent. He would go back into and through the Bulgarian lines for a week at a time and then meet me in Serres to report. His reports were both fascinating and accurate. I later in the day picked up Clark and Takki and took them back to Salonica. We were then using twenty-three agents, mainly civilians who had worked in the area for years and knew the people and language well (most of them spoke four or five different tongues).

All through June, I was chasing backwards and forwards between Salonica and Serres. I organised a dinner party at the White House and afterwards we went on to Madame Fannie's, this was a very select house and the girls beautiful. Every time it was a case of combining business with pleasure for I always came away with some useful information after a visit.

Reports from the front were bad, the French had retired from Evacli and our cavalry was sent into action near the Roupel Pass, they came under heavy fire and had to retire. The only bridge remaining to Serres was on the Orlako road and during one journey I was stopped halfway – the road was full of refugees.[7]

I then had a busy spell – I picked up five of our agents to drop off at Nigrita. From there I went to Akinos and sent for Yanni, our motor boat man, to bring the boat. When he arrived I loaded the agents into the boat and we went to Nehori. Then I went to Chai Agazi on a special job, while there, I also got hold of two Bulgarian deserters and had them put through a tough interrogation.

The street fighting continued during 1 and 2 September and I was kept busy running Pirie-Gordon and Whittall around the back streets from one point to another on official business.

By the 3rd the situation was calm and I went down the line to a spot 45 miles out of town with agents and pigeons. I stayed the night there and slept in the pigeon loft. As I always carried a plentiful supply of food and drink in the car things were not too bad at all. I was nearly always in civilian clothes, always with a car at my disposal, free from routine military control (for I had a permit,

---

7   Refugees are a principal source of intelligence in war and Dewhurst and his colleagues
    would have stopped to interview them on what they had seen.

signed by all the security chiefs in the area, which authorised me to pass any frontier, or guards by day or night, in civilian clothes, with a car without hindrance or search).

I then managed to spend a few quieter days in Salonica. But this calm was broken on the 14th, when a party of us, including Vignolle, the chief of French *Sûreté*, my chief Pirie-Gordon, an Italian *Sûreté* officer, a Russian liaison officer and Macrae, decided to paint the town. We wined and dined in style at Madame Fannie's she provided a choice assortment of her most beautiful female chattels, and a meal which was superb. The evening extended well into the early hours.

Aubrey Herbert[8], the well known authority on Turkey, who was serving with the Irish Guards, was the next passenger I had. This time we were off to Iribuozk where he was to meet the head Mufti of a band of *Comitajis* (these were mercenaries or brigands) who he wished to recruit. We met the head man all right, he was a Mohammedan, and we ate at his house. We had a bottle of gin with us which we offered to the old Mufti. He thought it was water and I've never seen one of his type get so merry. We stayed the night and left the next morning, with Aubrey Herbert feeling very satisfied with his trip.

In early November, Vignolle, Guys and Benwah of the French *Sûreté*, and Pirie Gordon and myself called at the Serbian HQ at Karalad. We had dinner in the mess of Colonel Tomich, and gave him the big news. A messenger had been caught in Salonica while carrying the pay roll and list of seventy-two Turkish and Bulgar

---

8   Traveller, diplomat, Conservative MP and intelligence officer who was a close friend of John Buchan and is thought to have been the inspiration for Richard Hannay's friend, Sandy Arbuthnot, who made his first appearance in the extract from *Greenmantle* included earlier. At the time he met Dewhurst, Herbert was investigating the possibility of Britain negotiating a separate peace with Turkey.

agents working in the Serbian lines. We immediately planned a round-up and each night for a week we made wholesale arrests. By the end of this time they were all arrested and spent the rest of the war in gaol at Malta.

On 10 November, Pirie-Gordon and I went out to interrogate some Turkish prisoners at a village between Hortreg and Stavros. This was the day when he nearly shot me, he was taking his pistol out of the holster when it went off and the bullet passed through my cap. Pirie-Gordon went very white from shock and all I can say is I'm lucky to be here to tell the tale.

oooooooooooooooooooooooooooooooooooooooooooooooooooooooooooooooooooooooooooooooooooo

Extracted from *Norman Dewhurst MC* by Norman Dewhurst (first published by H. J. Edmonds in 1968)

GO SPY THE LAND

GEORGE HILL

George Hill's ability as a spy and the leader of a team of saboteurs in Bolshevik Russia was legendary within MI6. Kim Philby described him in *My Silent War* as 'one of the few living Englishmen who had actually put sand in axle-boxes' a reference to the standard means of blocking railway lines by incapacitating trains.

Hill's adventures included using a swordstick in action against two German spies in the Russian town of Mogilev. He hurried back to his hotel to examine the blade, 'anxious to know what it looked like after its adventure. I had never run a man through before. It was not a gory sight. There was only a slight film of blood halfway up the blade and a dark stain at the tip.' He sounded distinctly disappointed.

Hill was born in Estonia, and grew up speaking a variety of languages fluently, including Russian. When Bulgaria entered the war on Germany's side, in October 1915, he was given a crash course in Bulgarian, taught to fly and sent to Greece, from where he flew agents across the Bulgarian lines. Later, in Russia, he worked alongside Sidney Reilly, assisted by a network of female agents they had hand-picked to run their safe houses; a group of train-watchers reporting on troop movements; a large network of couriers recruited by Hill to take the intelligence north to the British forces; and a

special operations 'wrecking gang' to sabotage Bolshevik lines of communication. Hill's description in this passage of a safe house full of young female
agents might have embarrassed even James Bond.

⁘⁘⁘

IT WAS DECIDED that Sidney Reilly and I should remain in
Moscow after the Allied Mission's departure. He was to carry
on his work against the Bolsheviks, and I was to continue my
activities in Ukrainia against the German Army and also keep my
courier service going.

I had already decided that I would not risk carrying a revolver,
for nine times out of ten a revolver is of no earthly use and will seldom get a man out of a tight corner. On the other hand, however
small it may be, it is a bulky thing and is easily found when one's
person is searched; it was illegal to carry firearms. I had decided to
take, just for my own comfort, my swordstick, though I knew that
under the circumstances in which I should live I would never use
it. Then I had a momentary but first-class attack of nerves; in half
an hour I should be a spy outside the law with no redress if caught,
just a summary trial and then up against a wall. What a fool I was
… bound to be caught. Why take off my uniform? It was a crazy
thing to do. What good could I do, anyway?

'Steady,' I said to myself, 'you are bound to feel like this. It is just
like going over the top, quite natural. Come on, get a move on or
you will never go.'

I went out by a different entrance from the one I had used in
entering, casually glanced round to see that I was not being followed, stepped into a cab and drove to the other end of Moscow.
Here I scrambled on to a tram which was already packed to suffo-
cation point and travelled by a roundabout way to yet another part
of the town where I rented a small flat.

It was a flat which had been selected by the chief of my courier service. He was a Russian cavalry officer who had served with great distinction in the early days of the war, a patriot, fearless, a first-class judge of men and as good an organiser as I could have wished for. It was essential to have a place where the couriers could come on return from their various missions, where they would rest for two or three nights in safety and where he could visit them daily. One of his acquaintances was a lady, the wife of one of his brother officers who had been killed early in the war. For reasons best known to herself she had taken to the oldest profession in the world, and had been making quite a fair living on the Tverskaya Ulitza, the Bond Street of Moscow. But she was a patriot, and she gladly undertook to put two rooms of her four-roomed flat exclusively at my friend's disposal, for which naturally he paid her a good rent. The value of such a flat was enormous. Even under the old regime she had been registered by the local police. Later she had duly registered her calling at the district commissariat, and the House Committee knew all about her. What was more natural than that unknown men should constantly be coming and going in and out of her flat? She was absolutely reliable and our weary couriers could rest in safety in one of our rooms there.

With a beating heart I rang the bell. A rather good-looking woman in a kimono answered the door. 'I am Mr Holtzmann,' I said. This was the name I had arranged to assume when using her flat.

'Ah, yes,' she admitted me and pointed to a door at the end of the corridor, and without more ado returned to her own room. I went into the room she had indicated, a small chamber with a bed and a telephone. First of all I called up the chief of my couriers.

'I am here,' I said, 'come round at once.'

Then I telephoned Reilly, warned him that in all probability a warrant for his arrest would also be shortly issued and advised him to make tracks for his secret lodgings. Then I put my hand under the bed by the pillow, and drew out a small trunk. In it was a complete change of clothes made to fit me. There were three or four dark blue Russian shirts which buttoned at the neck, some linen underclothing, a pair of cheap ready-made black trousers, peasant-made socks such as were on sale on the stalls in the market, a second-hand pair of top-boots and a peak cap which had already been well used. I dressed myself hastily. I put my English suit, underclothing, tie, socks and boots into the stove; I laid a match to the kindling wood and shut the stove door. Ten minutes later my London clothes were burned.

Presently Z, the chief of my couriers, arrived. He brought with him my new passport made out in the name of George Bergmann, the description on which tallied with my appearance. We had prepared and forged this passport some weeks before and tried it out by sending a volunteer with it from Moscow to Petrograd and back again. Thus recent seals and visas from the Cheka[9] gave it an appearance of authority.

Z had brought a cheap mackintosh, a hundred Russian cigarettes, and the latest reports from various of our agents, which I put into the bag, and then I left the flat as George Bergmann, looking very different already from the Mr Holtzmann that had entered less than an hour before.

Z and I had agreed that it would be better and safer that he should not know my future headquarters, but we arranged two other meeting places in case our present rendezvous was raided. Altogether I had eight secret flats or rooms in Moscow for the use of myself and my organisation, as well as a small wooden country residence 40 miles away, which was to be a final retreat and refuge if Moscow

---

9   Cheka is simply a phonetic rendition of the initials of the Bolshevik secret service, known as the Extraordinary Commission, in Russian: *Chrezvychaynaya Komissiya*

grew too hot for me or any of my agents. Each one of the places had to be kept going and had to have a completely plausible and natural *raison d'être* for its existence.

Feeling rather awkward in my new clothes, but much happier within, I decided to walk to the house where my new headquarters were fixed. This house was in the Zamoskaretchye district, situated on the south bank of the Moskva River, in the poorer quarter of the town.

Weeks before, when I had first realised that I might have to go underground, I had discussed the matter with my very competent and devoted secretary, Evelyn, who was *au courant* with all the work I had been doing. Evelyn was partly English, but had been educated in Russia, and besides English and Russian she knew German, French and Italian perfectly. She was a brilliant musician and could turn her hand to anything which required skill.

We had decided that our best chance of success was to become people of the lower middle class and to live an entirely double life. She had immediately obtained a situation as a school-teacher in one of the mushroom schools which had been founded by the Bolsheviks. This gave her the necessary papers and also the very coveted ration cards from the Bolshevik organisation; coveted because, without cards or enormous sums of money, it was impossible to get food.

Then, as a spinster teacher, she had rented a small four-roomed house, which she had furnished with the barest necessities, picking up sticks of furniture in the various markets of Moscow in the guise of a poor young woman. Everyone was selling furniture in order to be able to buy food.

It was essential that the people about us should be entirely trustworthy. Evelyn and I discussed the matter and decided to ask two friends of ours, girls of English birth but Russian upbringing, to join our organisation. Sally and Annie both jumped at the chance. They had brothers, one in the Machine-Gun Corps and the other in the tanks, fighting on the Western Front. Both had been wounded, but were back in France and the sisters were aching to do something.

Sally was one of the most beautiful girls I have ever seen. She had raven-black hair, a peach-like complexion and the most sensitive, pale, transparent hands. Annie, her sister, was not so good-looking, but was a plump, merry, good-natured soul. We had decided that Sally should become cook to this establishment of ours, and do all the housework, cooking and buying what was necessary. Annie was to start a dressmaking business. She was clever with her needle and could knock up blouses and re-make costumes. At a dressmaking establishment it was only natural that there would be people coming and going. We wanted another ally to run messages for me and deliver the parcels to Annie's customers. After a great deal of thought between us we decided to enrol a young Russian girl we knew, an orphan who had just reached the mature age of seventeen. Vi was a tall blonde with blue eyes, and the most appealing ways, and time proved that she was also full of pluck.

The girls had taken up their residence about a month earlier; Evelyn went to her school every morning at 8.30 and returned at 4. Annie was working up quite a good little business. Vi ran the errands, and Sally stood in food queues waiting her turn, scrubbed the floors of the house and did the cooking. They all had forged Russian passports, and never spoke anything but Russian.

I was to take up my residence in this house as a lodger. I had never been inside the house, but knew exactly where it was, had passed it many times, and knew all about it. It was a low, single-storied, white-walled building, in a block containing many other houses just like it. It had two great advantages, a front door opened on the street, and a back door led out into a large yard shared by the other houses around it, through which there was a separate entrance into the road. The wall at the end of the yard was low and, if necessary, one could easily slip over it.

I had decided to go in through the back entrance. As I reached the house and turned into the yard the light was already fading. Just before I reached the back door it was opened, a woman took three steps into the yard and then pitched a bucket of dirty water into a grated drain. I gasped. It was Sally, the beautiful Sally transformed into a barefooted slut who wore a begrimed white blouse and some sort of a skirt. Her hair straggled in a plait down her back, and her hands – her beautiful transparent hands – were red and swollen and the nails caked with dirt.

'Good evening,' I said in Russian. 'I am the lodger Bergmann, may I come in?'

'Yes,' she said, blowing her nose in the way noses were blown before handkerchiefs were invented, and added, 'I have a bad cold.'

I entered a tiny dark kitchen in which was a long typical Russian cooking-stove. The kitchen led into a tiny windowless hall with four doors, the front door being on the right-hand side. Another door led into the living-room, which had two double windows looking out on the street, and communicated with a long, narrow, one-windowed chamber in which I was to live. A communicating door led from my room into the girls' room, which was also the dressmaking establishment. From this room, too, a door led into the tiny hall.

Evelyn jumped up as I entered. 'Girls,' she called softly; 'he has come!' Annie and Vi bounded in, Sally slammed the back door and rushed into the living-room. We all looked at one another and grinned, feeling excited, unnatural and rather foolish.

<hr />

Extracted from *Go Spy the Land: Being the Adventures of IK8 of the British Secret Service* by George Hill (first published by Cassell and Co. in 1932 and republished by Biteback in 2014)

THE
LOOMING THREAT
OF RASPUTIN

J. D. SCALE

John Dymoke Scale, a 6 foot 4 inch Indian Army officer, was recruited by Cumming for his ability to speak Russian and posted to the MI I c Petrograd bureau. The British believed that the Russian monk Rasputin had persuaded the German-born Tsarina to get her husband to pull his troops out of the war. This extract from his memoirs covers the period up to the point when Scale and his colleagues devised a joint plot with a number of Russian aristocrats to torture Rasputin – in order to find out what he was doing – and then to kill him. Scale's involvement in the preparations for the operation were such that he had to be sent briefly to Romania to avoid being implicated but his MI I c colleague Oswald Rayner was present throughout the torture – a post-mortem found that Rasputin's testicles had been flattened with a hammer. Recent forensic evidence suggests that Rayner fired the shot which killed Rasputin.

Following the Bolshevik Revolution, Scale was sent to Stockholm to run agents into Russia, but he was eventually forced to leave Sweden after the police there discovered that, unbeknown to Scale, one of his agents had been murdering Bolshevik couriers and dumping their bodies around the Swedish countryside.

∞∞∞

I WAS ORDERED to Petrograd in August 1916 and arrived there on the last day of the month. The journey had been uneventful, but interesting, as it was my first trip through Scandinavia. As we landed at Bergen, we heard that Romania had entered the war on our side, excellent news, which in our ignorance we believed foreshadowed an early and successful issue in our favour. With Russia and Romania one continuous line of troops from the Baltic to the Danube an early victory seemed assured. Little did we imagine the terrible double debacle some of us were soon to witness.

It rained in Christiania and we were glad to get on to Stockholm, where we spent an unforgettable day. Gorgeous weather lured as out of the beautiful city, by steamer to Saltzobaden, a lovely summer resort a few miles from the capital. No sign of the world war was yet apparent here. The Rationing Scheme for Neutrals had not yet influenced the figure of the well fed Swede. Petrol too was obviously abundant for the glassy waters mirrored countless motor launches of every size and description. It was curious to realise that many of the diners in the restaurants were Germans, some of them possibly officers on leave from the front in France.

In peace-time frequent fast steamers made the trip to Petrograd direct from Stockholm. Now we had to travel up Sweden by rail to the north of the Gulf of Bothnia; a long tiresome journey, where the River Tornio, the frontier, was crossed by ferry, and we found ourselves at Hasparanda, the northern terminus of the Russian Railway in Finland. Although icons hung, as I remembered them, in the waiting rooms, the smell of stale incense, untanned leather and *makhorka* (tobacco) filled the air, Russian uniforms were everywhere and the Russian language was heard on all sides; it was not the Russia I had known. The people were taciturn, stolid and laughed seldom. I knew nothing then of Finnish character and history, and wondered that the effects of the war should have so altered things. Finland was Russia to me in those days.

On arriving in Petrograd I left the Foreign Office despatches I was carrying at the Embassy. The drive from the Embassy, which overlooks the broad stream of the Neva, to the Astoria Hotel, short though it was, gave me glimpses of some of the finest bits of the capital. We crossed a corner of the Field of Mars, now famous as the burial place of the 'Martyrs of the Revolution', a great open parade ground in front of the barracks of the Pavlofsky Guards. We turned into the Street of Pillions, where stood that treasure house of art, the Hermitage – the roof of its magnificent entrance supported on the bent shoulders of a row of colossal naked figures in dark grey polished marble. A few yards further on the street entered the Winter Palace Square, named after the imposing but ugly stretch of terracotta buildings on the right, while opposite these the fine semi-circular sweep of the General Staff and Foreign Office held the eye. Through its centre a great archway, crowned by a quadriga formed an exit from the square, and driving through this we crossed the Nevsky Prospekt, catching a glimpse of the Admiralty with its spire, a golden shimmering needle against the blue sky; while to the left the broad ribbon of this famous street lost itself in dim distance. In a couple of minutes my *izvoscheek* turned into the Square of St Isaac's, dominated by the great cathedral of that name. Here at a corner was the Astoria Hotel, while on the other side, across a small well laid-out public garden, stood the granite building of the German Embassy, massive and hideous as a prison, its windows boarded up since that first day of war, when it was ransacked by infuriated crowds.

The Astoria was a fine five-storied building, built round a large dining hall, down onto the coloured glass roof of which the windows of the inner rooms looked. It was German-owned and it had been opened just prior to the war. Marble stairs and plate glass windows, brilliant brass work and mahogany, thick red carpets and graceful palms, gave it a glow of comfort unknown in any other hotel in Petrograd. It had been taken over by the government at the outbreak of hostilities and was now the 'official' hotel, open only to diplomats, officers, and officials. It was managed by a Committee of Generals and an Admiral (the latter in charge of water, sanitation etc.) one of whom was always on duty in uniform, in the reception bureau. Always full, many people lived there indefinitely, in spite of a regulation, that no one save the diplomats and officials of allied powers, could stay there longer than a certain number of days. From lunch time till late at night its salons were kaleidoscopes of movement and colour. Cossacks, guardsmen, naval officers, in fact men in every Russian uniform imaginable, military and civil (most civilians in Russia wear uniform) sat at tables on stood in groups chatting with their women folk, often very beautiful women they were too, in wonderful clothes and jewellery. Here and there among the throng officers in the uniform of one or other of the Allied powers were conspicuous. A Romanian Military Mission had just arrived, and was the centre of new interest. No taciturnity or absence of smiles was noticeable here. In fact one could hardly recognise the airs played by the military band so loud was the buzz of talk and laughter. A cheery, careless place was the Astoria (a happy hunting ground for enemy agents too!) I was in Russia again at last, and the impression of gloom I had gained in Finland was dispelled. Dimly I sensed it was not quite the Russia I had known in 1912, but I put it down to the difference between cosmopolitan Petrograd, and super-Russian Moscow, and I went to sleep that first night undisturbed by the distant murmur of the swollen stream, so soon to break its banks and swamp everything.

It was many days before I learnt the intricacies of the passages leading to the office in the Russian General Staff where I worked. Through courtyards piled high with logs of silver birch (for heating the buildings in winter), up dark stone stairs, and along dim passages, I was continually finding myself in unknown regions. Like a Russian friend of mine, who when in doubt in London as to his direction, always returns to Trafalgar Square, I had a landmark. It was a large panelled room, more like a ball room than anything else, where white-headed generals and colonels of reserve sat at long tables, and through spectacles and large magnifying glasses, traced beautiful rasps while a full length painting of the Tsar in uniform, looked encouragingly down on them. This room was a thoroughfare for officers passing from one department to another, and its smell was the most arresting thing about it, it wafted down the corridors, and when I picked it up, I held to the line like a beagle, and knew I should get home. It was such a strange smell that I had to analyse it and I came to the conclusion it was a mixture of furniture polish, eucalyptus (most of the old gentlemen had continual colds) incense and oiled wrapping paper.

Our work was full of interest. We were the channel through which news of all movements of enemy troops were exchanged between the Russian and British War Staffs. Long cypher telegrams were continually arriving from London, containing the latest news from the front; these had to be decyphered and given to the Russian Staff, while summaries of news in Russian from all their fronts had to be translated, encyphered and sent to London. The Russian Intelligence was extremely good, and even during later times when everything else was chaotic the 'identification' (as the 'identifying' of enemy units is called) from the Russian fronts came through with surprising correctness and punctuality. We sometimes had trouble owing I think, to the 'sliminess' of the German General Staff. They naturally aimed at creating distrust between the military authorities of the two countries, and one of their aims was to make the Russians disbelieve the veracity of the British communiqués and to belittle our efforts, their method seemed to be as follows: Supposing the 40th German Division to have been almost annihilated in severe fighting on the British front, they at once withdrew the remnants, filled up the losses with fresh troops, and sent it *ventre à terre* across Europe to some quiet sector on the Russian front line, where it was identified (intentionally on the German part) within a few days of its reported annihilation by our troops in the West. I do not for a moment believe that they went to all this trouble solely with this object in view. Troops were wanted on the Russian front and this 'anti-British propaganda' worked in with their general plan of movement. But the result was apparent. The Russian General Staff were at first sceptical about our communiqués when this happened, but gradually took our statements to be nearer the truth than apparent German facts.

We worked in an atmosphere of tea. One always works like that in Russia, every Russian clerk drank glass after glass of tea while working, and the orderlies in each department of the War Office, as everywhere else, kept *samovars* at full blast, and only after long experience did our man realise I could not drink more than two glasses in a morning. The others were acclimatised to it, and not even the discovery of a bit of an old golosh in our *samovar* could deter them.

During my stay in Moscow in 1912–13, I had not come in touch with the Russian Army, and it was therefore in Petrograd that I gained my first experience of Russian military custom and etiquette. Unlike our practice (I talk of pre-war days) of getting into mufti on all possible occasions, the Russian officer wore uniform continually, and owing to the huge size of the Army, even in peace time, his day was one long round of giving and taking salutes. One might imagine that under war conditions, when almost every other person one met was in uniform, salute discipline would have grown slack. The opposite was the case. Every officer entering a restaurant or assembly, bowed to the company in general, and then clicking his heals and saluting the senior officer present, asked his permission to be seated. As he passed down the room he clicked his heels and bowed to each officer senior to him, and every officer junior to him rose from his seat and bowed. If a general entered a room every officer rose and stood till he was seated, or till he signed to them to be seated. Until the senior officer permitted it, no officer smoked, I remember the first time I noticed this. It was one evening in the large dining hall of the Astoria. I saw an officer rise from his seat and cross to where a famous Russian General was sitting. He stood to attention and I heard him say something. The General nodded and the movement of every officer in the room as he produced his cigarette case drew my attention to the fact that I was the only one smoking. When a junior tendered a verbal report to a senior, he stood at the salute the whole time he was speaking. Swords were always worn. At a dance or big dinner, no officer took his sword off, but if it was an informal affair he might do so with his host's permission. Some of the ranks were rather puzzling at first; for instance there were General-Admirals, there were Senior naval Officers with special duties on shore. A Staff Captain in the Army had nothing to do with the Staff, but was a rank between lieutenant and captain.

It was about the middle of November 1916 that a certain well known Englishman, Sir John Norton Griffiths, passed through Petrograd on his way to Romania on a special mission, naturally, at that time, of a secret nature. The Romanian campaign was going very badly, and there was great danger of the huge oil fields falling into German hands. The possession of this rich source of motive power, especially for her submarine campaign, together with the vast stores of grain, was an essential factor in German strategy, and the untimely entry of Romania into the war had been provoked through devious diplomatic channels by German intrigue to this very end. A large portion of the grain had already been captured as well as numerous herds of stock, as the German army had already overrun the western part of Wallachia as that region of Romania is called. Norton Griffiths was travelling post haste to prevent the seizing of the oilfields intact, and I eagerly volunteered to accompany him, if I could be spared. It was unluckily impossible to obtain permission in time from London, and disappointed, I saw him off alone on his difficult task.

German intrigue was becoming more intense daily. Enemy agents were busy hanging round the patient queues of hungry people waiting for the provisions that never came. Those agents were whispering of peace and hinting how to get it by creating disorder, rioting, etc.

The day had been a depressing one and things looked very black. Romania was collapsing, and Russia herself seemed weakening. The failure in communications; the shortness of food; the sinister influence which seemed to be clogging the war machine; Rasputin the drunken débauché influencing Russia's policy. What was to be the end of it all?

<hr />

This memoir is held by the Scale family and was kindly provided by his grandson Edward Harding-Newman

THE SCARLET
PIMPERNEL OF
PETROGRAD

PAUL DUKES & JOHN MERRETT

The British had a large number of agent networks inside Bolshevik Russia, some run by MIIc, which had a strong presence in Petrograd, and some by Captain Francis Cromie, the British Naval Attaché. But in August 1918, the collapse of an MIIc plot to overthrow the Bolshevik leadership and a failed attempt by anti-Bolsheviks to assassinate Lenin led to a Soviet crackdown on opposition forces which became known as the Red Terror. The British Embassy in Petrograd was attacked by Red Guards and Cromie was shot dead. Most of the MIIc officers were arrested and incarcerated.

One MIIc officer Gerald 'Jim' Gillespie remained at large and managed to put in place a fallback plan under which the agent networks were to be handed over to a member of the British expatriate community until Cumming could send in someone new to take over. The man Gillespie recruited to do this was John Merrett, the owner of a Petrograd engineering firm, who had no experience whatsoever as a spy but was to prove a remarkably good choice. Gillespie gave Merrett the details of the networks and the courier lines into Finland and left him with 200,000 roubles to fund the operations. Merrett soon found himself not just running the intelligence networks but also using the courier routes as escape lines to smuggle British citizens out of Russia and having to bribe members of the Cheka to give food to the Britons who were still in prison.

Eventually, Paul Dukes, a former concert pianist recruited by Cumming for his ability to speak Russian and merge into the background, was sent in to stitch the networks back together. But in the meantime Merrett was a heroic figure for many British expatriates, as one he rescued described:

'I asked Mr Merrett how he dared the risk of being arrested at every moment; he laughingly replied that while the Bolsheviks were busy arresting him at Moika, he was to be found in the country and when they were after him in the country, he was to be found somewhere else. When relating my adventures to my friends I always referred to him as the "Scarlet Pimpernel".'

The first letter is from Merrett himself applying to the Foreign Office for £3,000 compensation for money of his own that he was forced to spend on the networks and on rescuing British citizens. The second is from Dukes backing up the claim. They are followed by a passage from Dukes's book *Red Dusk and the Morrow* which describes Merrett operating in Russia, naming him as Marsh.

157 Palmerston Road
Bowes Park, N22
4 May 1920

To the Right Honourable,
The Principal Secretary of State for Foreign Affairs, Foreign Office.

My Lord,

This is an application to which, with great respect, I will ask you to give your consideration. It relates to events in Petrograd between September and December, 1918.

Although the statements which follow are, in large measure, capable of immediate corroboration, I am aware that the bases of my application are such as give me no legal or other material rights by which to enforce them. What, in fact, I hope to prove to your satisfaction is that there exists a sufficiently strong moral obligation to enable you after reading the following to find in my favour.

From 1909 until December, 1918, I lived in Petrograd, carrying on business till October, 1917, as an engineer, visiting England from time to time in connection with my business and by way of holidays.

I remained in Petrograd continuously from February 1915 until December 1918.

By living there so long, I naturally acquired an intimate knowledge of the country and its people, and this knowledge, by reason of my comparative obscurity, I was able to use to advantage at a time when the oppressive measures of the Bolsheviks made it vital for British residents and others to leave Russia.

My business was a prosperous one, but my fortune, with the exception of a few hundred pounds, remained in Russia, and was completely lost to me. A claim in no way concerned with the subject matter of this letter stands filed in my name at the Foreign Office and deals in detail with the remainder of my lost property.

It was a fortunate thing that my possessions were in Russia, because of the relief that could be therewith procured for persons imprisoned by the Bolsheviks and of the means it afforded for obtaining their release from prison and ultimately, in the majority of cases, from the country itself.

Although my services were used in a professional capacity by the Embassy and other government departments, the first connection I had with activities to be disapproved of by the Bolsheviks was immediately after the raid on the British Embassy and the arrest of the staff and shooting of Captain Cromie.

Monsieur D'Arcy, a prominent member of the French Mission, with whom I had been closely associated on work for the Allies, was imprisoned in the Peter Paul Fortress at the time the members of the British Embassy were arrested and placed there. He was released shortly after their arrival in prison, and immediately came to me and described the conditions under which they were forced to exist.

He asked me if it were not possible to arrange to get food and bedding to them, and suggested I should endeavour to raise a subscription amongst the Englishmen still free.

Monsieur D'Arcy's description of prison conditions and the treatment meted out to prisoners, demanded immediate action, and so, in order to avoid the delay which such a subscription would have involved, the necessary nucleus for a fund, namely, 10,000 Roubles, was supplied from my own resources.

With this money, and with the very able and willing co-operation of Captain Webster, of the American Red Cross, working under the protection of the Dutch Embassy, a kitchen was started, and food, as well as bedding and clean linen, supplied regularly to those in prison.

Apart from the members of the Embassy, British subjects in

general were being imprisoned, and as I was fortunate enough to avoid arrest, I was determined to do all in my power to alleviate the sufferings of the less fortunate.

Previously to this, I had assisted Mr Gillespie, the last of the intelligence officers, and on its becoming too dangerous for him to remain longer, I undertook at his request to keep on foot the various organisations, started by Captain Cromie and other British Officers.

These organisations, although formed originally for political and other work, were utilised by me for obtaining the release of those in difficulties, and getting them across the frontier in a variety of ways. The regular routes had become impossible.

On his departure, Mr Gillespie left me about 200,000 roubles to carry on with and this money was expended in, amongst others, the following ways:

(a)   Feeding and obtaining the release of those in prison.
(b)   Remunerating the various people connected with the organisations.
(c)   Providing the necessary funds for expenses on the journey of Englishmen I was able to assist out of the country.
(d)   Clearing up various outstanding matters in connection with former organisations.

The amount so left me was inadequate for prolonging the work and I had perforce to find the balance as best I could. This was done:

(a)   From my own resources.
(b)   By borrowing from friends on my personal guarantee.
(c)   From certain moneys deposited with me for safe-keeping and transfer, by those who were being assisted out of the country. These I had eventually to fall back upon through complete lack of funds.

The aggregate amounts supplied from these three sources, and, therefore, exclusive of the 200,000 Roubles supplied by Mr

Gillespie, amounted to about 120,000 Roubles, which was at that time equivalent to £3,000. That is the rate at which the money deposited with me was guaranteed to be transferred.

It was impossible to keep anything in the nature of record or accounts because of the danger from searches by Red Guards.

I am dependent on memory for these figures, because arrest and further suffering of the implicated would have been involved had any such records been discovered.

With regard to the sums deposited with me for safe-keeping and transfer, demands for repayment in pounds are now being made to me by the persons who left them with me. These persons are for the most part in straitened circumstances.

It is chiefly on account of these demands that I now make this appeal.

The number of persons I was instrumental in getting out of Russia was, I believe, two hundred and forty-seven.

I had arranged for the release of Monsieur D'Arcy, who had again been arrested, but unfortunately he was too ill to move and died shortly afterwards in the Butyrka prison in Moscow.

I would like to say that the whole of the work thus carried out was voluntary, and at no time did I solicit or receive any recognition or remuneration for services which entailed considerable danger to myself, and involved my actual arrest on one occasion by the Red Guards. Fortunately, I succeeded in escaping on my way to prison, and was thereafter only able to avoid re-arrest by adopting disguises and sleeping in ever changing and out of the way quarters.

I am, my Lord
Your most obedient servant
J. A. Merrett

18 Gordon Square
WC1

Under-Secretary of State, Foreign Office, SW1

My Lord,

   With reference to enclosed letter of Mr John Merrett, I beg to state that I am able to bear out in substance the assertions made therein. I met Mr Merrett for the first time in November 1918 in Petrograd. I found him continuing the work of Mr Gillespie, who was in government employ and who had been compelled to quit the country. At the same time he was engaged in enabling allied subjects, particularly British who were in difficulties and whom the Bolsheviks refused passes, to find means of crossing the frontier unobserved. I had the opportunity during a couple of weeks of observing Mr Merrett's work in this sphere. During this period he enabled nearly a dozen people to escape, providing them in some cases with money and paying the smugglers and others through whose agency the transmission over the frontier was effected. Mr Merrett was certainly acting under circumstances of grave personal danger; when I arrived in Petrograd I found him in hiding, changing his abode every night, in various disguises, and hotly chased by the agents of the Extraordinary Commission. After he had successfully effected his own escape from Russia an important official of the Petrograd Extraordinary Commission, by name Masloff, who was charged with Merrett's case, was expelled for letting the prey slip through his fingers.

   I formed the judgment during those days that Mr Merrett was actuated partly, perhaps, by the love of adventure but mainly by a sense of duty toward the British colony in Petrograd. There was at that time absolutely nobody left who was attending to their material wants or discovering means of communicating abroad. Mr Merrett, I believe, felt that he could not leave Petrograd until someone arrived, or some arrangements were made, for the continuation of the various activities for which he temporarily voluntarily assumed the responsibility.

So far as I am aware Mr Merrett was never directly employed by the British government – certainly not for this branch of work and the expenses of it he bore largely out of his own pocket. Only a few days after his escape to Finland his estate near Petrograd was pillaged by the Bolsheviks and everything destroyed. At the same time I know that nothing remained of his business and property in Petrograd.

I am not sure of the exact number of people whom Mr Merrett was instrumental in enabling to escape but from the assurances of many people in Petrograd it must have been very large indeed. Mr Merrett was of material assistance to myself in my early days in Petrograd – in fact, the work I carried on during 1919 was founded on what Merrett had been able to preserve of organisations which came to grief after the murder of Captain Crombie.

I regret that my reply to Your Lordship's enquiry of 31 May is so late. I have been in Poland for the past two months and the copy of Mr Merrett's letter was received by me only yesterday upon my return. I shall be happy to furnish any further information on the subject. Mr Merrett's claim appears to me just and moderate. Owing to his private capacity and the circumstances in which he worked very little is generally known of the great services he rendered in the autumn of 1918.

Your obedient Servant,
Paul Dukes

The above letters are held in the UK National Archives in file T 161/38

RED DUSK AND
THE MORROW

PAUL DUKES

Paul Dukes was first employed by British military intelligence to work on propaganda during the early part of the First World War when he was a concert
pianist at the Petrograd Conservatoire. In the wake of the Bolshevik Revolution and the subsequent forced departure of Cumming's men, he was called
in to Cumming's office at the top of Whitehall Court and recruited into MI I c.

Cumming told Dukes that he was to go back into Russia to pick up the
pieces of the abandoned British networks from Merrett, whom he refers to
here as Marsh. Dukes adopted many covers, even getting himself recruited
into the Bolshevik secret service, the Extraordinary Commission or Cheka.

Dukes helped Merrett escape and then took over the networks assisted
by his mistress Nadezhda Ivanovna Petrovskaya, a doctor and former revolutionary. She was a genuine member of the Bolshevik Party and had known
Lenin well enough to have visited him in prison posing as his fiancée when
he was arrested in St Petersburg in December 1895. Petrovskaya used the
covernames Mariya Ivanovna Semenova or Smirnova and is here mislead-
ingly described as Marsh's housekeeper.

I WAS AWAKENED rudely by a loud ring at the bell and sprang up, all alert. It was quarter to eight. Who, I asked myself, could the callers be? A search? Had the House Committee heard of the unregistered lodger? What should I say? I would say Stepanovna was a relative, I would complain rudely of being disturbed, I would bluster, I would flaunt my passport of the Extraordinary Commission. Or perhaps Stepanovna and Varia would somehow explain away my presence, for they knew the members of the committee. I began dressing hastily. I could hear Stepanovna and Varia conferring in the kitchen. Then they both shuffled along the passage to the door. I heard the door opened, first on the chain, and then a moment's silence.

At last the chain was removed. Someone was admitted and the door closed. I heard men's voices and boots tramping along the passage. Convinced now that a search was to be made I fished feverishly in my pockets to get out my passport for demonstration, when – into the room burst Melnikoff! Never was I so dumbfounded in my life! Melnikoff was dressed in other clothes than I had seen him in when we last parted and he wore spectacles which altered his appearance considerably. Behind him entered a huge fellow, a sort of Ilya Muromets,[10] whose stubble-covered face brimmed over with smiles beaming good-nature and jollity. This giant was dressed in a rough and ragged brown suit and in his hand he squeezed a dirty hat.

'Marsh,' observed Melnikoff, curtly, by way of introduction, smiling at my incredulity. We shook hands heartily all round while I still fumbled my passport. 'I was about to defy you with that!' I laughed, showing them the paper. 'Tell me, how the … I thought you were in prison!'

'Not quite!' Marsh exclaimed, dropping into English at once. 'I had a larky get-away! Slithered down a drainpipe outside the

---

10   Russian folk hero with supposedly super-human strength.

kitchen window into the next yard as the Reds came in at the front door. Shaved my beard at once.' He rubbed his chin. 'About time, by the way, I saw the barber again. The blighters are looking for me everywhere. I was held up one evening by one of their damned spies under a lamp-post. I screwed my face into a freak and asked him for a light. Then I knocked him down. And yesterday evening I was going into a yard on Sadovaya Street when under the arch I heard someone behind me say, 'Marsh!' I sprang round, just about to administer the same medicine, when I saw it was Melnikoff!'

'But how did you find me here?' I said.

'Ask Melnikoff.' I asked Melnikoff in Russian. He was nervous and impatient.

'Luck,' he replied. 'I guessed you might possibly be in Sergeiev-itch's flat and so you are. But listen, I can't stay here long. I'm being looked for, too. You can meet me safely at three this afternoon at the 15th communal eating-house in the Nevsky. You don't need a ticket to enter. I'll tell you everything then. Don't stay more than two nights in one place.'

'All right,' I said, 'three o'clock at the 15th eating-house.'

'And don't go to Vera's anymore,' he added as he hurried away. 'Something is wrong there. Goodbye.'

'Get dressed,' said Marsh when Melnikoff had gone, 'and I'll take you straight along to a place you can go to regularly. But rely mainly on Melnikoff, he's the cleverest card I ever saw.'

Stepanovna, beaming with pleasure and pride at having two Englishmen in her flat, and nervous at the same time on account of the circumstances, brought in tea, and I told Marsh of my mission to Russia. Though he had not been connected with intelligence organisations, he knew people who had, and mentioned the names of a number of persons whose aid might be re-enlisted. One or two occupied high positions in the Ministry of War and the Admiralty.

171

But there was a more pressing task on hand than intelligence. The Bolsheviks suspected Marsh of complicity, together with other Englishmen, in assisting Allied citizens who were refused passports to escape from the country secretly. Numerous arrests among foreigners were being made and Marsh had had a hair-breadth escape. But his wife had been seized in his stead as hostage, and this calamity filled him with concern.

Mrs Marsh was imprisoned at the notorious 2 Goróhovaya Street, the address of the Extraordinary Commission, and Marsh was awaiting the report of a man who had connections with the Commission as to the possibilities of effecting her escape.

'This man,' explained Marsh, 'was, I believe, an official of the *Okhrana* (the Tsar's personal secret police) before the revolution, and is doing some sort of clerical work in a Soviet institution now. The Bolsheviks are re-engaging Tsarist police agents for the Extraordinary Commission, so he has close connections there and knows most of what goes on. He is a liar and it is difficult to believe what he says, but,' (Marsh paused and rubbed his forefinger and thumb together to indicate that finance entered into the transaction), 'if you outbid the Bolsheviks, this fellow can do things, understand?'

Marsh put me up to the latest position of everything in Petrograd. He also said he would be able to find me lodging for a few nights until I had some settled mode of living. He had wide acquaintanceship in the city and many of his friends lived in a quiet, unobtrusive manner, working for a living in Soviet offices.

'Better be moving along now,' he said when we had finished tea. 'I'll go ahead because we mustn't walk together. Follow me in about five minutes, and you'll find me standing by the hoarding round the Kazan Cathedral.'

'The hoarding round the Kazan Cathedral? So you know that

hoarding, too?' I asked, recalling my intention of hiding in that very place.

'I certainly do,' he exclaimed. 'Spent the first night there after my get-away. Now I'll be off. When you see me shoot off from the hoarding follow me as far behind as you can. So long.'

'By the way,' I said, as he went out, 'that hoarding – it doesn't happen to be a regular shelter for – for homeless and destitute Englishmen or others, does it?'

'Not that I know of,' he laughed, 'Why?'

'Oh, nothing. I only wondered.'

I let Marsh out and heard his steps echoing down the stone staircase.

'I shall not be back tonight, Stepanovna,' I said, preparing to follow him. 'I can't tell you how grateful…'

'Oh, but Ivan Pavlovitch,' exclaimed the good woman, 'you can come here any time you like. If anything happens,' she added in a lower tone 'we'll say you belong to us. No one need know.'

'Well, well,' I said, 'but not tonight. Good-bye, good-bye.'

While Stepanovna and Varia let me out I had a vision of Dmitri standing at the kitchen door, stolidly munching a crust of black bread.

Outside the hoarding of the Kazan Cathedral I espied the huge figure of Marsh sitting on a stone. When he saw me over the way he rose and slouched along with his collar turned up, diving into side streets and avoiding the main thoroughfares. I followed at a distance. Eventually we came out to the Siennaya market, crossed it, and plunged into the maze of streets to the south. Marsh disappeared under an arch and, following his steps, I found myself in a dark, filthy, reeking yard with a back stair entrance on either hand. Marsh stood at the stairway on the left.

'Flat 5 on the second floor,' he said. 'We can go up together.'

The stairway was narrow and littered with rubbish. At a door with '5' chalked on it Marsh banged loudly three times with his fist, and it was opened by a woman, dressed plainly in black, who greeted Marsh with exclamations of welcome and relief.

'Aha, Maria,' he shouted boisterously, 'here we are, you see – not got me yet. And *won't* get me, unless I've got a pumpkin on my shoulders instead of a head!'

Maria was his housekeeper. She looked questioningly at me, obviously doubtful whether I ought to be admitted. Marsh howled with laughter. 'All right, Maria,' he cried, 'let him in. He's only my comrade – comrades in distress, and ha! ha! ha! "comrades" in looks, eh, Maria?'

Maria smiled curiously. 'Certainly "comrades" in looks,' she said, slowly.

'By the way,' asked Marsh, as we passed into an inner room, 'what name are you using?'

'Afirenko,' I said. 'But that's official. Tell Maria I'm called "Ivan Ilitch".'

Maria set the *samovar* and produced some black bread and butter.

'This flat,' said Marsh, with his mouth full, 'belonged to a business colleague of mine. The Reds seized him by mistake for someone else. Silly fool, nearly (here Marsh used a very unparliamentary expression) with funk when he got arrested. Sat in chokey three days and was told he was to be shot, when luckily for him the right man was collared. Then they let him out and I shipped him over the frontier. They'll forget all about him. In the daytime this is one of the safest places in town.'

The flat was almost devoid of furniture. A bare table stood in one room and a desk in another. An old couch and a few chairs made up the outfit. The windows were so dirty that they were quite opaque and admitted very little light from the narrow street. Although it was nearly midday an oil lamp burned on the table of the room we sat in. Electric light was becoming rarer and rarer and only burned for a few hours every evening.

Marsh sat and talked of his adventures and the work he had been doing for the Allied colonies. His country farm had been seized and pillaged, his city business was ruined, he had long been under suspicion and yet he refused to leave. But the arrest of his wife bore constantly on his mind. From time to time his boisterous flow of talk would suddenly cease. He would pass his hand over his brow, a far-away troubled look coming into his eyes.

'If only it were an ordinary prison,' he would say, 'if only they were human beings. But these…! By the way, will you come with me to see the Policeman? I am going to meet him in half an hour.' The 'Policeman' was the nickname by which we referred to the Tsarist official of whom Marsh had spoken in the morning. I reflected for a moment. Perhaps the Policeman might be useful to me later. I consented.

Telling Maria to look out for us both about that time next morning, we left the flat by the back entrance as we had entered it. Again Marsh walked ahead, and I followed his slouching figure at a distance as he wound in and out of side streets. The dwelling we were going to, he told me, was that of an ex-journalist, who was now engaged as a scribe in the Department of Public Works, and it was at the journalist's that he had arranged to meet the Policeman.

The journalist lived all alone in a flat in the Liteiny Prospekt. I watched Marsh disappear into the entrance and waited a moment to convince myself he was not being tracked. From the opposite sidewalk I saw him look back through the glass door, signalling that all was well within, so giving him time to mount the stairs I followed.

∞∞∞

Extracted from *Red Dusk and the Morrow: Adventures and Investigations in Soviet Russia* by Paul Dukes (first published by Doubleday, Page & Co. in 1922 and republished by Biteback in 2012)

The in-house MI6 cartoon of Agent ST1, Sidney Reilly, who was commissioned as an officer in the RAF before being sent into Russia.

SAFE HOUSE ON THE CHEREMETEFF PEREULOK

SIDNEY REILLY

The memoirs of Sidney Reilly, the so-called Ace of Spies, make for intriguing reading. The first half is Reilly's own account of his operations in Bolshevik Russia on behalf of MI1c, the organisation we now know as MI6. The second half is an account of the fallout from his final fatal mission to Russia by Pepita Bobadilla, an actress who married Reilly bigamously in 1923.

Reilly has been dismissed as a fantasist but there is nothing in his account of his operations in Russia or in his wife's account that does not accord with what we now know to be the truth. It is easy to understand the cynics' views. Getting to the truth can be difficult with Reilly. His activities – in government service, in business, and in love – have been exaggerated, but there is no doubt that he led a colourful life and believed very strongly, arguably too strongly for an intelligence officer, in the anti-Bolshevik cause. A former MI6 officer who looked after the service's archives once told me: 'He's been written off by historians by and large. But he has been greatly underrated. He was very, very good – a very able agent and a far more serious operator than the impression given by the myth. Historians do have this tendency to write off something that has been made to appear glamorous. He was unusual but I don't think he was glamorous. He was a bit of a crook, you could almost say, certainly sharp practice. But as an agent he was superb.'

'PASS, COMRADE RELINSKY,' said the Lett soldier on guard at the corner of the street.

I passed. The soldier did not trouble to examine my papers. He knew me. I was Comrade Relinsky of the *Cheka-Criminel* – a Communist and a Comrade. With the *canaille* in the street it was different. The papers of many of them would be found not to be in order. Fully half of them would be hauled off to the Butyrsky.

I turned into the Tverskoy Boulevard, ruinous, deserted, desolate, strewn with dirt and litter. It was a beautiful day in Moscow – the time Midsummer 1918.

A lean, pitiful scarecrow of an object, starved, emaciated, hungry, was standing at the corner of the Boulevard. He gave me one frightened glance when he heard the Lett address me as a comrade. Then he shuffled hastily away, pitifully trying to disguise his poor attempt at speed.

It was gloriously warm. The Boulevard was bathed in delightful sunlight. It seemed wrong somehow that the sun should shine and the world go on when here in Moscow so much shame was being wrought. Was heaven then indifferent? Could the sun look unblinkingly on the lurid sins of man?

Halfway down the Boulevard I passed another human wreck, an old, old man, with long silver hair and a straggling grey beard. He was crying. His shoulders shook with convulsive sobbing. The shameless tears trickled down his thin, furrowed old cheeks.

'What is the matter, *Dedushka*?' I asked him.

'I am hungry,' sobbed the old man. 'For two days I have stood in the queues and got no food. Lord, have mercy on us, what is to become of us all?'

At the next corner the usual food-queue was waiting. It had been there when I had passed in the morning, three hours before, long, silent, listless, apathetic, like a snake torpid with starvation. The people would come early and line up there, very early, because there was never enough bread to go round. Starvation menaced the city. There were far too many mouths to fill. But the Bolsheviks were steadily reducing the surplus population. Everywhere everything spoke of dearth and stagnation. The peasants got no profit from bringing food into the city. They were rewarded only by a sense of having done their duty. The reward was inadequate. The peasants tilled and sowed for themselves only. Moscow was a city of the damned.

Near the Cheremeteff Pereulok a fitful attempt was being made to clear the litter from the dirty streets. A gang of men and women were working there, men with well-bred, scholarly faces, women dignified and refined. By them, keeping guard, was a workman, covered in bandoliers and with a holster at either hip. They were members of the bourgeoisie; they had been stockbrokers, lawyers, schoolmistresses, when there had been stocks, laws and schools in Russia. Being bourgeoisie they were made to work for the new task-masters. They were tired, emaciated, starving, weary. It was great fun to keep them from the food-queues. A dead horse lay at one side of the road. It had dropped there from sheer exhaustion and starvation, when it had become too weak to go on. It had been left there. The carcass had now been there for several days.

The comrade with the bandoliers and the revolvers called a greeting to me for he knew me. I was Comrade Relinsky of the *Cheka-Criminel*. I returned his greeting and passed on, picking my way carefully over the filthy street.

The Cheremeteff Pereulok was in the shade. It was a relief to turn into it from the white glare of the main street. I stopped at No. 3. I turned round. Nobody else was in the street. I was unobserved.

I slipped into the house and mounted the stairs. They were dirty and covered with litter and stunk abominably. The whole house was deathly silent. It might have been deserted – in the hands of the housebreakers probably. As a matter of fact it was a large block of flats, more than two hundred altogether, and all of them were occupied by more than one family. I came to a halt before a door, listening and looking very carefully up and down the stairs before I knocked. The door opened about half an inch and the point of a nose might be seen peering round it.

'Is that you, Dagmara?' I asked.

'Monsieur Constantine?' There came the sound of a chain being removed, the door opened, and I slipped in. The door closed quietly behind me.

I was Constantine, Chief of the British Secret Intelligence Service in Soviet Russia.

Dagmara was Aleksandr Grammatikoff's niece and, as such, of course, perfectly well known to me, though I had not seen her since before the outbreak of the war. She was now a dancer at the Arts Theatre and shared a flat in the Cheremeteff Pereulok with two other young actresses, the Miles. Now among the colleagues of these young ladies at the Arts Theatre was Mademoiselle Friede, sister of no less a personage than Colonel Friede, who at that time was Chief of the Bolshevik Staff in Moscow. It became obvious at once of what use Dagmara could be to me and why I wanted an introduction to the charming Mlle Friede.

It was no surprise to me to learn that Mlle Friede and indeed her brother, the Bolshevik Chief of Staff, were not Bolsheviks. Most of Moscow was anti-Communist. The town swarmed with White

Russians. Many of them were in the employment of the Bolshevik authorities. By the granting of extraordinary privileges, particularly in the all important matter of rations, the Bolsheviks were endeavouring to increase their membership. People slipped into the Communist Party very easily. I saw the advisability of becoming a member myself.

My great purpose at present was of course to secure copies of those confidential military documents which passed through the hands of Colonel Friede. And as it happened the Colonel's sister was not only a close friend of the Miles sisters but frequently visited them at their flat in the Cheremeteff Pereulok. These young ladies were entirely on my side, and it was arranged that I should meet Mlle Friede there. The meeting was a great success. When I was sure of Mlle Friede, I unfolded my proposition to her, namely that her brother should secure me copies of all documents which passed through his hands. Mlle Friede greeted the suggestion with joy, and assured me that her brother was only too anxious to be able to strike a blow against Bolshevism.

I had one or two surreptitious meetings with Friede, and when we were each assured of the other's bona fides, he became my most willing collaborator. All communiques from the Archangel front, from the Korniloff front, from the Koltchak front passed through his hands. All army orders, all military plans, all confidential documents relating to the army fell within his province, and many a copy of a highly confidential document he handled was read in England before the original was in the hands of the officer to whom it was addressed.

The house in Cheremeteff Pereulok was a large place, containing no fewer than 200 flats, and some of these were of the largest size. The flat for example, occupied by the Miles sisters, which was on the third floor, was altogether too spacious for the young ladies who occupied it, and rooms of it were let to two sub-tenants, an ex-government official and a professor of music. These interesting young ladies had a regular visitor, whom they knew as Sidney Georgevitch, officially described as Relinsky of the *Cheka-Criminel*.

What more natural than that the young artistes should be visited by a close friend of theirs, Mlle Friede, also of the Arts Theatre? The young ladies were apparently very much attached and the visits were of daily occurrence. Mlle Friede would bring her portfolio with her, and no doubt the young ladies met for the purpose of practising triolets together under the guidance of the music master.

Yes, but portfolios may be made to carry many more things than a pianoforte score. Mlle Friede lived with her brother in a flat not very far away. Every evening he would bring home copies of the Bolshevik despatches and orders. The following morning she brought them round to the Cheremeteff Pereulok, where they were duly handed over to me.

In fact the flat in Cheremeteff Pereulok was my headquarters in Moscow and the Miles sisters, Friede and Dagmara K. were among my most loyal and devoted collaborators.

And thus it was that I was absolutely *au courant* with everything that was happening on all the Bolshevik fronts, and was enabled to get a correct orientation of the political and military position of the regime. Some of these communiqués were in the highest degree humorous and characteristic, as when the young Red General Sabline telegraphed: 'Our *canaille* has ratted again, and we have been obliged to yield Red Hill.'

My own official reports to my superiors in London always took one form. Beneath their national apathy the great mass of the Russian people longed to be delivered from their oppressors. Give Russia a popular government and once more she would show a united front to the Germans. In any case, Bolshevism was a far worse enemy than Germany, a hideous cancer striking at the very root of civilisation.

It was pretty obvious that, if they could only be made to co-operate, the anti-Bolsheviks could seize the reins of power with ease. Numerically they were far superior to their enemies. But they were leaderless. The Russians are useless without a leader. Without a leader they will stand and let themselves be slaughtered like so many sheep. I was positive that the terror could be wiped out in an hour, and that I myself could do it. And why not? A Corsican lieutenant of artillery trod out the embers of the French Revolution. Surely a British espionage agent, with so many factors on his side, could make himself master of Moscow?

Extracted from *Adventures of a British Master Spy: The Memoirs of Sidney Reilly* by Sidney Reilly (first published by Harper & Brothers in 1933 and due to be published by Biteback in 2014)

THE SPY WHO SAVED 10,000 JEWS

HUBERT POLLACK

I first heard the name Frank Foley in 1995. I was working on a book about Britain's spies and interviewed two former MI6 officers who looked after the Service's archives. At the end of our conversation, I asked them if there was anything they wanted to tell me, to bring out into the open.

There was. Two of their former officers deserved to be better known than they were – an unusual suggestion from an organisation as secretive as MI6. One was Sidney Cotton, who appears in the next chapter, the other was Frank Foley, the Service's bureau chief in '30s Berlin, who was still held up to new recruits as a brilliant agent-runner but whose main claim to fame was that he had saved tens of thousands of Jews from the Nazis.

'One of the most interesting things about Foley was that normally to be a good case officer you need to be a bit of a shit,' one of the former MI6 officers said; agent-runners might sometimes have to drop an agent, or put him in a position where he was forced to do something he didn't want to do, or worse. 'But Foley managed to be a brilliant case officer and a near saint. Schindler pales into insignificance alongside his work on getting Jews out of Germany. He was a very able man, who never got the recognition he deserved.'

It seemed unlikely that someone might have saved tens of thousands of Jews and no one knew anything about him, but I set out to find out more about Foley and eventually wrote his biography, collecting first-hand testimony by a number of living witnesses which persuaded *Yad Vashem*, the Israeli Holocaust memorial organisation, to name him as Righteous Among the Nations.

It was well deserved. The cases here would have been relatively routine for Foley. He also went into concentration camps to get Jews out and in the wake of the *Kristallnacht* pogroms of November 1938, when all Jewish men were being taken to concentration camps, he hid four or five in his flat every night, providing them with the documentation they needed to escape, in most cases visas, in some false passports.

This remarkable testimony comes from one of Foley's own agents. Hubert Pollack not only worked for MI6 but also with *Mossad le Aliyah Beth*, the Zionist organisation which smuggled Jews into Palestine.

M Y WORK WAS for the most part secret and brought me into contact with political agents of different sorts. This limits my freedom of writing. I will therefore limit myself to giving a few sketches.

Captain Frank Foley, formerly British Passport Control Officer in Berlin, deserved the gratitude of tens of thousands of Jews whom he saved from Germany. He was one of the few Englishmen in Germany who was never taken in by Nazi trickery, and thus one of the few British officials in Berlin whose mission was a success.

Not all, but the more important British embassies have a section which has the nondescript title of British Passport Control Office. The role of this department is to oversee the granting of visas of entry into British territory for those without British passports. The

British Passport Control Officer (PCO) completely controls who does and does not receive a visa, not the Consulate. An unhappy Consul-General cannot appeal the PCO's decision; not to the ambassador, the Foreign Minister or even to the Prime Minister. He can of course try but no one is in a position to overturn a decision of the British Passport Control Officer or to demand that he must issue a visa.

The Passport Control Office does not have a completely free hand in the granting or refusal of visas. It has to abide by the visa regulations for the United Kingdom, its colonies, protectorates and mandates. These laws are not all the same. Their respective sympathy to immigrants is quite different and their management varies with respect to political developments. But this management is greatly influenced by the way in which a PCO deals with the cases that come in and then forwards them to the responsible central administrations (where their agreement is necessary).

It is probably commonly known that Captain Foley sent an urgent telegram to Mr Eric Mills, the Commissioner for Migration of the Palestine Government, pleading for a number of blank certificates for the most urgent cases, and that Mr Mills complied with this request. It is less well known, that Mr Mills, in confirmation of the receipt of these certificates, received a telegram that simply read: 'God bless you. Foley.'

Thus did this man deal with his 'cases'.

I have been too often in a position where I have had to tell men who effusively thanked me for a life-saving immigration visa to Trinidad, South Rhodesia, India or Great Britain: 'Go to Tiergartenstrasse 17 and thank Captain Foley. You owe him your visa, not me.' Did any of the men take this as seriously as it was meant to be taken? I doubt it. I was for them the Jew, and the 'other guy' was the *Goy*. And that was – very, very regrettably – true.

Our work together rested on the basis of completely reciprocal trust. Of course, I had to earn this trust at first. Before my time at the *Hilfsverein*,[11] when I was a practising independent emigration consultant, I never brought a case before Captain Foley that did not correspond to the appropriate regulations. With me, there were no falsified thousand-pound-accounts[12] or similar tricks. As soon as Captain Foley was clear about that, our co-operation became easy. As I was then entrusted by the *Hilfsverein* with the handling of all of the questions concerning the British Passport position, Wilfred Israel[13] inducted me in this capacity especially with Captain Foley. With that, I was a *persona gratissima*. That forced me, of course, to be particularly careful and thorough in the treatment of my cases, and my connections proved to be useful to me in more than one instance. There were also cases in which I did not deem it advisable to take the responsibility myself. I will recount two of them here, because the manner of their treatment by Captain Foley is characteristic. This is the way in which he treated all similar 'problematic' requests.

Dr H, a gynaecologist from an industrial city in Saxony, was introduced to me as someone who wanted to emigrate to Palestine by his relative, a Berlin Zionist. Everything was in the best order. The taxes were paid, the lift was packed. The currency acceptance was ready to be called up. One thousand pounds was allocated. The only black spot was the criminal record. He had been jailed

---

11   *Hilfsverein der Deutschen Juden*, literally the Assistance Organisation for German Jews, helped Jews to get out of Germany.

12   Anyone emigrating to Palestine had to deposit £1,000 in a bank account to provide sufficient funds for living expenses when they initially arrived there. Ironically, Foley himself frequently found ways around this rule.

13   Wilfred Israel was the owner of one of the largest Berlin department stores and prominent member of the *Hilfsverein*. He was the model for Bernhard Landauer in Christopher Isherwood's *Goodbye to Berlin*.

for carrying out an abortion. A rather hopeless affair. I asked for the details. According to the doctor, who made a good personal impression, it was a biased judgment in order to eliminate a successful Jewish and socialist competitor. I reported to Captain Foley and stated the case to him without any taking any specific position on the case. He listened to everything, looked through the filled-out request papers, and asked me if I had the impression that the man regularly performed abortions as a business practice. When I said no, he asked me to leave the application with him and to get him a copy of the judgment, which I did. When I went to the Passport Office on another matter two days later, Captain Foley asked me into his office: 'This is undoubtedly a clear anti-Semitic motivated judgment without any certain proof. I would like to see your client, but alone.' After a very thorough discussion with Captain Foley, Dr H returned. A few weeks later he went to Palestine. Today, he practises somewhere in that country. In spite of his time in prison for giving an abortion he had no problem obtaining both permission to immigrate and a licence to practise medicine. That was how Captain Foley worked.

The second is a *Hilfsverein* case. *Fräulein* N came to my office direct from prison, having been held for communist activity. She was a lovely, lively girl of about twenty years. Not one of those unbearably hysterical or intellectually warped female 'communists' who could be found in the different youth organisations, including Zionist clubs. The father of her child, who was born in prison, had obtained permission for her to join him in Southern Rhodesia. He had a residence permit and sufficient income to live on. But she still needed a visa. Inquiries to the *Hilfsverein's* Hamburg office, which originated the case, and unofficial inquiries elsewhere confirmed the excellent personal impression. Unfortunately that cost us a couple of days, and there was a Gestapo deadline on emigration. The concentration camp was beckoning.[14] So the papers were completed and sent to Captain Foley along with the letter from the authorities in Southern Rhodesia. But the issuing of a visa is at the discretion of the Passport Control Officer. I brought the papers out and laid them on the table.

'How old is the young lady today?'

'Twenty.'

'She was in prison for two years, therefore she was eighteen when she was sentenced. How do you say it in German? *Jugendeselei* [the folly of youth]. That's what it looks like to me. Or do you believe that the young woman will be active as a communist in Rhodesia?'

'Hardly.'

'Then send her to me. Is the child written down in the passport?'

'Yes.'

'Excellent. Goodbye.'

After a very long discussion with Captain Foley, *Fräulein* N came back to me with a passport with a visa. Twelve hours before the expiration of the Gestapo deadline she departed from Bremen.

The day after she left, at around 1 p.m., my telephone rang at the *Hilfsverein*. Since during office hours all calls from government officials or representatives of other Jewish organisations were passed to me, I was not surprised when my secretary handed me the telephone with the announcement:

'Gestapo.'

'Yes?'

'This is the secret police. Are you personally responsible for the case of N?'

'Yes, sir.'

'Where is the woman?'

---

14 Jews released from jail were normally taken straight to a concentration camp.

'On board Dutch steamship so-and-so somewhere between the Bremen docks and Rotterdam. But if you have to know precisely you should ask the *Grenzpolizei* at the Bremen docks. They will obviously know much far better than I.'

'Departed yesterday from Bremen. The report is of course in front of me. I wanted just to be convinced that everything is in order and see if you were nervous. Heil Hitler.'

We worked under such conditions – and became accustomed to them.

Both of the cases mentioned above contain the 'problematic' elements: a) a prison sentence for something that is also a crime under British law, b) communist activity. Both times a Passport Control Officer of less humane disposition would not have taken the responsibility or risk of granting a visa and would have stuck to the letter of the law and denied the request, leaving the unfortunate applicant to be sent to a concentration camp. Captain Foley took the responsibility. What drove him to that was that nobility of origin, disposition, and education, which makes a man in such a post feel that power was given to him in order to help the helpless: *noblesse oblige*.

People who do not know Captain Foley, or only know him superficially, might think that I am exaggerating or that, from some sort of reasons, I am celebrating him in an unjustified manner. This would be a huge miscalculation. The number of Jews saved from Germany would be smaller by tens of thousands of people – yes, that's right, tens of thousands – if instead of Captain Foley, a 'diligent official' had sat in his position. There is no word of Jewish gratitude to this man that would be exaggerated.

After the November Pogrom of 1938 and the mass arrests, a wild rush on all of the foreign representatives set in. Everyone was hoping for a miracle and a visa. The British Passport Control Officer was so overrun for two days, that the work became impossible. Then Captain Foley created order. He was not only a man who, like all of his personal co-workers, worked often and thoroughly. He could also organise.

The three night commissionaires from the embassy on the Wilhelmstrasse were transferred to Tiergartenstrasse. They organised the visitors in rows of four, queuing from the street, through the front garden, up the staircase and into the waiting room. The commissionaires could not speak German. They were very polite – but also energetic. They wore uniforms decorated with many medals from the previous war and they were '*Goys*'.

As a result, an exemplary order took hold, although the November and December weather was horrible and the anxiety of the visitors very high. For people who had no time to wait, Captain Foley wrote *Laisser-Passer* with his own hand. In this way, we, the representatives of the Jewish organisations, could move quickly and freely.

Captain Foley saw the Nazis not only at official or semi-official luncheons, parties and parades. He often walked or used the tram instead of taking his car to his office, and thus in half an hour saw more of real Nazi-dom than in hours spent at official dinners. From his windows, he could watch the constant growth of the German War Office buildings. Finally, the crowds of both German and Jewish victims of the Third Reich who came to him were most instructive. He knew the Nazis and how to handle them.

One morning when I entered the waiting room of the British Passport Control Office there was a tall, well-dressed, intelligent looking German who presented his passport and an application for a visa to Captain Foley. He spoke fluent English without the least trace of a German accent. Captain Foley looked at the man closely and looked at the passport. Then he took a pencil, put a line through the application, wrote 'Refused' on it and said in German 'Sorry. I am unable to grant you a visa.'

The German, still in English, began to bluster and showed a letter from a well-known English firm, adding that he understood that the British Home Office had granted a permit on his behalf. Capt. Foley replied: 'Yes, I have received the permit. It entitles me to grant you a visa, but it does not bind me to do so.' He declined, in all civility, to give any reason why he would not issue the visa. But as the door of his room closed behind the German, he commented in an undertone. 'We do not want spies in England.'

Then Capt Foley turned to the matter in hand, and forty-eight hours later a young Jew left Sachsenhausen concentration camp for a British colony.

Extracted from *Was nicht in den Archiven steht: Captain Foley, der Mensch, und andere Berichte* by Hubert Pollack (held at the Yad Vashem archives, file reference YVS 01/17) and from a Pollack article titled 'Captain Foley Knew the Nazis' (published in the *Palestine Post*, 29 June 1941)

SIDNEY COTTON: THE MI6 PIONEER OF PHOTO-RECONNAISSANCE

JOHN GODFREY

The Second World War established signals intelligence and air photography as the two most valuable methods of gathering information on enemy military activity. Before the war, the RAF's reluctance to undertake aerial intelligence missions over Europe had led the Air Section of MI6 to create its own photo-reconnaissance organisation. Sidney Cotton, an Australian pilot, carried out a number of missions, some in co-operation with the French, to photograph border areas of Germany and Italian-occupied territory in the Mediterranean and East Africa. The first flight over Germany came in March 1939, when using a Leica camera Cotton photographed Mannheim. During July and August 1939, Cotton flew his Lockheed 12A deep into German territory, under cover as a businessman and amateur pilot, photographing a number of locations of interest to British intelligence, including Berlin and the German naval base at Wilhelmshafen. John Weaver, a member of Cotton's unit, described how shortly before the outbreak of war, Cotton flew to Berlin's Tempelhof airport. 'Goering and his lieutenants were there. Seeing the aircraft, they made enquiries as to whom it belonged. On finding out, they approached Cotton for a flight and asked where he would take them. Cotton said: "I have a dear old aunt who lives in such an area and if you have no objections we could fly over there." It was agreed and off they set. But what they did not know was that dear old Sidney was pressing the tit the whole time, taking photographs.'

Here Admiral Sir John Godfrey, Director of Naval Intelligence (DNI) for the early part of the war, and the man who brought Ian Fleming into the intelligence world, describes Cotton's importance, and the Air Chiefs' pathetic response.

><><><><><><><><><><><><><><><><><><><><><><><><><><><><><><><><><><><><><><><><><

MOST SECRET

NID 003580/41

13.9.41

Employment of Mr Cotton and Development of Aerial Photographic Reconnaissance

COTTON'S CAREER

Cotton served in the RNAS in the last war. He has over 5,000 hours total flying time in over 150 different types, including Blenheim, Spitfires, Lockheed, Douglas, etc. Since the last war he has been employed on civil aviation work and from 1919–24 was engaged on air photographic survey work in Newfoundland and Labrador and later worked on development in air photography for surveying.

He has been connected in his business with development in air survey work and has an almost unrivalled knowledge of the operational problems involved in air photography and a considerable technical knowledge of the latest types of equipment now in use by the RAF and Fleet Air Arm.

DNI first met him in April 1939 when, with the help of the Admiralty, he was provided with a Lockheed aircraft and did excellent service under C, carrying out a number of important air photographic flights over Germany, Sardinia, the Dodecanese, Italian East Africa, the West Irish coast, etc.

Immediately before the war, he was able to obtain valuable information regarding air concentrations near the German coast, and a week before war started he flew ever Wilhelmshaven and obtained the only photographs of this area in those very critical days.

His methods of obtaining photographs from anything between 20,000 and 30,000 feet and so escaping detection was brought to the attention of the Air Staff at C's urging, with a view to his being provided with an aircraft of suitable type for this work.

The Air Staff were not very forthcoming and raised objections to him, but at the same time, they were not themselves able to produce anything which satisfied our reconnaissance needs.

It was not until five months after the war started (in February 1940) that his merits were appreciated by certain of the Air Staff and, with a certain amount of surreptitious assistance from the Admiralty, he was provided with a Spitfire aircraft carrying extra petrol and carried out extremely valuable work on the Western Front.

He gradually, and with much opposition from the Air Staff, managed to expand his activities and formed a small unit based at Heston, with another in France, near Paris. These two units of Spitfires gave most excellent service, those in France being the means of obtaining most valuable intelligence from high-altitude photography at a time when the Blenheim aircraft there were being lost in ever increasing numbers when engaged on photographic work at lower altitudes.

Just prior to the collapse of France he managed, with the assistance of General Joseph Vuillemin (Chief of the French Air Staff) to establish a small unit on the French Mediterranean coast, from where most valuable flights were made over Italian ports, without interference.

Later he continued to expand his unit from Heston, developing the Spitfire aircraft for still greater ranges and improved results of nearly 2,000 miles was obtained, despite the assertions of the Air Ministry technicians that such results were not feasible.

In June 1940, having built up the high-altitude photographic organisation from nothing to a unit of the utmost value to all the services, he was dismissed his post and deprived of his temporary commission as a commander as Wing Commander in the RAFVR. His honorary commission was terminated in March 1941.

Since June 1940, he has worked as a civilian on various propositions connected with improvements in aviation, particularly with a scheme for night bomber interception involving searchlights mounted in aircraft. In this he has collaborated with technicians from the RAF.

He has been employed once again by C's organisation in fitting out ex-Norwegian seaplanes for use in landing agents, etc., from Malta.

In addition, he is interested commercially in the supply of Sidcot heaters to aero engines, in the Sidcot flying suit which he designed and produced and which is now the standard RAF suit, and in various other aircraft accessories.

From the very beginning of the war, Cotton has had an uphill struggle in his efforts to persuade the Air Staff to accept his ideas and to allow him to develop them.

He is very intolerant of routine procedure and the resultant delays and was apt to speak his mind rather too freely in discussion with Senior Air Force officers.

As a result, he was labelled unorthodox and alienated himself with some of the Air Staff. Perhaps the initial mistake was in putting him in charge to develop a new organisation instead of using him in a technical capacity. He has little, if any, executive ability.

The Air Staff opinion of Cotton is that he is a line-shooter, racketeer and salesman, who does not deliver the goods.

A line-shooter he certainly is but he has delivered the goods most loyally as far as we are concerned and has been the driving force in the development of air intelligence from photography. Since he left the unit there has been little, if any, further development on the lines he so successfully started, and we are now no better off for air reconnaissance than we were a year ago.

Our present air photographic reconnaissance is not satisfactory, except for the comparatively short range work covering the invasion ports, Western Baltic and as far south as Gironde.

Beyond these limits, and in the Mediterranean, West Africa, Norway, (north of Trondheim), and in all other parts of the world, it is negligible despite every effort on our part to improve it.

Pressure has been brought to bear through the medium of the Joint Intelligence Committee. Letters have been written. Promises have been made by the Air Staff and not fulfilled. Aircraft allocated for the work have been diverted to other duties. In fact, the Air Staff have shown a lamentable lack of appreciation of the importance of air photographic intelligence.

We are not alone in complaining. The Army Staff are of a parallel opinion. There is no good reason for this neglect.

The Ministry of Aircraft Production (MAP) is constantly blamed for not producing sufficient high-performance aircraft for this work. This Ministry refutes the accusation and says aircraft have been constructed for use for photographic purposes and that the fault lies with the Air Ministry. New types have been promised and reputedly given the highest priority, but somehow or other they do not appear.

Proposals have been put up that the Navy should develop and operate its own air intelligence units, particularly in the Mediterranean theatre, as that is the only way we shall get what we require. These proposals have produced no result so far, although they have been supported by the Operations and Plans Divisions and the Assistant Chiefs of Naval Staff.

I still maintain that we shall eventually have to take over the operation of our own photographic reconnaissance units and that such a man as Cotton would be invaluable to help us to develop it.

He need not, and indeed should not, in my opinion, be given control of any such organisation, but his experience, ideas, and intimate knowledge of all the operational problems involved are unrivalled.

The Air Staff will refuse to allow Cotton to use any RAF facilities if they can, but I challenge the right of anybody to dictate to the Admiralty who it may or may not employ in any capacity. We have always been jealous of our independence as a service and we must keep up that tradition.

In any case, such victimisation (there is no other word to describe it) of an individual who accomplished so much and who is so wholeheartedly intent on doing his utmost in his 'unorthodox' way to help in the defeat of an extremely unorthodox enemy is most unjust.

There is not a scrap of evidence, other than vague charges, none of which are as yet substantiated to support the veto put on him.

It is of interest that despite the complete ban on Cotton which the Air Ministry has imposed and which includes an order that he is not to visit any RAF establishment or aerodrome, he has recently been called in by Bomber Command and Fighter Command, as well as by the air side of C's organisation to help them in various ways.

It appears that he is still to be on call when any troubles arise and expected to give the Air Staff the benefit of his experience and technical ability, although this involves special authority each time for him to visit the necessary station.

During the past few days, he has been called to the Polebrook bomber aerodrome where [US Army Air Force Flying] Fortresses are operated to help with such problem as condensation trails, frosted up windscreens and so on, problems with which his work with high-altitude Spitfires has made him familiar. At Fighter Command HQ recently, he was called in by the Air Operations Commander-in-Chief for consultation in connection with his development, in collaboration with Wing-Commander William Helmore of MAP, of the new 'Turbine' light for night interception work, which is now being extensively fitted, although turned down by the Air Staff some months ago.

J. H. GODFREY
DNI
13.9.41.

Note: Since writing the above, the original letter to support Cotton's statements that he is actively collaborating with Air Commands and MAP in the development of his patents for the fitting of searchlights in aircraft for night interception and in the various other ways mentioned above have been seen by an officer of my staff.

∞∞

The above report by Godfrey is held at the UK National Archives in file ADM 223/464

MI9 AND COLDITZ

M. R. D. FOOT & J. M. LANGLEY

MI9, the organisation which taught Allied aircrew how to evade capture and assisted British prisoners-of-war to escape from German prison camps, was set up in December 1939 under Major Norman Crockatt; initially, it had the twin role of helping British and Allied prisoners or evaders escape from behind enemy lines and of controlling the interrogation of enemy prisoners-of-war. In December 1941, the interrogation of enemy prisoners was split off to become the responsibility of MI19 under Crockatt and from then on MI9, headed by Jimmy Langley, one of the authors of this book, dealt solely with running escape lines for Allied escapers and evaders and collecting intelligence from them, not just when they returned to the UK, but even while they remained in the camps. Some of the most famous, if not always the most successful, escapes were from Colditz.

I N SOME PARTICULARLY escape-minded camps, notably Oflag IVc at Colditz, the tunnellers were able to levy timber from everybody's bed boards. Prisoners slept in rough wooden bunks, containing anything up to ten short crosswise timber planks; it was soon proved that people could sleep quite soundly on three, and the tunnellers took the rest. The original beds at Colditz were metal; replaced in mid-war by the Germans when they discovered that their prisoners were turning inessential parts of their beds into tools.

Peter Allan of the Cameron Highlanders, an excellent German speaker, was smuggled out of the fortress in a *paillasse*, and got clear away from the neighbourhood; his German was indeed good enough for him to accept a lift from an SS officer, who drove him a hundred miles towards Vienna, There Allan's money ran out, and so did his luck. He appealed to the United States consul; but was unable to persuade that cautious diplomat that he was a genuine British escaper, not a Gestapo provocateur fishing for an excuse to close the consulate down. He fell asleep on a park bench, broke down under interrogation from a passing policeman, and was back at Colditz doing his month's solitary a fortnight after he left.

Reid and Barry meanwhile were deep in their second attempt to get out of Colditz by tunnel. On 29/30 May 1941 they, six other British officers – including Colonel German, the Senior British Officer – and four Poles slipped into a tunnel that began in the prisoners' canteen. The Germans had just locked the canteen, with a new type of lock they thought insurmountable. Reid had no trouble dismounting it, and thought moreover he had bribed a sentry near the tunnel's exit: he had paid over 100 Reichsmarks, and another 400 were to follow after he had gone. Unhappily for the escapers, the sentry told his superiors, and they were arrested one by one as they crawled out onto the lawn. The sentry got a fortnight's leave, but the remaining 400 Reichsmarks of MI9's money remained available for other attempts.

Several of the Colditz escapers are justly famous, and the whole camp would have agreed with the opinion of one of them, that 'imprisonment was a spur to new achievement,' and that 'the real escaper is more than a man equipped with compass, maps, papers, disguise and a plan. He has an inner confidence, a serenity of spirit which make him a Pilgrim.' When it was Airey Neave's turn to go to Colditz, after an eastabout escape from Thorn had petered out too soon, he found that 'it was stimulating to live in this hive of industry,' for 'success can only be achieved by a minute mastery of detail and a study of the mind and methods of the enemy.'

Two old Wykehamists, gifted to an unusual degree with that intelligent pertinacity which is one of the schools hallmarks, who were in the same regiment – the King's Royal Rifle Corps – escaped together from Stalag XXd at Posen on 28 May 1941, by hiding successfully in the rubbish dump: two subalterns, Michael Sinclair, 19, and Edward Davies-Scourfield, 22, who got out with their major, Ronnie Littledale, 39. Though the Nazis had annexed western Poland, its Germanisation was still far from complete, and these escapers got a great deal of help from the Poles: one of the joys of escaping in Poland was that the population was so strongly anti-German. They were passed on to Warsaw, where they spent several months in an Englishwoman's flat, frequently being entertained to more or less formal dinners by a succession of hosts, and engaged in incessant discussions about when it would be safe to move on and in what direction. Eventually, in January 1942, they cast up in Sofia, where the Bulgarian police promised them asylum and then promptly sold them to the Gestapo. Littledale and Sinclair escaped again on 17 January, from a train near Vienna; Sinclair was almost at once recaptured, but Littledale was at large for nearly six months more, in Bohemia. They all met again eventually, in Colditz.

In that castle-full of professional escapers, a hard core of escape-minded characters was provided by three-score Dutch colonial officers, cheerful, strong, seasoned men whose military bearing put the British to some shame. As a mild form of goon-baiting, the British tended to straggle onto parade, hatless and dishevelled, while the Dutch were always punctual and immaculate. The two nationalities agreed to pool their resources for escaping. Most of the Dutch spoke fluent German, which few Englishmen there but Michael Sinclair could manage; hence the idea of pairing a Dutch and a British officer for an escape. By 1942, the escape committee was well provided with keys and could gain access to any part of the castle, even the French, even the Poles had agreed to co-ordinate their escape attempts with the rest, and some serious work could begin.

Pat Reid, a captain in the Royal Army Service Corps, was in charge of escape planning from January 1941, and had Airey Neave as his deputy from August. He organised a regular, permanent, twenty-four-hour watch on the enemy, in which all the British prisoners were glad enough to join. This did not only mean that a cry of 'Goons up' heralded every German guard's entrance to the prisoners' courtyard, or to a particular staircase in it; it meant that every sentry's beat, every arc-light's timetable, the entire routine of the garrison were studied as intensely as any young lover ever watched the movements of the beloved: the enemy's methods received such painstaking attention that no chink in his restraining armour could go unspotted.

The Poles took the lead in lock-forcing; the British learned from them fast. Squadron-Leader Brian Paddon became particularly expert. Reid, who was an engineer in civil life, had an eye for how buildings are put together, which led him to discover a disused passageway that ended in an attic over the Germans' guardhouse. This part of the castle included their officers' mess. Through this passage he sent out, on 5 January 1942, Neave and a Dutch officer Tony Luteyn, dressed in home-made German officers' uniforms. Their cardboard leggings would not have looked well after a rainstorm, but they passed after dark. Neave, with Etonian self-assurance, returned the salute of the sentry outside the guardroom door, and they strolled away down a side path towards the married quarters. By the time Reid had finished closing up their exit behind them, his watchers were able to tell him that the getaway had at least started well. In fact, they got clear away; survived a check at Ulm by walking out of a government office by a back door and another at Singen close to the Swiss frontier by bluff; and in little more than forty-eight hours were safely on Swiss soil.

Their absence was covered at the frequent Colditz 'Appels' – roll calls, at which the guards painstakingly counted and recounted an often shifting mob of prisoners – by a couple of Reid's ghosts, officers whom the Germans wrongly believed to have left the camp (two devoted men, Flight-Lieutenant J. W. Best and Lieutenant M. E. Harvey, RN, 'ghosted' in Colditz for eleven months on end. Next night another pair left by the same route: J. Hyde-Thompson of the Durham Light Infantry and another Dutchman, Lieutenant Donkers. They came unstuck at Ulm main line station. The girl ticket clerk, suspicious already of two vaguely odd-looking Dutch electricians who had booked to Singen on the previous evening, jibbed at being asked for tickets to the same station by a similar pair, and called for the station police, to whom the escapers soon confessed their true identity. Reid had not tried to cover up for four: Colditz was already aware. He decided that 'from now on, no more than two escapers at a time would travel the same route,' a sensible precaution.

There was a constant coming and going through those castle gates, officially; and of course all these sorties provided opportunities for prisoners to try unofficial exits as well. Michael Sinclair had bad sinus trouble; the commandant, a stickler for convention, saw that he was sent out for treatment by a specialist in Leipzig. There, on 2 June 1942, Sinclair eluded his escort. Reid had provided him with a forged *Ausweis* (identity card) that enabled him to travel by train, and enough of MI9's money for his fare to France. He turned his tunic inside out and discarded his cap, so with his thorough command of German he could easily pass as a civilian. He had got as far as Cologne before he was detected at an extra strict control of papers, following on an air raid the night before.

Paddon, whom no lock could hold, decided in his own words that 'he travels best who travels alone' when caught with a Polish fellow escaper on Leipzig station, while both were posing as Belgian forced labourers. They had skipped from a military hospital near Dresden, to which they had been sent from Colditz for treatment. On June 1942, he left Colditz officially again, to face a court-martial at Thorn for the crime of insulting a German NCO. Colditz sent one of its sharpest sergeants to keep an eye on him, and he was seen into a cell at Thorn. By morning, the bird had flown. Some RAF sergeants, including a friend of Paddon's, had a route to Stettin ready, his need was greater than theirs, they put him on it and he was in Sweden in a week. Paddon's nickname, 'Never-a-dull-moment' was well earned. He had a force and gaiety of manner that was all but irresistible, except to camp guards, and used it with effect on the crew of the first Swedish ship he found. Not everybody was so fortunate. Flight-Lieutenant H H Vivian for example walked out of Stalag Luft III at Sagan at the end of September 1942 disguised as a medical orderly. He hunted in vain for a ship successively at Danzig, Stettin, Stralsund and Sassnitz. Discouraged, he decided to abandon the attempt to cross the Baltic and to try his luck west-about instead. He had a set of false papers that was invalid outside north Germany, so he destroyed them; went to Berlin by train; and had the bad luck to fall at once into a police control he could not pass with no papers at all.

Another half-successful walk out from Sagan had been made

a few days earlier by Flight-Lieutenant A. van Rood, dressed as a *Hundeführer*, a guard-dog handler. He got right down to the Swiss frontier, but was arrested before he could cross it; re-escaped in Leipzig on the way back; and was almost immediately recaptured. Such walks out were dreamed of at Colditz, but seldom secured. Reid himself escaped thence on 14 October 1942 with Hank Wardle of the Canadian air force, who had long been his closest helper; Ronnie Littledale; and one of Colditz's rare naval officers, Billie Stephens, a survivor of the great raid on St Nazaire. This inter-service and international team climbed out through a barred window – cutting the bars with an MI9 saw – and managed to slip across various brilliantly lighted pathways while sentries' backs were turned. They then succeeded in climbing down the moat, and with infinite difficulty scrambled out through a cellar flue. All four were in Switzerland within a week.

〜〜〜〜〜〜〜〜〜〜〜〜〜〜〜〜〜〜〜〜〜〜〜〜〜〜〜〜〜〜〜〜〜〜

Extracted from *MI9: Escape and Evasion 1939–1945* by M. R. D. Foot & J. M. Langley (first published by Bodley Head in 1979 and republished by Biteback in 2011)

LITTLE CYCLONE:
THE GIRL WHO STARTED
THE COMET LINE

AIREY NEAVE

Andrée de Jongh was a young artist in Brussels when German troops marched into Belgium in May 1941. Her father dubbed her 'the Little Cyclone', because she was so determined to make things happen. Inspired by Edith Cavell, the British nurse shot dead by the Germans during the First World War, the 24-year-old de Jongh nursed wounded Allied troops. She then set up the Comet Line to smuggle trapped soldiers and airmen through France and across the Pyrenees into Spain. When the first group never arrived, the 'Little Cyclone' did the job herself. She turned up at the British consulate in Bilbao in August 1941 with two Scottish soldiers and insisted she could bring many more. MI6 was convinced she was a German spy. But the 'Little Cyclone' got her way and the escape line she created smuggled more than five hundred Allied servicemen to safety. Such heroism came at an enormous cost. One hundred and fifty-six members of the Comet Line died, the majority of them in Nazi concentration camps. This passage covers a period following a number of arrests, including those of de Jongh and her father Frédéric. By now, the line had been taken over by Elvire de Greef (Tante Go).

<hr />

OR TANTE GO, too, these were sad days. The Line recovered fitfully after Franco's arrest. She fretted in the villa at Anglet. There seemed little left but memories. She was the doyenne of the Line. Only she was left of those historic personalities from France and Belgium who had so much helped the Allied cause. She had delighted in her work of commanding the troops of the South. She was still young-looking, forceful and clever. But, as she mused in the villa on winter nights, her world seemed to have changed. She was filled with frustration and annoyance. Her green eyes expressed impatience. What was everyone waiting for? Everywhere Occupied Europe waited tensely for signs from over the Channel.

On 28 March 1944 came poignant news for the watchers at Anglet. Frédéric de Jongh, alias Paul, the frail and gentle schoolmaster, was led from his cell at Fresnes to Mont-Valérien. He understood his own impractical, scholarly nature. He had been ill-equipped to follow the dynamic Dédée.[15] But he loved her. He had no regrets. He was proud to have stayed the course. Before he died he was received into the Church.

In his last hours he asked to be with Robert Aylé and Aimable Fouquerel, the masseur of the Rue Oudinot. They sat at the same table and wrote their final letters. And then, on a fine morning at dawn, before Paris had gone to work or children were ready for school, the Belgian and the two Frenchmen died together, smiling.

Paul had been his daughter's most faithful servant. He was a martyr of the Line. And every year, on 28 March, the children of the

<hr />

15   His nickname for Andrée de Jongh, adopted by the Line as her codename.

Ecole Frédéric de Jongh in Brussels place flowers on his memorial and sing La Brabançonne.

Tante Go had little time for grief at her countryman's death. Already the fleets of the Allied Air Force swept across the skies to France in preparation for the great landing. Though it was the dawn of their liberation, Tante Go and her family worked on. The Line resumed, and parties of airmen, led by Florentino, went to Spain, but the savage bombing of road and rail communications made it unsafe to bring more than a few from Paris. It was not worth the risk. Orders came from London to concentrate the men in groups in Belgium and Central France.

By the Sherwood plan, the airmen were gathered from their hiding-places by the few remaining helpers and grouped in forests. Over a hundred hid in the forest of Fretteval near Châteaudun, and as many camped out in the thick woods of the Ardennes. There they stayed, in their 'camps', until their liberation in August and September, 1944. They were supplied with food and clothing by parachute or by audacious black marketeering. Their morale was sustained by the stirring news of the Allied advance brought by agents dropped to them. As a result of this skilful operation, hardly a man was lost when the Allies finally broke through and rescued them. It was a fit ending to the great Comet Line.

Tante Go heard the furious bombing by day and night as she continued to keep contact with her organisation. The escape line was virtually at an end, but a few parties still went over the Pyrenees at the very moment of invasion. Then came the great battle of Normandy.

Tante Go was irrepressible. She had already sent Janine across the mountains for safety, but she and Monsieur de Greef continued their underground exploits to the very last. When there were no airmen, they took to espionage. Three times she crossed the familiar frontier, in person, carrying secret details of German dispositions. The British begged her not to return. She had been very gallant, they said. Why risk all when the war was nearly over? But Tante Go would have none of it. She would see the beginning and the end of this immortal story. And in those last days there was a fantastic incident in the best tradition of the Line.

Florentino had climbed unceasingly to and fro for three years from St Jean de Luz to the lowlands on the Spanish side. He had helped to bring through over two hundred airmen to safety. After the landing in Normandy, he still marched nimbly over the frontier, crossing the Bidassoa, and skirting the Trois Couronnes until he could see the Spanish coast. It was a month after D-Day that he made his last passage, taking with him, instead of airmen, minute pieces of paper, messages for Allied Intelligence. After delivering them, he set off as usual on return to France.

At three o'clock in the morning, Florentino had crossed the Bidassoa and was descending to Urrugne. Suddenly in the night there was the rapid fire of an automatic weapon. He fell, with one leg shattered and bleeding. He felt a furious pain, but, alert as ever, he took from his tunic the secret papers which he was carrying and slipped them beneath a boulder. Then, despite the agony of his leg, he began to roll over and over in the darkness down a slope. The shouts of Germans came nearer. In the end they found him. They stood over him asking questions.

He did not reply. He bore his pain in silence as, with difficulty, they carried him to a frontier post. From there he was taken by car to the Police Headquarters at Hendaye. He was lifted clumsily from the car and laid on the floor of the office.

'Name?'

Florentino lay with his eyes closed. There was no answer. They asked him in French and Spanish and in the Basque language through interpreters. Not a word would he speak. After scratching their heads, the Germans dispatched him to the civilian hospital at Bayonne. One of his legs was hideously fractured, the bone broken in a hundred pieces.

The news reached Tante Go. She was mad for action, and responded with her old fire. Within twenty-four hours she had, through numerous contacts and friends, acquired full details of the incident. She knew where Florentino was lying in the hospital. She knew the ward and the number of his bed.

Beside Florentino lay a young Frenchman injured in a recent bombardment. When Tante Go had discovered his name, she planned to visit him, bringing him a parcel of cakes and fruit. One morning she boldly entered the ward, walked to the young man's bed, and stood beside him.

Florentino did not move. He gave no sign of recognition. For half an hour Tante Go sat beside him talking to the young man, who was delighted with his visitor. Then, as she rose to go, she dropped her handbag. As she bent down between the beds to pick it up, she whispered in Spanish:

'Two o'clock.'

Still Florentino did not move. He lay there like a man in a dream. He had spoken little, even to the nuns who tended his wound. He was determined to give no information to anyone.

At two o'clock there was noise and commotion at the far end of his ward. Loud voices in German frightened the patients. Three stern-looking men stood arguing with the Sisters of Mercy.

'He cannot be moved. It would be dangerous!' cried the nuns.

The men brushed aside these protests. One of them waved a paper. The others rudely pushed past the nuns. Their hats still remained firmly on their heads, as was the custom of the Gestapo. They marched up to Florentino's bed and informed him in German, of which he understood not a word, that he was to be transferred to another hospital.

Florentino remained impassive, his big, gnarled hands resting on the sheets. His lined, weatherbeaten face was without expression. A stretcher was brought, and with much ado he was hastily lifted on to it. The men carried him from the ward. The voices of the Sisters of Mercy had risen in anger:

'You brutes!' screamed one of them, sobbing.

As they carried Florentino from the entrance to a waiting ambulance, the whole staff of the hospital gathered at the door. There were cries of:

'Barbarians!'

'So that is how you treat wounded! You wait till the Allies get here!'

'Have you no mercy on this poor man?'

The Gestapo was in a hurry, and handled the stretcher roughly, to shouts of:

'Los! Los! Schnell!'

Their behaviour, even for the Gestapo, was brutal and outrageous. The faces of all three bore an unpleasant sneer. Their hair was cropped. Their eyes stared fiercely.

Their sinister appearance seemed not to affect Florentino. He was bundled into the ambulance like a sack of flour. He must have suffered agony, but he said not a word. After a last display of bad manners and guttural shouting, the ambulance drew out of the courtyard of the hospital and disappeared. The tearful group of nuns wrung their hands as they stood on the steps. The taciturn, brown-skinned Florentino had been their favourite.

Despite the jolting of the ambulance as it sped along the road to Anglet, Florentino was grinning broadly. The Gestapo had now removed their hats, and shook each other by the hand. They offered

Florentino a welcome glass of cognac, which he drained immediately. They no longer spoke German, and the scowl had disappeared from their faces. Florentino had easily recognised their leader. It was the gallant *l'Oncle*, the husband of Tante Go, and two of his friends.

As a result of his position as interpreter in the *Mairie* at Anglet, Monsieur de Greef had concocted and forged an order from the Gestapo for the transfer of Florentino from Bayonne to Biarritz. Armed with these documents, he had requisitioned one of the municipal ambulances of Bayonne.

The rescue of Florentino took only twenty minutes. Within the same period of time he was safely hidden in a house on the outskirts of the village of Anglet. It was here that in a few weeks he was liberated by the Allies he had served so well.

<hr />

Extracted from *Little Cyclone: The Girl Who Started The Comet Line* by Airey Neave (published by Biteback in 2013)

A POLISH SPY
IN ALGIERS

MIECZYSLAW ZYGFRYD
SLOWIKOWSKI

Polish intelligence provided MI6 with a large number of agents and copious intelligence during the Second World War. The intelligence from the
Poles, which included material from Germany, France and Poland itself led
to no fewer than 22,000 MI6 reports, including the bulk of the intelligence
on the development of the V1 and V2 'flying bombs' at Peenemünde as
well as details of German aircraft, tank and submarine development. The
relationship with the Poles was handled by Wilfred 'Biffy' Dunderdale, the
former MI1c bureau chief in Paris who was known to the Poles as 'Wilski'.

Mieczyslaw Zygfryd Slowikowski (codename Rygor) was one of the most
productive Polish intelligence officers. He first went to France where he
set up the Interallié agent network which produced exceptional reporting
on German armed forces in both France and Belgium. In mid-1941, he was
sent to Algiers where he set up Agency Africa, a network of agents which
provided the bulk of the Allied intelligence for Torch, the Allied invasion of
North Africa. Working undercover as the owner of a porridge factory, he

built up an extensive network stretching from Tunis to Dakar, which in a remarkably short space of time penetrated all of the targets Slowikowski had been given. On the eve of the Allied landings, there was not a single division, fort, coastal battery or airport which had not been reported on in detail.

He passed the intelligence back to London and also on to the Americans via Robert Murphy, the American representative in North Africa, whose consuls were wrongly credited after the war with providing the intelligence which in fact came from Slowikowski's agents.

This passage sees him going to London after the successful Torch landings where he discovers that his bosses in Polish intelligence have no interest whatsoever in his work and were merely a post-box for Dunderdale and MI6 which valued it extremely highly. He was appointed OBE and settled in Britain after the war.

I HAD ARRIVED later than usual at the Rubens Hotel.[16] Major Jan Zychon (codename JANIO) said that the British wanted to have a chat with me. I should report immediately to Commander Wilfred Dunderdale (WILSKI), British Intelligence's chief liaison officer with our section, who awaited me in his office. One of our young officers took me there. Turning left at the hotel exit, it was only a few minutes' walk along Buckingham Palace Road.

Commander Dunderdale received me at once and ordered an officer to assemble all his personnel. Meanwhile, in perfect Russian, he expressed his pleasure at being able to meet me in person. Praising my work highly, he said that the head of the British Secret Intelligence Service was recommending me to the War Office for a high British decoration.

After a while the room began to fill up with army and naval officers,

---

16   Wartime headquarters of Polish intelligence.

who, presumably, were in some way involved with the activities of Agency Africa and in the preparation of Operation Torch. Commander Dunderdale said, 'Gentlemen! I am privileged to introduce Mr Rygor whose work is very familiar to you' (followed by applause). He then introduced the officers individually. His welcome made me speechless, especially after my lukewarm reception at the Rubens. After a short while the officers left and I was alone with their chief.

Dunderdale said: 'Sir, you were brought to London at the insistence of General Menzies, the head of the British secret service,[17] who wishes to have your report on the internal situation in French North Africa. Our officers there lack your experience in these matters, and most of their estimates are obviously second-hand.'

He expressed his confidence in my judgement and added that the General would like to have my appreciation of the situation there. This would be used in his next report to the Prime Minister, who needed it prior to his conference with President Roosevelt, to take place somewhere this month, and which would include a discussion of the North African problem. As time was short, we should get down to work. He called his secretary who took down in shorthand his English translation of my verbal report in Russian. It encompassed, among other questions:

1. A general outline of internal politics in French North Africa prior to the Allied landings on 8 November 1942.

2. The development of the internal political situation after the landings and the role played by Darlan[18] and other French leaders.

---

17   Stewart Menzies took over as C in November 1939. He retired in 1953.

18   Admiral François Darlan, commander-in-chief of the French Navy before the war. He joined the Vichy government, serving briefly as Prime Minister. Darlan was in Algiers when the Allies invaded in November 1942 and ordered French troops to cease resistance. But many Frenchmen still regarded him as a traitor and, on 24 December 1942, he was assassinated.

3. The orientation and actions of political parties and movements, i.e. 'La Resistance' and 'Combat'.

4. The background to Darlan's assassination on 24 December 1942, and an account of the French royalist party.

I also answered Dunderdale's questions concerning various French personalities. Finally, my own opinion was expressed and the names of several prominent Frenchmen suggested for influential positions. I emphasized that this should be treated as an interim period until power in French North Africa was turned over to the Free French under de Gaulle's undisputed leadership. My report was derived from the information collected by our Agency and represented a cross-section of opinion.

Our conversation was interrupted by a telephone call from General Menzies, inquiring whether the report was ready. Dunderdale assured him that it would be ready in less than half an hour and that, in his opinion, it was interesting, penetrating and clear-sighted.

A short while later our prolonged chat ended. The verbal report was ready. Dunderdale asked me to prepare a written memorandum on our conversation as soon as possible. I knew that he was pressed for time: nevertheless he did not want our meeting to terminate abruptly. He promised to show me, in the near future, the huge map of North Africa hanging at the War Office with all my Intelligence information marked on it from which Operation Torch was planned. This inevitably reminded me of Colonel Solborg's description of his own visit there. Dunderdale escorted me to the door. Shaking my hand, he added, 'I'm sorry that you are not British – for what you have done for Britain, you wouldn't have to work again for the rest of your life!'

I left in a daze. The contrast between the importance attached to our work by the British and the sheer indifference shown by our General Staff was staggering. Quite obviously Central Office had nothing to do with the decision to bring me to London. It was the British, and not the Poles, who were interested in someone capable of helping prepare Churchill's meeting with Roosevelt. It proved that Central Office was only acting as translators and postmen for Agency Africa's messages, which went to General Menzies, and they had not even bothered to analyse my reports. Ironically, although the Poles were instrumental in bringing about Torch, they knew nothing about its planning whatsoever!

The implications of Commander Dunderdale's remarks were sinking in. I had never thought of myself as a British agent but had fondly imagined that I was working for the Polish General Staff. JANIO would have some explaining to do. Preoccupied with my thoughts, I missed the hotel and found myself outside a small cinema. Distracted, I entered, unaware that it showed mainly newsreels, and those from the Eastern Front. The audience were enthusiastically applauding the shots of 'Uncle Joe'. I left, in an even more confused state, and returned to my hotel room to brood in solitude.

I had more than sufficient time at my disposal to grill JANIO for an explanation of our relationship with our British hosts. While he skilfully wove his way round the questions, I pinned him down on my secret report detailing my discussions with Colonel Solborg.[19] He had read it but had, at the time, dismissed it as 'an unauthorized venture into grand strategy'. He admitted that Operation Torch had developed in an identical way and that he had been wrong to destroy it. He added: 'The Polish General Staff are not interested in the existence of Agency Africa. It neither occupies itself with operational matters nor has it been advised on them by the Anglo-American Joint Chiefs of Staffs. Furthermore, it hasn't asked about them.'

---

19   Colonel Robert A. Solborg, representative of the US intelligence chief General William Donovan, head of the Office of Strategic Services, forerunner of the CIA.

This was a clear and unambiguous reply; everything had been answered; only the British and the Americans were interested in my work. Our Foreign Office were not much better either. Despite my continual memoranda, they had no conception of the political situation in Algiers. As late as April 1943, we received a message from Count Raczynski's office stating: 'Do not link yourselves with de Gaulle. The Commander-in-Chief backs General Giraud'.

My visit to London was very disillusioning. At least the witch-hunt for those responsible for the Polish debacle in 1939 had been abandoned. Possibly this was due to the realisation that the French had suffered an even greater defeat. In the event, thousands of files, collected with such fervour in our Paris days, now lay, thankfully, forgotten.

I felt uneasy and began keeping to my hotel room. My protracted stay was unexpected, I was sick of doing nothing, especially as it seemed that my mission was accomplished. I missed the excitement and the nervous tension. I longed to return to the African sun, to my friends, to the service and, above all, to my family. The delay was blamed on obtaining permission from General Giraud. The French were now in the saddle and apparently had no further need for the Poles in North Africa. The new 'official' agency would take much longer to form that the secret one!

One good thing, however, was my growing friendship with JANIO. He appeared to be alone. Possibly he had a wife somewhere in Poland but he did not tell me and I did not ask. His solitude reminded me of Maciej Ciezki, but his lack of friends amongst the Rubens staff remained a mystery. Gradually a picture of him emerged.

JANIO never refused anyone a favour. Typically, he once told me, 'Any person may become useful one day – you never know who and when!' Coming from Polish peasant stock, he was as cunning as he was shrewd. Well educated, he had fought for Poland's freedom since his youth. Somehow he had become entangled in intelligence and, quite instinctively, became one of its best proponents.

Before the war he had run an agency on North and Central Germany from the Polish town of Bydgoszcz and his achievements were extraordinary. The separation of East Prussia from the rest of Germany forced the Germans to come to an agreement by which they could send passenger and freight trains through the Polish Corridor. JANIO's men had come to a financial arrangement with some Germans whereby a Polish expert was 'allowed' on to their train at the first station in Polish territory. He opened certain letters, and even shipments of *Wehrmacht* weaponry, photographed them, then left at the last stop before the border crossing. These operations provided much valuable information.

After the Polish defeat in 1939, JANIO made his way to France where he obtained valuable information on the German navy from his pre-war agents whom he had planted in various *Kriegsmarine* garrisons and naval bases on the Baltic and the North Sea. With the fall of France, he came to Britain where the Polish Army was being rebuilt under British auspices. The British soon remembered that he was responsible for their information on German battleships and were eager to co-operate with him again.

JANIO confided to me that he was in trouble. He was receiving anonymous letters containing threats and slanderous accusations concerning his alleged pro-German sympathies and even allegations of treason. He was duly interviewed by the Military Prosecutor and cleared of any suspicion. The two letter-writers, former intelligence officers who had been removed from their posts at the Rubens, were exposed, arrested and sentenced to a term of confinement. Later,

JANIO, not wishing the gossip to continue, asked to be relieved of his duties and to be sent to the Front. He was killed at Monte Cassino in 1944.

∞∞

Extracted from *Codename Rygor: The Spy Behind the Allied Victory in North Africa* by Mieczyslaw Zygfryd Slowikowski (first published by Windrush Press in 1988 and republished by Biteback in 2010)

THEY FOUGHT ALONE

MAURICE BUCKMASTER

The role played during the Second World War by the guerrilla forces[20] of the French Resistance and by the British Special Operations Executive (SOE) officers and agents who worked alongside them is widely understood. But their critical role ahead of D-Day is only rarely recognised and is certainly far less known. There were a number of Allied special operations forces on the ground in France, of which those run by F Section of SOE were by far the most numerous. It ran more than eighty 'Circuits' or groups of resistance fighters, each with an organiser sent in from the F Section headquarters in Baker St, London, based just a few yards from the supposed home of fictional detective Sherlock Holmes.

The head of F Section was Maurice Buckmaster, who was thirty-seven at the start of the war and had been a teacher, a merchant banker, the head of the French office of the Ford Motor Company and then head of its European operations. He was fluent in French and after being commissioned into the Intelligence Corps he was appointed head of F Section.

In recent years, it has become fashionable to blame Maurice Buckmaster

---

20 There were two main French sections in SOE: the Gaullist Free French 'R/F Section' and 'F Section', which dealt with non-Gaullist resistance groups, including the communist Maquis.

for the deaths of SOE agents who were killed as a direct result of German infiltration of F Section's 'Circuits'. There is no doubt that F Section suffered substantial losses and that a relatively small number of its 'Circuits' (eight out of a total of eighty-six) were dismantled and turned back against the British under German control. Buckmaster cannot entirely escape blame for that, although he was certainly not solely responsible. But the losses need to be kept in perspective. F Section had at least 425 agents in France of whom 104 died, with only around twenty dying as a direct result of the German penetration of the eight 'Circuits'.

Those sent in from England were told before they went in that their life expectancy, in a country where Nazi surveillance was far more intense than it was in any other country in occupied Europe, was just six weeks. In such circumstances, it would have been odd indeed if the Germans had not managed to track down some of the SOE agents.

The original revelations of the German successes, made in the late '50s, led to the commissioning of an official history of SOE in France authored by Professor M. R. D. Foot and it is worth quoting his conclusions: 'Not only did F Section staff do all for the best; they did all that could be reasonably expected of them, given whom they were up against. There was far too much going on at once for every Circuit to get the minute care it deserved.'

It has been argued that Buckmaster failed to pick up telltale signs from the radio communications with his agents that they had been captured. The omission of important security groups which ought to have been seen as signs that the agents had been captured and were being played back against the British were missed. Certainly they were, but not by Buckmaster. Spotting those issues was not his job. The more pertinent criticism is that when told of such problems by Leo Marks, the head of SOE coding, he ignored them. While there is substance to such claims, it is clear from Marks's admirably honest From Silk to Cyanide that the reality is more nuanced than it might at first seem.

It is true that Buckmaster was sometimes reluctant to accept that an agent had been blown, but not always without justification. Even the best agents occasionally failed to send security checks or sent the wrong ones. It is clear from the Marks account that Buckmaster's failing was more a reluctance to give up on his agents and in the case of at least two of the better known casualties, Gilbert Norman and Noor Inyat Khan, Buckmaster insisted on continuing to communicate with them in the hope it would keep them alive.

Notwithstanding the failures, there were fifty active Circuits, all under the control of London, in place when it really mattered ahead of D-Day when they mounted a coordinated campaign of sabotage of railways, bridges, and German supply and ammunition dumps. They also destroyed telephone exchanges, an important element which ensured that German communications had to be sent by wireless transmissions that could be intercepted by the British and the messages deciphered at Bletchley Park. The work of the communist Maquis in mounting guerrilla attacks on German troops, delaying their arrival in Normandy and thereby enabling the Allies to establish a vital bridgehead, has never been properly recognised, not even in France. None of these operations would have been possible on such a scale without Buckmaster.

∞∞

THE BOTTOM OF the rowing boat grated on the deserted beach. Harry Morgan narrowed his eyes as he inspected the line of dunes for signs of the *Milice* or other unwanted visitors; there was no one. He gave the boatman a wave and vaulted, case in hand, onto the soft sand. At once he drew his revolver from his pocket and strolled warily up the beach. If the captain was to be relied on, he should be a mile or two from the town of St Tropez on the Côte d'Azur. At this time, October 1941, this coastline was still unmolested by the Germans and Harry expected a trouble-free trip. It was now three in the morning. He passed through the cactus-infested dunes on to the harsh gravel of the foreshore. Within a few minutes he could see the outlines of a farmhouse; he decided not to approach it to avoid the howling of dogs which he particularly feared. Instead he cut up through a pine grove and soon found himself a pine-board hut where the cork-cutters kept their tools. He lay down there to rest for a couple of hours, not wanting to enter the town at so conspicuous an hour.

Bearing in mind my instructions to find out what had happened in Marseilles, Harry decided to make his way straight to that city. Later that day he was sitting comfortably in a second class compartment as the train bore him along the rugged Provencal coastline.

'*Vos papiers, Monsieur.*' A member of the *Milice* stood in the door of the compartment.

Harry handed up his papers.

'Where are you going?'

'To Marseilles.'

'For what purpose?'

'Business.'

The policeman handed back his papers. '*Bien, Monsieur.*'

Upon reaching Marseilles, Harry decided to go carefully. He took a room in a commercial hotel in the business district under his cover name of Monsieur Nulli, wine salesman. Casual travellers were, of course, quite unremarkable in so busy a port as Marseilles and a feeling of security soon reassured Harry. He spent a certain amount of time loitering around the *Tabacs* and bars of the old quarter which had added to its reputation for toughness another for defiance. Already its narrow and ill-smelling streets hid many refugees on the run from the Nazis in the occupied zone and it was a brave member of the *Milice* who dared to venture into the quarter alone. Occasionally an over-zealous *sous-officier* attempted some kind of a search, but a pail of slops might inadvertently be tipped over him or a wardrobe slide unaided down a steep staircase at him. The *Vieux Port* remained strictly Free French. Eventually, exasperated by its continued resistance, the Germans were to blow it up, but that was not yet.

Nagged by a small pain in his side which he discounted as mere nerves, Harry began cautiously to question various contacts – the small lawyer whose practice was in the poorer quarter, the railwaymen who worked the shunting service along the quays and similar trustworthy people – about their willingness to participate in a clandestine ring; this ring was later led by a group who took the corporate name of the Palestine Express by virtue of their common Jewish origin. They did valuable work and remained undiscovered till after the liberation. Harry was somewhat surprised that those whom he approached were at first very suspicious of him and when he was able to win their confidence he asked them what made them so apprehensive. They answered, cryptically, 'Rumours'.

The house where our wireless operator was supposed to be working was at number twelve bis Rue de la Colline Noire. Harry scouted round the area, largely at night, taking drinks in the tiny *bistros* of the quarter and keeping his ears open. He had to exercise the greatest tact in his inquiries, for he knew that if anyone suspected him of being a police spy – whether counter-espionage or routine detective – the people of the *Vieux Port* would give him short shrift.

Soon it became clear that he would have to abandon his circumspect approach and make boldly for the wireless operator's den. If he had been blown, there was nothing for it: Harry would have to take his chance that the *Milice* had abandoned their watch on the house.

The Rue de la Colline Noire was a dark alley between cliffs of black houses, the entrances to which were up narrow stairs beside the shops forming the ground floor. Prostitutes hung about the doorways and seamen of many nations and origins moved silently up the street. The pain in his side was really worrying Harry now and he pressed his hand to it as he pushed through the knot of whores at the door of number twelve, ignoring the cries of 'Hallo, cheri,' which greeted him. A very fat woman a-jangle with cheap jewellery met him on the first landing.

'*Bonsoir, monsieur,*' she said in an inquisitive tone.

'*Je viens de la part de Monsieur Gaston,*' Harry said.

The woman looked sharply up the dark stairs which led to the second floor.

'Send him up,' a voice said.

Suspiciously, the woman removed her body and allowed Harry to pass. He hesitated, somehow alarmed by the tempo of the words which had just been spoken, and then went up the stairs. He looked back over his shoulder and saw that the fat woman had resumed her massive station barring the way down.

In the shadows on the top floor was a man. Harry had left his revolver with the lawyer, who had put it in his strong box. Once the danger of the actual landing was completed an agent might well find his revolver an embarrassment, since the times when, engaged on jobs of this kind, he would have to fight his way out, were outnumbered by those when he might be searched. A revolver would, of course, betray him when otherwise he could expect to bluff his way out.

The man in the shadows said: '*Tu viens de la part de Gaston?*'

'Yes.'

'Come in, please.'

Harry went past the man through the door into the attic. It was in darkness.

'I'll turn on the light,' the man behind him said, clicking the switch.

Three members of the *Milice* with drawn machine pistols faced Harry across the narrow attic.

He was quickly handcuffed. He had the presence of mind to protest most vigorously at this treatment.

'I will call my lawyer,' he shouted. 'I'll have the law on you. You won't get away with this.'

'We are the law,' said the chief of the *Milice*. 'Take him down.'

As Harry was led away through the streets of the *Vieux Port*, there were boos and catcalls from the inhabitants. '*Sa-lauds! Sa-lauds! Sa-lauds!*' they chanted at the *Milice*.

Harry was driven in a Black Maria to the police headquarters.

'Now then, Monsieur Nulli, what were you doing in that house?'

'I refuse to answer any questions until I have spoken to my lawyer.'

'There will be time for that,' sighed the detective.

'I am a sick man. I need a doctor. My friend Gaston told me I could find one in the Rue de la Colline Noire – suddenly I am arrested. Should a man be arrested for being ill? I will write to the Marshal himself about this. It is an outrage. Have you the Marshal's permission to detain me?'

'We do not need…'

'I demand to see my lawyer. I am a sick man. I need a doctor.'

'We will telephone…'

'I am losing my faith in the Republic…'

'What did you want in the Rue de la Colline Noire?'

'A doctor. I am a…'

'You are a sick man, we understand that,' the detective shouted. 'How are you sick? What is wrong with you?'

Suddenly Harry remembered the pain in his side; at once a twinge went through him.

'Here,' he said, 'feel this.'

The detective apprehensively placed his hand on Harry's side.

'Can you feel it? The palpitation. It's terrible.'

By this time, Harry had everyone in the police station rushing about, phoning the lawyer in the *Vieux Port* and trying to get hold of a doctor. Nevertheless, in spite of having somewhat distracted the interest of his captors, Harry knew that sooner or later they would begin to interrogate him in earnest; the quicker he could get away from them the better. For the moment, however, no opportunity presented itself. At this time Vichy had a number of plainclothes Gestapo men working for them; Harry knew he must clear out before he was handed over to them.

The 'palpitation' seemed to have impressed the detective, for within half an hour a doctor was shown into the cell where Harry had been locked. He examined Harry and a frown came over his face when Harry explained about the pain in his side.

'We must get you to hospital at once,' was the verdict.

'That is impossible,' said the detective. 'This man is a terrorist.'

'He must go to hospital. I will phone about a bed. He must be operated on at once.'

'I refuse to allow him to go to hospital in Marseilles,' persisted the detective. 'He has friends here. He might walk out of the hospital.'

'My dear sir,' replied the doctor, 'if this man walked out of hospital he would not get very far. He has appendicitis.'

Harry listened to this diagnosis with considerable trepidation; he seemed unwittingly to have brought more on himself than he had bargained for. Within an hour he was in an ambulance with the detective and the doctor on the way to Aix-en-Provence. The doctor told him that the hospital there was excellent. Harry lay on the stretcher in the ambulance and closed his eyes, thinking; he knew that Aix also contained the headquarters of the *Milice* for the district. The people in Marseilles had told him of men being taken to Aix for questioning. They arrived in Aix at four in the morning. Harry was put to bed in a private room with a guard on the door.

'We'll soon have you right,' the doctor assured him. 'We'll have that appendix out in no time.'

At eight they came for him. He was put on a trolley and wheeled down the corridor to a waiting room outside the operating theatre. He was wearing pyjamas with his mackintosh over them instead of a dressing gown. The guard had been refused entry to the operating theatre.

'Do you think he will walk away in the middle of the operation?' the doctor snapped indignantly.

When the trolley had halted, the doctor and the surgeon went into the vestibule for a short consultation. Harry could see them talking through a round observation hole, their backs to him. He was alone. He knew it was now or never; once he had been operated upon he would have to lie powerless while the *Milice* checked his papers and found them to be forged. He might well go straight from his convalescence to his death. Silently he swung his legs to the ground and slipped out of the room. He could not go back the way they had come for fear of the guard, so he took a passage which ran at right angles to it. He must find some clothes. Now he had a stroke of luck – searching with frenzied calm for signs of discarded clothing, he saw through an open door a room which the painters used to keep their overalls and equipment. Within seconds he had slipped on a paint-stained overall and paint-drenched espadrilles, snatched up a pot and a ladder and hurried on his way. So far there was no outcry, but it must come any second. He realised that the front door would be alerted. He must find the back stairs.

'Stop him! Stop the assassin!'

There it was. Harry heard running footsteps behind him. The passage along which he was walking seemed endless. He turned and began to walk back towards his pursuers. Not recognising him, the detective and the doctor and the guard and a nurse came tearing past towards the front stairs. He made room for them to pass and proceeded to the service stairs. A few seconds later, still with his ladder and his pot of paint, he walked out of the hospital into the streets of Aix. Stabs of pain bit into his side as he boarded a tram for the suburbs of the town.

Finally he managed to get aboard a train for Narbonne, through the agencies of a railway employee who smuggled him into the engine's fuse box. Throughout the history of the Resistance the railwaymen were, almost one hundred per cent, the keenest and most resolute resisters. Their strong sense of comradeship and their fierce independence were alike unquenchable. At Narbonne, Harry's railwayman put him in contact with a dentist who was already involved in an escape-route, and from there he was taken down to the foothills of the Pyrenees. In mid-December, in the company of a Pyrenean guide and still suffering the agonising pains of appendicitis, Harry Morgan walked over the Pyrenees into Spain.

Extracted from *They Fought Alone: The True Story of SOE's Agents in Wartime France* by Maurice Buckmaster (first published by Odhams in 1958 and republished by Biteback in 2014)

A BRITISH SECRET AGENT WITH THE RESISTANCE

RICHARD HESLOP

Richard Heslop's brilliant account of the work of an SOE officer controlling resistance operations in German-occupied France is one of the
most stirring special operations memoirs ever written. Beginning with
this exhilarating opening featuring what was clearly one of the most trau-
matic moments of Heslop's life, the pace never slackens. Xavier, the title
of the book, was Heslop's fieldname on the ground in France. He was one
of Buckmaster's men, codenamed Marksman and the leader of the SOE
Circuit of the same name which operated in the area between Lyon and
the Swiss border, but his false documents listed him as René Garrat, and
under that name he worked in a French factory by day while leading or
plotting the attacks on the Germans by night.

THE JOB WHICH led to my most disturbing incident as a British agent started quite simply when I met one of the many dozens of resistance men I had worked with in the Angers area. I saw him in a bar, and as we sat over a coffee one morning in mid-1943, he told me that he could let me have all the future train movements for months to come, every ammunition train, every troop train, every food train, which had been planned with characteristic German efficiency and listed in one slim file which rested in a steel drawer inside the movement control office at Le Mans station.

I was, of course, instantly aware of the value of this information. Armed with it, I could brief the Royal Air Force to attack the trains and could let the saboteurs in the groups know when food trains were passing so that they could be derailed and the goods taken into the secret stores of the Resistance. How, I asked, were these plans to reach me?

'Monsieur, I have a contact at Le Mans who is a movements control officer. He can tell you where they are kept and you can come in and get them.'

That was all very well, I told him – but what about guards, locked doors and so on? And if he worked there, why couldn't he collect the papers?

He explained that there was only one guard on at nights, a Frenchman, and that he could be tempted away by the offer of a couple of brandies in a bar close by the offices. He would leave a shutter open in a ground-floor room and the window unlocked so I could come in that way. There would be no problem. As for locked doors, he would give me wax impressions of the only key I would need which opened the door from the room with the open shutters into the room where the file was kept, but he would even try to keep that unlocked for the night I would make my burglary.

'I cannot take the file out as I am a Frenchman. Every Frenchman is searched when they leave the offices and I could not risk smuggling the papers through myself,' he told me.

But there was another snag. If the file disappeared, the Germans would know that it had been stolen and they would change the whole of the schedule. If I took the file, I asked my contact, could he smuggle it back the following day without being discovered?

'Yes, they don't search people going in. If you photograph the documents and let me have them back in a day or so, then I can cover up for that length of time. If a German asks to see the file I can put him off by pretending that another officer is looking at it, and put it back later without anyone knowing that it has been out of the office.'

That settled all my inquiries. He told me when I could have the impression of the key and I made arrangements for this to be picked up. I also arranged that he would give the date on which the raid could be made to another contact I would send to him.

I received the impression of the key a few days later and, as I was working legitimately as a lathe operator in a factory making tungsten drills – perfect cover for me – I was able to make my own key from the wax impression. I was ready for the burglary from then on. I was told the day by a courier who reached me at Angers and I arranged to be taken by van out to Le Mans. The driver knew nothing of the job I was on, just that I wanted transport there and back. I dressed in my dark-blue overalls and my black beret; as they would help to conceal me in the dark, got into the van and was driven off. At 11 p.m., the time arranged, I was hiding in the shadows by the offices, when I saw my contact come out and chat to a guard who had been paying little interest in his job of sentry. After a few minutes the two moved off towards the café, from which I could hear, distantly, the clatter of glasses and the hum of talk.

I waited for the two to get out of my sight and then, with my heart beating heavily at the thought of my coming burglary and the chances of being captured, strolled over to the offices and to the shutters.

The shutters opened at a touch and without any noise – he must have oiled them. The window, too, was opened as he had promised and I pulled myself up into the dark, quiet room. I stood listening for steps, but all I heard were the voices from the café. I pulled my .45 revolver out, carried it in one hand after pushing off the safety catch, and took out a pencil-slim electric torch from another pocket.

I eased myself quietly across the room to the door which led into the office where the files were kept, and leaned my shoulder against it as I turned the handle. That, too, was open and there was no need for my key. I opened this slowly – again there was no noise – entered the room and closed the door behind me. I switched my torch on, shone it on to the floor and took two paces towards the files.

Then, all at once, the lights in the room came on and a girl's voice ordered:

'Stay where you are, don't move.' I swung to my left and saw a pretty young girl of twenty-three or twenty-four standing there dressed in a white blouse and a blue skirt. In her right hand she held a pistol which was pointing straight at me, but wavering so much that the muzzle seemed to be blurred. I fired from the hip. She fired at the same time. Her shot hit the ceiling, mine hit her in the left breast, and I had the crazy thought that my pistol instructor would have been proud of me. The heavy .45 bullet flung her across the room and she crashed on her back on the floor. She gasped and started to moan, and the blood seeped into her trim white blouse.

I should have shot her in the head, snatched the plans and run before the noise of the shots brought searchers. But I was sickened because I had shot a pretty girl, so I put my gun down, knelt on the floor beside her and cradled her head in my lap. I stayed like that for some minutes, as the girl gasped her last breaths, and then died.

Shocked, I still held her for another minute or two. I laid her down gently, picked up the two guns and switched the lights off. I leaned against the wall and thought for a moment that I was going to be sick. The room reeked of gunpowder and mingled with it was a trace of the girl's perfume. I can smell it even now. I pulled myself together and then realised that the blast from my .45 must have been heard a long way off. But I heard no shouts, no running feet. Automatically I turned to the right file, switched on my torch and brought out the plans which I tucked into one of my big, overall pockets. I stepped over the body of the girl, walked to the door, went into the next office and stood by the open window. I looked out, saw no one, and the only sounds were those from the bar. I dropped to the ground and ran into the darkness towards the van which was tucked away a few streets off.

I stopped, panting. It was only then that I realised I had committed a murder. I leaned against a wall catching my breath, as the shock of this hit me for the first time. Murder was a frightening word at any time. But to have committed a murder oneself, and that of a pretty girl, was enough to turn one's senses. I wanted to run, run anywhere, but I fought the panic that rose in me and forced myself to be calm.

Then another thought came into my mind. How the hell did that girl know I was going to be there? Who had talked and who was she? Had my contact betrayed me? What had happened and how was I going to escape being caught and tried?

But reason told me that the Germans could not trace me for I had left no fingerprints and they would not be too thorough just because a slip of a girl had been killed. I would photograph the plans and have them delivered back to my man as we had planned. And in the meantime I would try to find out the identity of the girl.

I was driven back to Angers and dropped at my house. The next day I arranged for the plans to be photographed and asked for information to be obtained for me on the previous night's events.

I heard within a few hours that the girl, who was named Marthe – I never did know more than that – was a recent recruit to the *Milice*, the French plainclothes equivalent of the Gestapo. Her boyfriend worked at the movement control and by chance overheard my contact discussing my coming raid on their offices. The boyfriend told Marthe about this as an interesting anecdote – he was a loyal Frenchman – not realising his girl was a member of the *Milice*.

Marthe was young and eager and, I presumed, had sought to impress her new chief by catching a thief single-handed. It was her misfortune to meet a fully armed and trained British army officer instead of a frightened, unarmed French thief. I felt a little better when I knew that the girl was an enemy of France. But I shall never forget that I was forced to kill a girl. Until now no one has known I was Marthe's killer – not even SOE. I was too ashamed.

As it was, the plans were not as vital as I had been led to believe. They were useful, but only covered a small section of the future movements of the railways through Le Mans junction. The Germans hunted the murderer, checks were made in Le Mans, but no one, outside my contact at the control office, found out the killer.

The final reaction set in a couple of days after her death. I could not stop trembling, I could not eat. I was very tensed up and preoccupied for many days. At night I lay awake, hearing again the sound of her cries as she lay dying, and smelling again the fresh, exciting perfume she had worn. I was remorseful and wondered why the hell I had wanted to become a British agent. How, I asked myself, had I managed to become an assassin?

Extracted from *Xavier: A British Secret Agent With The French Resistance* by Richard Heslop (first published by Rupert Hart-Davis in 1970 and republished by Biteback in 2014)

BLETCHLEY PARK AND THE D-DAY DECEPTION

MICHAEL SMITH

The extent to which the codebreakers of Bletchley Park influenced the outcome of the war is truly astonishing. Historians generally accept that the intelligence they provided cut as much as two years off the length of the war, saving hundreds of thousands of lives on all sides.

While wars are won by troops on the frontline, men with bayonets fixed, aircrew risking their lives in the sky and naval forces at risk of being blown out of the water at any moment, the assistance they had from Bletchley Park included the critical intelligence on the locations of the U-Boat 'Wolf Packs' during the Battle of the Atlantic; the details of Rommel's plans in North Africa and a stranglehold on his supplies; Hitler's plans to continue fighting in Italy, a critical mistake which allowed the Allies to keep large numbers of German troops tied down there and away from the D-Day invasion; the detailed plans of the German defences in Normandy; and Hitler's orders to his generals throughout the invasion of Europe. But arguably Bletchley Park's most important contribution was to the D-Day deception which ensured the Allied invasion forces secured a vital foothold in Normandy.

B LETCHLEY PARK WAS now playing a critical role in a large number of different military operations around the world. One of the most important of these, arguably one of the best intelligence operations of all time, was the Double Cross System.

MI5 had managed to arrest the majority of German spies who arrived in Britain and was using them to feed false intelligence back to the *Abwehr*, German military intelligence. The operation was run by the Double Cross Committee, made up of representatives of MI5, MI6 and the three armed forces, which decided what information should be fed back to the Germans. By the beginning of 1941, it was clear that the double agents could be used to deceive the Germans, to provide them with misleading information that would give Allied forces an advantage on the battlefield.

Much of the material passed to the Germans was 'chickenfeed', genuine but unimportant information that would give the *Abwehr* a feel that its agents were doing something and had access to real intelligence without telling them anything really harmful. But mixed among this were key pieces of specious or misleading information designed to build up a false picture of what the British were doing.

The phoney intelligence reports were sent by wireless, or in some cases letters, under the control of MI5 agent handlers. While the *Abwehr*'s responses to the double agents' reports and the 'shopping list' of information the Germans asked for helped the Double Cross Committee to work out what the Germans did and did not know, it did not reveal whether or not the reports, and therefore the misleading intelligence picture they were building up, was believed in Berlin. The only way of finding that out was by deciphering the messages passed between the *Abwehr* outstations in Paris, Madrid, Lisbon and Belgrade and their bosses back in Berlin. But these links all used the *Abwehr* Enigma machine, which was a much more complex system than those that were being broken at Bletchley Park.

It had four rotors rather than three and they turned over in a thoroughly unpredictable way, frequently in tandem. Hut 6, the section which broke the German army and air force Enigma ciphers, had looked at the *Abwehr* Enigma early in 1941 but had not seen any way to unravel it, so the problem was handed over to the Enigma research section run by Dilly Knox, one of the greatest of Britain's codebreakers in both the First and Second World War. It was down to Knox that Britain had even tried to break Enigma and without his expertise, it is far from clear that the Poles would have given the British codebreakers the vital information they needed to break it. At the beginning of December 1941, Knox did what no one else had managed to do. He found a way to break the *Abwehr* Enigma. The first of the messages, known collectively as ISK for Illicit Signals Knox, was sent to MI5 and MI6 on Christmas Day 1941.

The value of the ISK messages to the Double Cross system is impossible to overstate. They alone gave the Double Cross Committee the absolute certainty that the Germans believed the false intelligence they were being fed and showed whether or not individual double agents were trusted or under suspicion, in which case steps could be taken to remedy the situation.

By the spring of 1942, the information collected from the Bletchley Park decrypts had built up such a good picture of *Abwehr* operations in the UK that MI5 was able to state categorically that it now controlled all of the German agents operating in Britain. The Double Cross Committee could begin building up a false picture of the Allied forces that would take part in the D-Day invasion and trick the Germans into putting their troops in the wrong place.

The Double Cross deception, codenamed *Fortitude South*, evolved rapidly as the D-Day preparations built up during the early months of 1944, but the bare bones of the plan remained the same. The Germans were to be given false intelligence that would make them conclude that the Normandy landings were a feint attack aimed at drawing German forces away from the main thrust of the Allied invasion, which would be against the Pas de Calais. This would ensure that the bulk of the German forces would be held back from the Normandy beaches, allowing the Allies time to establish a foothold in northern France from which they could break out south towards Paris and east towards Germany.

A completely mythical formation, the First United States Army Group (FUSAG), was created. It was supposedly commanded by General George Patton, a hero of the invasion of Sicily and a man whom the Germans would believe must be heavily involved in the invasion of Europe. The plan had FUSAG based across East Anglia and south-eastern England and it was vital that the agents' reports were coordinated to make it look as if this was the case, and to downplay the mass of troops waiting in the south and south-west to attack the German defences in Normandy.

The most spectacularly useful of the wireless agents deployed in the *Fortitude South* deception plan was the Spaniard Juan Pujol Garcia, codename *Garbo*. He was an accomplished fraudster who originally approached the MI6 station in Madrid only to be rejected as an obvious charlatan. Undaunted, he offered his services to the German *Abwehr* and agreed to go to England as a German spy. He then went not to London but to Lisbon where, armed with an out-of-date copy of *Jane's Fighting Ships* and a *Blue Guide to Great Britain*, he began feeding false intelligence to the Germans for cash. His messages were intercepted by the British who, concerned that he might discredit their own operation, brought him to the UK and began running him back at the Germans under British control. *Garbo*'s network of agents, all of them completely fictitious, was so large and had become so vital to the overall deception picture that virtually everything had to be closely coordinated on a day-to-day basis. The most important of the other agents who, in the parlance of the Double Cross Committee, 'came up for D-Day' was the triple agent *Brutus*. Roman Garby-Czerniawski, a Pole, had led the *Inter-allié* network in France and, once it was uncovered, volunteered to work for the *Abwehr* in London in order to save the other members of his group from execution. On arrival in Britain, he immediately told the authorities of his mission and was turned against the Germans. Two others should be mentioned as important to *Fortitude South*: the Yugoslav Dusko Popov, codenamed *Tricycle*, and *Treasure,* Natalie 'Lily' Sergueiev, a French citizen born in Russia whose family fled in the wake of the Bolshevik revolution.

These four were the main agents used to build up *Fortitude South*, the false picture of the intended target of D-Day. *Tricycle* and *Brutus*, who was supposedly a member of a Polish unit attached to FUSAG, provided an order of battle for the fictitious formation so comprehensive that the Germans were not just supplied with details of individual units, strengths and locations, they were even given reproductions of the insignia supposedly painted on the side of the FUSAG vehicles.

Treasure's role was to report from the West Country that there were very few troops there, further pushing the Germans towards the view that the main thrust of the attack would be against the Pas de Calais. But she came close to blowing the whole plan. Sent to Lisbon to collect a radio set from the *Abwehr*, she told a former acquaintance she met in the street that she was now working for the British secret service. When she returned to London, she confessed to considering warning the *Abwehr* as retribution for the British refusal to allow her to bring her dog to the UK without going through quarantine. She was swiftly retired and replaced by an MI5 operator imitating her distinctive method of sending morse and her loquacious messages. For several months after D-Day, the *Treasure* character – although not the agent herself – was kept active for no other reason than that her messages were so long-winded that Bletchley Park was able to follow them through the *Abwehr* communications network and use them as cribs, streams of known plain language which would help them decrypt the ciphers. Denys Page, who was in charge of breaking the *Abwehr* hand ciphers, said the cribs supplied by *Treasure* and *Brutus* had 'absolutely saved our bacon' after the Germans introduced more secure systems during 1944.

But by far the most important and complex role was played by *Garbo*. At one point, he had a network of twenty-seven supposed agents, some of whom still survived from his freelance period before the British recruited him. They included a Swiss businessman based in Bootle who had reported 'drunken orgies and slack morals in amusement centres' in Liverpool and an enthusiastic Venzuelan living in Glasgow who had noted the willingness of Clydeside dockers to 'do anything for a litre of wine'. The Swiss businessman died of cancer in the autumn of 1942. But his widow continued working for *Garbo*, becoming virtually his personal assistant. The Venezuelan also grew in stature, becoming *Garbo*'s official deputy and developing his own ring of agents in Scotland, one of whom was an ardent communist who actually believed he was working for the Soviet Union. The *Abwehr* codenamed this group of agents the Benedict Network. *Garbo*'s mistress, a secretary working in the offices of the War Cabinet, provided useful opportunities for valuable pillow talk. She, like the wireless operator, believed that her lover was a Spanish Republican. *Garbo* had also successfully set up a large network of agents in Wales, mostly Welsh Nationalists but led by an ex-seaman, 'a thoroughly undesirable character' who was working for purely mercenary reasons. At this point, it is probably worth reminding the reader that none of these people actually existed.

Nevertheless, they all contributed to the German complete confidence in *Garbo* as their most reliable source for intelligence on the Allied plans and set the scene for his key role in *Fortitude*. The German belief in the existence of FUSAG was steadily built up by a number of means apart from false reports from the double agents. Dummy invasion craft nicknamed 'Big Bobs' were left out in the open in east coast ports and mobile wireless vehicles travelled around south-east England broadcasting messages from a number of different locations to fool the German radio interception units.

So fantastic was *Garbo*'s story that it would have been virtually impossible to imagine that the Germans would believe anything he said if it were not for the fact that Knox had broken the *Abwehr* Enigma. The deciphered Enigma messages between the *Abwehr* headquarters and *Garbo*'s controller in Madrid were vital to the prosecution of the D-Day deception from its very conception and now they confirmed that the Germans were still completely fooled. This was not just because *Garbo*'s story carefully fitted in with all the other detail being sent by *Brutus*, *Tricycle*, *Treasure* and the other double-agents. It was also because it fitted in completely with what the Germans were expecting, and that was known in detail as a result of the intercepts of messages between Hitler and Field Marshal Gerd von Rundstedt, the German commander in France.

Throughout April and into May a series of high-level messages broken at Bletchley reaffirmed that the Germans believed the main British attack would be on the Pas de Calais, although there were also worrying occasional suggestions of an additional attack on Normandy. Concerns over the German mentions of Normandy led to a decision on 18 May to go all out on the *Fortitude South* deception pointing to the main Allied landing being on the Pas de Calais.

In the early hours of 6 June 1944 – D-Day – *Garbo* made repeated attempts to warn his *Abwehr* controller that the Allied forces were on their way. This move was agreed by Allied commanders on the basis that it would be too late for the Germans to do anything about it but would ensure that they still believed in *Garbo* as their best-informed secret agent after the invasion had begun. As predicted it only served to increase the Germans' trust in him and paved the way for the next stage of the deception. Shortly after midnight on 9 June, as the Allied advance faltered and with the elite 1st SS *Panzer* division on its way from the Pas de Calais, together with another armoured division, to reinforce the German defences in Normandy, *Garbo* sent his most important message about the D-Day landings. Three of his agents were reporting troops massed across East Anglia and Kent and large numbers of troop and tank transporters waiting in the eastern ports.

> After personal consultation on 8 June in London with my agents *Donny*, *Dick*
> and *Derrick*, whose reports I sent today, I am of the opinion, in view of the
> strong troop concentrations in south-east and east England, that these opera-
> tions are a diversionary manoeuvre designed to draw off enemy reserves in order
> to make an attack at another place. In view of the continued air attacks on the
> concentration area mentioned, which is a strategically favourable position for
> this, it may very probably take place in the Pas de Calais area.

Garbo's warning went straight to Hitler who ordered the two divisions back to the Pas de Calais to defend against what he expected to be the main invasion thrust and awarded Garbo the Iron Cross. Had the two divisions continued to Normandy, the Allies might well have been thrown back into the sea. Bill Williams, Montgomery's intelligence officer during the invasion of Europe, said the D-Day deception, codenamed *Fortitude South*, might have had to be aborted if it were not for the breaking of the *Abwehr* Enigma messages.

The staff branch responsible for deception and cover plans, was more dependent on *Ultra*[21] than any of the rest of us. It was the only source revealing the enemy's reaction to a cover plan. Without *Ultra* we should never have known. In the case of *Fortitude South*, it is arguable that without *Ultra* confirmation that it was selling, it might have been dropped.

Without Knox, and the breaking of the *Abwehr* Enigma, the D-Day deception would simply not have been possible, but he would never know that. He was terminally ill in December 1941 when he made the crucial break. He died in February 1943, sixteen months before the most important of his many remarkable achievements played its indispensable role in ensuring the success of the D-Day landings.

Extracted from *The Secrets of Station X: How the Bletchley Park Codebreakers Helped Win the War* by Michael Smith (published by Biteback in 2011)

---

21   *Ultra* was the codeword used to indicate the intelligence produce of deciphered high-grade enemy ciphers like Enigma.

GARBO:
THE STAR OF THE
DOUBLE CROSS SYSTEM

JUAN PUJOL GARCIA

There is no doubt that Garbo was the most valuable of the Double Cross agents, the star of the show and the agent in whom the *Abwehr* put its most faith. He describes here how, having persuaded the Germans to recruit him as an agent, he then contacted the Americans and through them the British. It was a timely reappearance and, given the original British dismissal of his merits as an agent, a very fortunate one. They had intercepted his messages to the *Abwehr* and had become extremely concerned that an uncontrolled agent, evidently believed by the Germans but reporting nonsense, might cause havoc with their deception operations. They were very grateful to find him and brought him to the UK to meet Tommy Harris, his new MI5 controller.

I HAD SMUGGLED the $3,000 that Federico [the German agent-handler] had given me in Madrid into Portugal without any trouble. I had rolled the money up tightly and slid it into a rubber sheath, then I had cut a tube of toothpaste open at the bottom end, emptied out all the toothpaste, inserted the notes and rolled the bottom of the tube up to look as if it were half empty. I couldn't get all the money in one tube, so I had put the rest of the 100-denomination notes into a tube of shaving cream using the same method. It was perfect camouflage and I had no problems at the Fuentes de Oñoro checkpoint at the border.

With this money I now bought a Baedeker tourist guide to England, Bradshaw's railway timetable and a large map of Great Britain, and retired to Cascais to study them in detail.

Then, in October 1941, I sent my first message to the Germans from Cascais, although, as far as Federico was concerned, I was already in England; it was quite a long message.

In invisible ink, I told them that before leaving Portugal I had posted the key to a safety box in the Espírito Santo bank to the German Embassy in Lisbon, with instructions that they should send it to Federico at the German Embassy in Madrid. I went on to explain that on arriving in Britain, I had got talking to the KLM pilot who flew us in to London and had become very friendly with him, introducing myself as a Catalan political exile who had had to flee because of my political views. I had then persuaded the KLM pilot to take my Spanish mail to the Espírito Santo bank in Lisbon on a regular basis. In my letter I also said that he had not at first been too keen to help, perhaps because he suspected something, but that I had assured him that none of my envelopes would be stuck down so he could always see for himself what the contents were; my letters were meant, I had explained to him, to give my fellow Catalan patriots information about other Catalans in exile in England.

I had also told the pilot, I said to the Germans, that this, my first letter, would merely be informing my fellow Catalans in Spain of my arrival in the British Isles. Finally, I suggested to the Germans that I was thinking of going to live near Lake Windermere in the centre of Britain because I had heard that there were a fairly large number of troops stationed up there.

I had had to devise this ploy about the KLM pilot because, as I was still living in Portugal, there was absolutely no possibility of my letters being franked by the British Post Office. So this, my first letter, consisted, on the surface in ordinary visible ink, of an enthusiastic account of England by a passionate Catalan democrat with all the information for the Germans written in between the lines in invisible ink.

I had become a real German spy.

I sent three messages to the Germans from inside Portugal (purporting to come from England), all of which were worded with the care and attention worthy of the most adroit German field agent. I tried hard to introduce new information gradually and to be cautious when I mentioned the new contacts I had recruited to help me. In my first message I told them that I had found three people who would continue to supply me with further information, whom I had made my subagents: one in Glasgow, one in Liverpool and one from the West Country. The naivety with which I told them the facts I had discovered probably contributed to the conviction that I really was in London.

In the second message, I said that I'd been offered a job at the BBC and was about to accept. I also said that I'd heard that the navy was carrying out landing-craft manoeuvres on Lake Windermere and described in detail how I had grappled with a whole string of obstacles.

The third message, which as always was a complete invention, had a unique impact, although it was not until much later that I learned of the stir it caused in the British secret service.

In this third message I said that a convoy of five ships had left Liverpool for Malta, although neither the date nor the number of ships actually tallied exactly with my message. But the coincidence was sufficiently close for the British to think that a German agent was loose in England.

This worried the British enormously, especially when they were able to confirm that the Germans had carried out an aerial reconnaissance of the projected route and of Malta's Valletta Harbour. Who was this agent? Where was he getting all this information from that endangered British security?

The British were going crazy looking for me as they had no idea where I was and, indeed, whether I existed at all. Cyril Mills told me later that he was in Portugal at the time and that he had mentioned to the intelligence gatherers in Lisbon and to those in Madrid that the German agent Arabel could have come from either of those cities. If so, how had he got into Britain? Everyone in Britain was hunting for me and trying to discover how I was getting information through to Madrid.

So much of this reads like a fairy story that it will not come as a surprise to readers to learn that it was this third message which led to the British accepting me, and which eventually enabled me to become both the Germans' top spy Arabel and MI5's counter-spy Garbo.

While I was in Portugal I received only one message from the *Abwehr*; this asked for more detailed and weightier reports on troop sightings and movements. From this I gathered that my coded messages were neither as good nor as consistent as had been expected. The farce was coming to an end. Apart from the risks that my continued presence in Lisbon posed, I was extremely worried because

I did not know what to do or say in order to keep my operation running efficiently. I had never been to England and my knowledge of English was confined to a fleeting study of the language during my schooldays. And what of my military knowledge? I didn't have any idea about the composition of a foreign army, let alone the British military set-up. Given my inability to obtain direct British contacts, I therefore decided to abandon the whole operation and disappear from Europe altogether. But before doing so I thought I'd have one last try and risk all on the play of a card.

I went to the American Embassy in Lisbon. The United States, it must be remembered, had just come into the war as a new belligerent against Germany, Italy and Japan. It must have been during one of the first days of February 1942 when I walked in and asked to speak to either the military or the naval attaché.

This time around my luck held. I was met by an official who, after I had been frisked by the marine on duty, ushered me into the naval attaché's office to meet Lieutenant Demorest.

I cannot tell you what a relief it was to be able to sit opposite someone who was in a position to make decisions, even though I was aware that his powers were limited. I began to unburden myself by telling him about my attempt to contact the British in Madrid, my rejection and then my resolution, fired by *amour propre*, to obtain some practical and useful information that would capture their imagination, vindicate my humiliation and enhance myself in their estimation so that they would believe that I was motivated by a desire to defend democracy.

I briefly outlined my contacts with the Germans and mentioned that they had given me invisible ink, a code book and money; I told him about my trip to Portugal, my second attempt to contact the British through their Lisbon Embassy, my second rebuff, my resolution to press on with work begun and, finally, my last desperate move of coming to see him; I said that if that too failed, then all the work I had done so far would come to nought.

Demorest showed keen interest right from the very beginning and seemed amazed by my story. He asked me for proof, which I proceeded to give him. For the first time there seemed to be a distinct possibility that I had found the right person; at last, someone was going to help me to complete the mission I had set myself. It was precisely while I was telling him my story that its full implication struck me: I started to realise the potential value of the trick I had begun to play on the Third Reich.

Demorest asked for two days in which to follow up my story, confer with his British colleagues and convince them that they must get in touch with me. He gave me his phone number and urged me to be very careful and to avoid going out unless I had to.

Then Demorest evidently tried to make his British counterpart, Captain Benson, see that he had nothing to lose by telling his superiors that this alleged agent wanted to hand over some invisible ink and a code book, and he advised Benson that he must act swiftly as I had either to continue with the game or stop altogether.

Someone in England had already had the perception to suspect that the spy they were hunting for was probably the same person as the freelance agent at large in Portugal, so some days later Captain Benson asked Demorest to give me his phone number. I then telephoned Benson, who arranged for me to meet Gene Risso-Gill, an MI6 officer in Lisbon, on the terrace of a refreshments shop overlooking the beach at Estoril. Three days later Risso-Gill telephoned me to say that he had received instructions that I should be taken to London.

Old Risso-Gill was a most polite and elegant gentleman with a dark complexion and a short thick beard, who overwhelmed me with his affability. He seemed delighted to hear about my adventures, laughed heartily and immediately began to plan how I could leave Lisbon in secret, without alerting German informers in the aliens department or the border police. Sometime later he came around to my place to tell me that a four-ship convoy that was heading for Gibraltar lay in the Tagus and that he had arranged for me to leave on one of the ships the following evening. I was not to take any luggage but to give him the invisible ink and the code book and he would see that they reached London. It was my one chance to travel in safety, so I had better be quick about sorting out my Portuguese affairs.

I left Estoril at five o'clock the next afternoon for an unknown destination; I had to trust that the British would indeed get me to London from Gibraltar, but did not know how, when or in what capacity I would travel there and couldn't help wondering what treatment the British would have in store for me on arrival. Risso-Gill seemed to read my thoughts, for he kept reassuring me during the short walk down to the harbour.

It will only be a short journey, he said, no need to worry. All I had to do was to board the ship right behind him and then go straight to the crew's dining room when he gave the signal; the captain had precise instructions what to do with me when we reached Gibraltar: he was to hand me over to two officers, who would provide me with money and find me somewhere to stay.

My legs were shaking as I walked up the gangway past the Portuguese policeman at the top. Risso-Gill said something to him, then led me down to the captain's cabin. The captain told Risso-Gill to warn me not to talk to any of the crew, but to have dinner with them and then go straight to my bunk, which the quartermaster would find for me as he knew of my arrival.

After Risso-Gill had left the ship, I went down to the crew's mess; so far all the arrangements for my departure from Portugal had been faultless, which increased my confidence.

Sometime after supper, when I was lying on my bunk, I heard the bang and rattle of the engines as the ship slipped her moorings. Early next morning one of the crew tapped me on the shoulder and made signs for me to follow him to the mess for breakfast. Afterwards he signalled for me to follow him up on deck for a breath of fresh air.

It was a beautiful day; we seemed to be sailing 12 miles or so off the Portuguese coast, gently cruising along in convoy with three other merchantmen. The fresh air did me good, for I had found it rather claustrophobic shut up down below and had not much cared for the smell, which made me feel sick. At about ten o'clock an alarm went off, everybody raced to action stations and a sailor threw a life jacket at my feet, indicating that I should put it on. Were we in danger? Had they spotted an enemy submarine or a plane? Then I realised that this was not a genuine emergency, just a practice drill.

We coasted along the shore for twenty-four hours and then, very early the next morning, I heard the ship's engines stop. When I went on deck I found the Rock of Gibraltar towering overhead. At about 8 a.m. a small boat approached and two officers stepped on board. The captain sent a sailor to bring me to his cabin and there introduced me to the two officers, who both spoke Spanish: one said he was a port official and the other that he had been instructed by London to look after me. I took leave of the captain and followed them into the small boat; we landed and walked unchallenged through the passport police check and customs and headed straight for a restaurant. Over a large English breakfast, I was informed by one of the officers that there was a room at my disposal for my own exclusive use and that I could come and go as I pleased. He then handed me a wad of sterling notes and suggested that I buy some clothes as he knew I had brought no luggage whatsoever with me, not even a change of clothes. He ended by telling me that

I might have to wait for two or three days before getting a plane for London, as I would be travelling on an unscheduled flight.

He then took me to my room, gave me his telephone number in case I needed it and said that he would call as soon as he knew when I was leaving.

I spent the whole morning exploring Gibraltar, which I found to be a huddle of small shops, restaurants and hotels all along one main street, the adjoining small alleys leading to the harbour being of little import. I bought some underclothes and a Spanish newspaper and sat in a café. After lunch in a restaurant, I spent most of the afternoon watching some people play tennis who seemed to be naval officers and their wives. The truth is that there wasn't much to see in Gibraltar; it is not endowed with many tourist attractions and most people only go there to buy things because they are cheap and duty free.

I visited a large nightclub cum coffee house filled to the brim with soldiers listening to a Spanish all-girl band, but the din was so great that I couldn't hear the music. I didn't see any fights, but was told that scuffles frequently broke out between the soldiers and the sailors.

Two days later I left Gibraltar in an extremely uncomfortable military plane that had no seats, just long benches, which made me think that it was meant for transporting paratroopers. There were two other passengers, but we were never introduced, nor did we speak to each other throughout the long eight-hour journey. They were carrying mail so were probably diplomats or special couriers.

In order to avoid German fighter planes, we headed far out into the Atlantic and so did not reach Plymouth until late afternoon, when we arrived tired and hungry as all we had had during the flight was tea. I don't think I've ever drunk so much tea in all my life as I did during that long, cold journey, not even during the London

Blitz when we used to spend hours on end in underground shelters. I must have had more than twenty cups in a desperate attempt to keep myself warm.

I caught a glimpse of Plymouth from the plane and was suddenly acutely aware that I was away from home and about to enter an alien land. Would the English be friendly toward me? Would they believe my story about the tussles I had had with their embassies in Lisbon and Madrid, which showed how inefficiently these places were being run? Would they understand my motives for all that I had done and honestly believe that I wished to work for the good of mankind?

I thought about the city states of ancient Greece, of Cleisthenes's Athens, or Pericles and of the beginnings of democracy. I reiterated to myself my firm belief that individuals should have a say in their own government and knew that I had been right to put all my efforts into upholding such a doctrine. I entered England full of restless anticipation. What would my future hold?

My first recollection of England on that calm, clear day in April 1942, as I walked down the steps of the plane, was of the terrible cold – cold outside and icy fear inside. At the bottom of the steps, stood two officers from MI5 who would shape my destiny. The one who introduced himself as Mr Grey didn't speak a word of Spanish; I didn't say anything to him in my faltering English. The other, Tomás Harris, whom everyone called Tommy, spoke perfect Spanish.

Extracted from *Operation Garbo: The Personal Story of the Most Successful Spy of World War II* by Juan Pujol Garcia & Nigel West (first published by Weidenfeld & Nicolson in 1985 and republished by Biteback in 2011)

THE RECRUITMENT OF DOUBLE AGENT TREASURE

KENNETH BENTON

Kenneth Benton served in MI6 from 1937 through to 1968 in a number of roles, including head of station in Rome, Madrid, Lima and Rio de Janeiro and Director Latin America, when his proposal that the Service instigate a coup in Paraguay was turned down. After the war, he became a thriller writer creating fictional MI6 officer Peter Craig, but here we focus on one of his own real-life intelligence coups, the recruitment in July 1943, of Lily Sergueiev, codenamed Treasure.

Benton served from 1941 to 1943 as the MI6 officer in charge of counter-espionage in Madrid, identifying a total of nineteen *Abwehr* agents, including the talkative Treasure who was to prove one of the most useful double agents so far as the codebreakers were concerned. Her reluctance to use one word when a dozen would do was deployed by the Twenty Committee to feed long streams of information to the *Abwehr* that were specifically designed to help Bletchley Park to break into the Nazi ciphers.

Benton recalled how Treasure, a 'walk-in', who had been working for the *Abwehr*, first flounced into his offices insisting that he recruit her to work for MI6. She subsequently returned carrying a terrier called Frisson and insisted the dog be allowed to go to England with her and be made exempt from UK quarantine restrictions.

His reports on his subsequent interviews with Treasure are a model of their kind, giving extensive detail of her potential value and possible pitfalls and, recognising that she would be part of a much larger operation, correctly asking for instructions as to how to proceed.

'She became a very useful agent, and was one of those who, to use the jargon of the time, "came up for D-Day",' he later recalled. But she appears never to have forgiven him for the inevitable demise of her dog. 'She wrote a book, in French, about her experiences and freely criticised some of her British acquaintances,' Benton said. 'She described me as "*très anglais*", and from her that was not a compliment.'

<hr />

SPAIN
C. E.
17.7.43
Natalie Sergueiev

Owing to lack of time the earlier part of the subject's story follows by next bag. It is very briefly as follows:

In 1933, at a time when she was genuinely interested in the Hitler movement, she met Felix Dassel, a German journalist in Berlin. She continued to see him at long intervals during the next four years, when he assisted her in writing articles for publication in French newspapers. In 1937 he asked her cover the Civil War in Spain, but soon showed that he wanted SIS [Secret Intelligence Service] information rather than straight journalism. He finally explained to her that he was working for the [German] SIS and they parted. After the armistice in 1940, she was stuck in France and saw no means of getting out. She conceived the idea of getting sent on some mission for Dassel to some place outside Nazi influence. He later saw her in Paris, had her trained to some extent in intelligence methods and proposed that she should go first to Syria, then after the Allied invasion of Syria, she was to go to Australia. This also fell through and finally she was handed over to Major Kliemann[22] of: 2, Rue Villa Boileau, Paris XVI. This was in October 1941.

This house is under the name of Yvonne Delidaise, who is Kliemann's mistress. Her brother Richard, living at Rue de Lonchamp 723, Meuilly, undertook the task of training her in W/T[23] and she was later trained at 77, Rue de l'Assumption (corner of Rue du Dr Blanche). This was in October 1942. She explains that her training was frequently interrupted, plans changed, and altogether her employers seem to have used very slipshod methods.

It was decided in June 1942 that she should definitely try to attain entrance to the UK. When in Vichy, where she had to apply for an exit visa, she took the opportunity of travelling to Algiers, where her sister, Madame Sauty de Chalon is living. She made contact here (14.10.42) with a friend of her sister's named Pierre Jourdain, employed in the Algiers Naval Intelligence Division, who had just left the service in disgust.

She confided her secret plans of double-crossing the Germans to Jourdain. If, as is probable, he is now back in his former position, he could confirm this.

She finally arrived in Spain with a French passport in order, and came to Madrid, where, according to her instructions, she telephoned to Luis Miret of Nrvaes 55 (telephone no. 512420) and

---

22   Major Emil Kliemann, *Abwehr* deputy head of station in Paris.

23   Wireless Telegraphy i.e. the use of a radio transmitter.

reported her arrival, saying that she was CANUTO. She had been told that she was to have no contact with this man, but the next day a young German arrived at the hotel and asked for Miss Canuto. She happened to hear his inquiry and spoke to him. He had how-ever no instructions for her and told her to continue to report, but in writing. She has also written to Miguel Ottono, Auritsen Borda, Valle de Bastan, Erraisu, enclosing a letter for Kliemann written in secret ink and addressed: Gary.

She has a further cover address in Lisbon,

Rodolfo MORGENER (an Austrian)

Rua Joaquin Antonio de Aguiar 35, 3°, Left.

Telephone: 52030

She is to report at this address when she arrives in Lisbon and give her address. She will probably be visited by Kliemann in Lis-bon before she leaves and he may give her a W/T set. When she expressed herself horrified at the idea of trying to take a W/T set into England in her luggage they replied that they might give her one disguised as a gramophone; they had tried that once and it had come off.

She has Esc. 20,000 and the original plan was that she should first apply for her visa for the UK in Lisbon and not Madrid. Her employers had apparently not realised that she could not get into Portugal without having some visa of destination.

She pointed out that her valid French passport with French exit and Spanish entry visas must surely arouse misgivings, but was told that she could, alternatively, say that she had been smuggled across the frontier by Pascual of Hendaye.

The two letters, which she believes we have had delivered in Algiers for her, are, she states, merely a notification to her sister of the fact that she is in Spain and trying to get out.

The secret ink is used as follows: Melt one of two small pieces of material in the flame of a match without turning it black. Dip the end of a toothpick repeatedly into the molten material and allow to solidify, until a blob of hard material has been formed on the end of the toothpick. This is used dry on ordinary writing paper after the latter has been rubbed all over with dry cotton wool in order to raise the fibres very slightly. She does not know the developer.

The main directives which the Germans gave her, after training her in the recognition of aeroplanes, military uniforms etc., are written in a solution of lemon juice in water on the attached two sheets of notepaper. The Germans had told her to memorise all her Instructions, but when they finally began to train her intensively during the last day or two before her leaving Paris, they tried to cram her mind with so much new and unfamiliar material that on her own initiative she wrote out the main details.

She is perfectly prepared to play as CEA[24] and will delay her departure here or in Lisbon as long as you wish so that contact can be made with Kliemann under our control.

Request instructions as early as possible.

SPAIN
C. E.
28.7.43
Redacted of 17.7.43

The following is in extenuation of my para 2. At the time subject met DASSEL she was touring round Central Europe mostly by bicycle and writing articles in the *Wandervogel* style for *Le Jour*.

---

24   Counter-Espionage Agent.

A collection of letters written by her friends was published about this time (1934).

In 1936, she arrived in Berlin on a tour which she was making for the purpose of writing up the *Kraft Durch Freude* organisation. DASSEL asked her to go to Czechoslovakia and obtain stories on Czech political figures. She did this and subsequently returned to Paris.

The following year DASSEL met her in Paris and asked her if she would agree to cover the Spanish Civil War for him. She went to Spain and began to send in her stories, but after a time he showed her that she was not sending in the right type of material. She went to Paris to meet him. He explained to her that he was working for the German Intelligence Service and that he expected her to cover the war from the intelligence angle. She would not agree to this and severed her connections with him.

This part of the story is admittedly puzzling since it is difficult to see what practical value her reports, even from the intelligence angle, could have had for the German Intelligence Service. A more detailed interrogation of subject regarding the exact directives she had received from DASSEL would probably clear this point up.

Next year, in 1938, she conceived the idea of cycling from Paris to Saigon. She had reached Aleppo when the war broke out.

Subject at once went to Beyrouth and took a course of training as nurse. She was still there when the Armistice was declared, upon which she returned to Paris.

She states that as soon as there seemed any hope of British resistance continuing she determined to leave occupied Europe and join the Allied Nations. Her first step was to write to DASSEL, who soon afterwards visited Paris. She told him that she wanted to work for the Axis and suggested that in view of her language qualifications – her English is very good – she should be trained and sent abroad.

She succeeded, in spite of the fact that she had rejected his proposals in Spain, in convincing him of her bona fides. She was invited to visit Berlin, in January 1941.

Subject states that Kliemann often visits Portugal as representative of the German Chamber of Commerce at Paris, and adds that Kliemann was sometimes referred to as Kielburg. This seems to show that Kliemann is definitely identical with Glist K-11 although she thinks his name is Johann not Emil. He carries a ring with the initials JK engraved on it.

Kliemann was on friendly terms with Major Genty, aged forty-six, an aviation officer who was formerly in Belgrade, married to a Polish woman aged about twenty-three. This is presumably the new Vichy consul General at Tangier. Genty sponsored subject's application to the Vichy authorities for permission to enter the Free Zone. Kliemann said that Genty did not form part of his organisation but acted as a friend only.

Subject states that Yvonne Delidaise visited Madrid on 25.3.43 when she stayed at the Palace Hotel with a woman representative of the Paris firm of Heim Jeunes Filles and tried unsuccessfully to enter Portugal. She does not know if they were engaged on a mission for Kliemann. (This is partly confirmed by our lists.) Delidaise is described as aged twenty-six, interpreter, and arrived at the Hotel in the company of Renee Marty.

I am awaiting your further Instructions regarding subject's movements. In my opinion she would make a useful CEA and for this reason I consider it important that she should encounter some delay and difficulty in proceeding to the UK.

She has written to Kliemann reporting that she feels we are not entirely satisfied with her story of having bought her passport and asking urgently for a suitable address where she could have obtained it. She has also reported that her cousin Dr Hill is interceding on her behalf. It would give real air of vraisemblance to the affair if you could send her a telegram purporting to come from Dr Hill informing her that her visa has been authorised. Her address here is at Pension Argentina, Avenida Jose Antonio, sixty-four.

Should be grateful for instructions by telegraph as to whether you wish her to ask Kliemann to meet her, and where.

∞∞∞

The above memos by Benton on the recruitment of Treasure are held at the UK National Archives in file KV 2/464

After the war, MI6 discovered that not only was Treasure working for the *Abwehr* and for MI5/MI6, she had also been an NKVD[25] agent throughout that period.

---

25   The Soviet Foreign Intelligence Service was part of the Soviet secret service, the Peoples' Commissariat for Internal Affairs, or NKVD (*Narodnyy Komissariat Vnutrennikh Del*), from 1934 until 1954 when it became part of the Committee for State Security, the KGB (*Komitet gosudarstvennoy bezopasnosti*). The KGB was dissolved in 1991 when the Russian Foreign Intelligence Service, or SVR (*Sluzhba vneshney razvedki*), was set up.

THE TORTURE OF THE WHITE RABBIT

TOMMY YEO-THOMAS

F. F. E. 'Tommy' Yeo-Thomas worked for a Paris fashion house before World War Two. He escaped to Britain after the fall of France in May 1940 and was recruited into the SOE's Gaullist Free French 'R/F Section' where as deputy head of the section he liaised with the *Bureau Central de Renseignements et d'Action* (BCRA), the Free French Intelligence Service. He parachuted into France on three separate occasions, the last time in February 1944, when he was arrested and tortured by the Gestapo. He was taken to Fresnes prison where he met up with one of his own men, Captain Desmond Ellis Hubble, whom he had recruited into the Free French Section. They were eventually taken to Buchenwald concentration camp where they entertained themselves playing chess on Hubble's pocket chess set, which he had somehow managed to persuade the Gestapo to return to him after his interrogation. Yeo-Thomas would survive Buchenwald, but sadly as Yeo-Thomas describes below in an understandably bitter letter to his boss Lieutenant-Colonel L H 'Dizzy' Dismore smuggled out of Buchenwald, Hubble did not. Yeo-Thomas was awarded the George Cross and awarded the Military Cross with Bar.

14 September 1944.

My dear Dizzy,

These are 'famous last words' I am afraid, but one has to face death one day or another so I will not moan, and get down to brass tacks.

I will not attempt to make a report on my journey except to say that up to the very moment of my arrest it had been a success and I had got things cracking and woken up a number of slumberers. I was quite pleased with things – I took every precaution and neglected nothing – my capture was due to one of those incidents one cannot provide for – I had so much work that I was overwhelmed so I asked PIC to provide me with a sure dependable *agent de liaison*, and he gave me a young chap called Guy, whom I renamed Antonin. He worked for me for a week, and then got caught; how I do not know, but in any case, he had an appointment with me at 11 a.m. on Tuesday 21 March by the Metro Passy and brought the Gestapo with him. He was obviously unable to withstand bullying and very quickly gave in to questioning. I was caught coming around a corner and had not an earthly chance, being collared and handcuffed before I could say 'knife'. I was badly beaten up in the car on the way to Gestapo HQ, arriving there with a twisted nose and a head about twice its normal size. I was then subjected to four days continuous grilling, being beaten up and also being put into a bath of icy cold water, legs and arms chained, and held head downwards under water until almost drowned, then pulled out and asked if I had anything to say. This I underwent six times but I managed to hold out and gave nothing away. Not a single arrest was made as a sequel to my capture. The only trouble was that the party who was lodging me got arrested and will have to be compensated for losing liberty and home.

I was interrogated for about two months, but dodged everything. I was offered freedom if I would hand over Bingen – some hopes – I nearly lost my left arm as a result of the tortures, as I got blood poisoning through my wrist, being cut to the bone by chains and remaining unattended with handcuffs biting into them for about six days. Apart from that I was kept in solitary confinement for four months at Fresnes. I was very unpopular as a Britisher and one of the German NCOs, a *Feldwebel* [Sergeant], was particularly glad at every opportunity of punching me or slapping my face. He gave me three weeks of glasshouse in a darkened cell, without mattress, blankets, deprived of all means of washing, and with about a half pound of bread per day as sole food. I was pretty weak when I came out, had lost about two and a half stone in weight, I was sent to Compiegne on 17 July, whilst there recuperated a bit and had arranged an escape together with a chap well known to Passy[26] and the BCRA and got sent to Weimar on the eve of escaping. The other chap succeeded. Bad luck for me.

The journey here was an eventful one, it took eight days. The first man I ran into when being entrained was Hessel[27] of the BCRA and the second was Hubble. We had various adventures all were handcuffed the whole time, nineteen men in one compartment and eighteen in another. We could not move being packed like sardines. The gates of the compartments were padlocked and we had very little air, no food had been provided for. We were given one day's rations which had to last five days, luckily I had some Red Cross parcels or we would have starved. The train was bombed and machine-gunned on the way and we had a very narrow shave. Our escorts ran and left us helpless, had

---

26 André Dewavrin of the BCRA, codenamed Colonel Passy.

27 Lieutenant Stephane Hessel. He also survived Buchenwald.

the train caught fire we would have burned like trapped rats. We
had to stop at Saarbrücken for three days in a punishment and
reprisals camp, and were beaten up on arrival. As usual I seemed
to attract particular attention and got well and truly slapped and
cuffed. We were confined for three days and nights, thirty-seven
of us in a hut 9 feet by 7 feet. It was Hell. We then came on to this
place Buchenwald. On the way our escorts plundered and stole
practically all our effects. Never believe a word about German
honesty, they are the biggest thieves, liars, bullies and cowards I
have ever met. In addition they delight in torturing people and
gloat over it. Upon arrival, which took place at about midnight,
we were locked up in the disinfection quarters and next morning
were very nearly hanged summarily, but temporarily reprieved.
We were stripped, completely shorn and dressed in prison rags,
losing our few remaining belongings, and sixteen of us, including
Hubble were told to report to a certain place. We never saw them
again and found out that they were hung without trial on the night
11/12 September. They have been cremated so no trace remains of
them. We are now awaiting our turn. There are one hundred and
seventy airmen (British and American) brought down and captured in France, but they are being treated as Terror Fliers and
sleeping in the open, living under appalling conditions in viola-
tion of all conventions. They ought to be treated as PoWs. Men
die like flies here. I sent a message to you through Geneva. I hope
you received it, but have no means of telling. The bearer of this
letter will give you all details so I will not say more – whatever he
tells you is Gospel truth. He is no romancer, and he will never be
able to really do justice to the horrors perpetrated here. For God's
sake Dizzy, see to it that our people never let themselves be softened towards the German people, or there will be another war
in fifteen years time and all our lives will have been sacrificed in

vain. I leave it to you and others to see that retribution is fierce. It will never be fierce enough.

Yeo-Thomas

The above letter is held at the UK National Archives in file ADM 223/481

PREPARING THE GROUND FOR JAMES BOND

IAN FLEMING

The creator of Britain's most famous secret agent was recruited into naval intelligence shortly before the Second World War to be the Personal Assistant to Admiral John Godfrey, the Director of Naval Intelligence (DNI). Godfrey had consulted his First World War counterpart, Admiral Reginald 'Blinker' Hall, on what he should do. Hall relied heavily on his own PA, Claude Serocold, a raffish playboy stockbroker, and told Godfrey to find someone similar. Godfrey consulted his friend Montagu Norman, the Governor of the Bank of England, who promised to find the right man. He found Ian Fleming.

Fleming joined the Naval Intelligence Division as Godfrey's PA shortly before the war, with the designation of 17F. It is often suggested that he was 'just in naval intelligence' and therefore knew very little about the ways of MI6. Nothing could be further from the truth. Fleming was Godfrey's link into the secret world, liaising on his behalf with MI6 and Government Code and Cipher School (GC&CS) at Bletchley Park, as well as the Special Operations Executive. He was also the new DNI's 'ideas man' and Godfrey made no secret of the fact that he relied heavily on Fleming as the author of many of his most important memos and reports, a point made clear by the gravity of the last two passages in this collection of Fleming's official writing.

In his post-war memoirs, Godfrey said: 'Ian Fleming's work and mine were inextricably intermingled. His command of English ensured that everything I wrote was to the point, was devoid of ambiguity and worded in a way that appealed to the Americans.'

There were no fancy frills in Fleming's writing.

∞∞

DUTIES OF PA TO THE DNI

At the end of the war, Fleming wrote the job specification for his successors, including as a key requirement the ability to carry out 'confidential missions' on behalf of his boss.

In wartime much use is made by the DNI of civilian contacts outside Whitehall and a large proportion of his contacts in his own Division are with civilians in naval uniform.

In the last war, the DNI found it convenient to canalise the majority of those through a senior RNVR officer, who acted as his Personal Assistant. This officer had command of three languages and widespread outside interests and contacts. As a result, 'bright' suggestions by the many brilliant civilians working with a junior rank in the naval Intelligence Division (NID) often received more encouragement than if they had gone through the normal Head of Section-Deputy DNI channel to the DNI. In fact the DNI found his PA of use in most matters not directly connected with the naval Service.

This officer was also a convenient channel for confidential matters connected with subversive organisations and for undertaking confidential missions abroad, either alone or with the DNI.

The DNI also found it convenient to have an officer not connected with ordinary sectional duties to represent him on inter-service and inter-departmental committees at a level not requiring his presence or that of the Deputy Director of Naval Intelligence (DDNI).

It is recommended that such an appointment should also be created in future wars and that the officer holding it should be chosen with considerable care and, if possible, retain his appointment throughout the war and thus ensure continuity in the handling of particularly confidential matters.

At the end of the job specification, Godfrey noted that it was 'a very great appreciation of his own job by Ian Fleming, who carried out the duties of PA to DNI throughout the Second World War with outstanding success.'

OPERATION RUTHLESS

One of Fleming's earliest proposals for a 'confidential mission' was in September 1940 and was inspired by Alan Turing, who was then leading Bletchley Park's efforts to break the German naval Enigma ciphers. Turing hoped Fleming might be able to devise a cunning plan to 'pinch' a naval Enigma machine and its settings, which were more complex than the German Army and Air Force equivalents. Fleming put forward a proposal for a daring operation, Operation Ruthless, to capture a small German vessel that would have an Enigma ('the Loot') on board, detailing the men required for the mission and pencilling in his own name alongside the requirement for a 'word-perfect German speaker'. To the intense disappointment of both Turing and Fleming, the operation never took place.

DNI

I suggest we obtain the loot by the following means:

1. Obtain from Air Ministry an air-worthy German bomber.

2. Pick a tough crew of five, including a pilot, W/T operator and word-perfect German speaker. Dress them in German Air Force uniform, add blood and bandages to suit.

3. Crash plane in the Channel after making SOS to rescue service in plain language.

4. Once aboard rescue boat, shoot German crew, dump overboard, bring rescue boat back to English port.

In order to increase the chances of capturing an R or M Boat with its richer booty, the crash might be staged in mid-Channel. The Germans would presumably employ one of this type for the longer and more hazardous journey.

F

GODFREY'S BATTLES WITH C

The armed forces intelligence branches spent much of the war complaining about the standard of intelligence produced by MI6, sometimes with good reason but mostly out of prejudice and ignorance. MI6 reporting throughout the war was far better than it was ever given credit for, and military, naval and in particular air intelligence frequently rubbished reports that would later turn out to be entirely accurate. The early reports on the German development of the VI rockets were just one example, with the RAF refusing to believe them and declining to bomb the Peenemünde rocket base until it was too late.

The full extent of the role played by MI6 in providing actionable intelligence during the Second World War remains concealed, in large part as a result of the determination of MI6 chiefs to keep everything they did secret. In their defence, this was based on the entirely sensible principle that agents who worked for them only did so because they believed their identities would never be revealed.

Godfrey criticised MI6 on a regular basis. This letter of complaint, written by Fleming for Godfrey, but signed personally by Fleming with the initial F, is a case in point.

It is clear from our conversation this morning on the subject of a plan for coast-watching in Central America that liaison between our two departments is still not as perfect as it might be.

As regards this particular plan, as I see it, the procedure should have been that the officer who composed it should in the first instance have approached Colonel [John] Cordeaux or Commander [Christopher] Arnold-Forster on the subject, and they would probably have referred him to our South American Section and to the OIC[28] who are the experts on the habits and routines of the U-boats.

Your representative could then have examined the details of our present naval reporting organisation in Central America and he would have heard the operational comments on the scheme which I have enclosed in my letter of 18 July. With this basis of practical knowledge a memorandum from him suggesting possible means of patching up, with the help of the Secret Intelligence Service (SIS), the holes in our reporting organisation would have been extremely valuable.

I had hoped that the appointment of Colonel Cordeaux would have created a machinery for seeing that this sort of problem would have been simplified on the above lines, but gather that his duties as Head of the North European area are likely to reduce his value as our primary link with your department on naval matters. The fact that Cordeaux has had to absent himself for so long from his naval duties raised the question as to whether his main usefulness to you is going to depend on his relationships with the NID or

---

28   The Admiralty's Operational Intelligence Centre.

on his production duties in the SIS. This is a point which I think requires clarification both for my own information and to correct the impression which appears to exist amongst the other naval officers in your department; for instance, I understand that Captain Russell is to deputise for Colonel Cordeaux in his absence but is at the same time extremely chary of making decisions when he is away, and the fact that Colonel Cordeaux has arranged for all naval matters to be canalised through him or his deputy has tended to put a curb on the initiative of other members of the naval Section.

Curiously enough, Cordeaux's appointment has thus in some respects lessened the direct liaison between our departments on a lower level. This tendency has not been so apparent during his absence in Stockholm and things are now working fairly normally again, i.e. Arnold-Forster is in direct touch with DDNI, Fleming, and Heads of Sections, and Commander [name redacted] is always available. Captain Russell maintains his daily visits as previously.

I should greatly deplore any weakening of the liaison on this level. The fact that these channels were not used by Commander [Kenneth] Cohen in forwarding his memorandum has been largely responsible, for the confusion which subsequently resulted.

I would be very grateful if you could think over the points I have raised and let me have your views. The issue in a nutshell is whether Colonel Cordeaux can combine his production duties for a certain part of Europe with the task of satisfying his day-to-day Admiralty requirements from your organisation throughout the world.

F

SAVING MI6 FOR BOND

Despite the numerous letters of complaint over MI6 operations he wrote for Godfrey it is clear that Fleming's personal position was much more supportive of C, whose title would be converted to M in the Bond books.

Up until the start of the war, C had always been a naval officer. The use of the letter C derived originally from the initial of the Service's founder Commander Mansfield Cumming RN, although it was soon taken as standing for the 'Chief' or head of the Service. The tradition, which also began with Cumming, that C always signed his memos in green ink stemmed from naval practice. Cumming was replaced by Admiral Hugh Sinclair, but when Sinclair died in November 1939, he was replaced by his deputy Stewart Menzies, a senior army officer, leaving the Navy with its nose out of joint.

Godfrey, supported by the First Sea Lord Admiral Sir Dudley Pound, put together a plan for a separate naval secret service that would rival MI6, with the ultimate intention of replacing it. But Churchill demurred and ordered an inquiry which found that MI6 was actually much better than the armed forces seemed to believe, putting an end to any hope of an independent naval secret service.

Fleming stood up to Godfrey and agreed with the inquiry's positive assessment of MI6. The Navy should concentrate on getting more naval representation inside MI6, with a staff officer attached to C as his personal assistant, the role he provided for Godfrey. He appears to have been eyeing the job up for himself. But Godfrey was not about to let Fleming go and it was given to a Royal Navy officer already serving in MI6, Christopher Arnold-Forster.

Nevertheless, Fleming's intervention saved MI6 and ensured that it would go on to enjoy a hallowed place among the world's intelligence services, in many ways as a direct result of his later creation of the Service's most famous officer, a man with the same rank and service affiliation as Fleming – Commander James Bond RNVR.

I am sorry to say that I think this report very reasonable. As to the individuals concerned, the points made also seem just, but in any reorganisation which might be necessary there is a grave danger, as with all reorganisation, of 'letting the baby out with the bath water'.

I think that the infusion of new blood into the existing organisation would be better than chopping off hoary but experienced heads. This process of infiltration has presumably been going on since the beginning of the war, and it could be expedited at any moment, particularly by the War Office, who have trained personnel in such sections as MI(R).[29]

I should imagine that if MI(R) and certain NID personnel were drafted on to the existing organisation, the result would be to revitalise the whole.

Probably in order to get the best out of Colonel A. M. Craig, Arnold-Forster and [Captain Edward] Hastings, it would be a good thing for all three to have young Staff Officers-cum-Secretaries attached to them. It would probably be a good thing if 'C' himself had such an individual.

F

BOND'S FUTURE MISSIONS

In a draft memorandum to the head of the Joint Intelligence Committee in April 1944, Fleming pointed out the new threats facing the intelligence services in a post-war world. For reasons that are unclear, when the files were released to the National Archives in May 2008, Fleming's assessment of what those threats might be was removed on the grounds of national security. Precisely what the risk to national security might have been

---

29 Military Intelligence section which was a War Office predecessor of the Special Operations Executive.

sixty-four years after Fleming drafted the memo is difficult to comprehend. But given Fleming's emphasis on the acquisition of high-tech intelligence, it is tempting to imagine that – alongside the obvious dangers posed by the Soviet Union and Communist China, and the industrial nations' need for oil – he already saw egomaniac scientists dreaming up diabolical schemes for world domination as one of those threats. At any event, he argued that human spies were the only real way of obtaining the intelligence that would be required and urged that MI6 concentrate on recruiting highly trained agents capable of obtaining it, paving the way for the first appearance, in 1953, of James Bond.

1. With reference to your A/J/7 of 17 April 1944, I entirely agree with the desirability of providing C with all possible indications of the lines along which we shall probably require him to concentrate in peace time.

2. It is a difficult task, but I think even at this early date I can put forward the following firm requirements:

As the first priority we shall require high-grade technical intelligence on weapon development by the major powers.

This will particularly apply to radar, new explosives and fuels, the use of magnetic, acoustic and other principles for the direction and firing of underwater weapons, and remote control flight of aircraft or missiles, submarine, torpedo, and mine development in all its branches, will require constant attention.

The end of one war generally provides the writing on the wall for the weapons which will be used in the next one, and the above seem to cover the present lines of research and development.

The Admiralty will continue to require intelligence affecting sea power generally. The size of navies will probably be ascertainable by other means, i.e. through Naval Attachés, the Press, Photographic

Reconnaissance Units, etc., but movements or projected movements of major units will be important even in peacetime, unless they are notified openly by the country concerned. Really high-grade information on naval construction and design will be necessary as will be details of commercial design and invention which may herald alterations in naval architecture, motive power, etc. Naval air intelligence will be a most important new field which was hardly touched upon by intelligence before this war.

Development, design and strengths in midget underwater craft of all kinds will be an important and troublesome commitment, since these craft can be built and manned even by minor naval powers. Their existence would entail very heavy expenditure on port defences throughout the Empire.

Topographical and beach information in protected areas, including any clues as to the establishment of new naval bases, aerodromes and arsenals.

3. As regards priorities between countries or regions it is of course impossible at this date to foresee which may be the aggressor nations of the future.

[The remainder of paragraph 3 and the following two paragraphs were redacted from the file in 2008 on the grounds of national security]

6. In addition to the above there will of course be the main Empire danger spots which have always existed but these are largely a matter for diplomatic and overt channels. Such localities are Spanish Morocco, the Dardanelles, the Suez Canal, the Middle-East oilfields and the Gulf of Maracaibo in Venezuela.

[Paragraph 7 was also redacted on the grounds of national security]

8. I have made this appreciation as broad as possible, but I would repeat that our first and really paramount requirement will

be first-class technical information along the line suggested in my para 2. Whatever the success of our future GC&CS this type of technical information is seldom the subject of W/T communication and I urge that highly trained agents for this field of enquiry should be selected and strategically disposed as soon as possible after the war.

F

The above documents are held at the UK National Archives in files ADM 223/851 and ADM 223/464

THE SAD CASE OF
JAN MAŠEK

BOB STEERS

Bob Steers served in the British Army's Intelligence Corps in the immediate post-war years. In 1948, he was sent to the Austrian capital Vienna, then divided into five sectors, British, American, French, Russian and International, the last controlled alternately by each of the four Allied powers on a monthly basis. Vienna became one of the major espionage capitals of the world, a situation vividly portrayed in the Graham Greene-scripted film *The Third Man*, later turned into a novel. Steers was a member of Field Security Section Vienna, where he worked for much of the time for MI6. This story demonstrates the point already made about agent handlers having to be prepared to be brutal. Agents sometimes have to be burned, although often, as here, it is not always clear whether their loss was a matter of necessity or stupidity.

DURING THE ALLIED Occupation of Austria (1945–55) the country was, like Germany, divided into the British, American, Soviet and French zones. Although it was military government, as far as the Western forces were concerned, there was very little interference of the civil authorities in the running of their country, in fact, in 1949 there were democratic elections, the various political parties, even the communists, having complete freedom to express themselves.

Having spent just over a year in the beautiful province of Carinthia I was posted to Field Security Vienna in 1950. The Austrian capital, like Berlin, was some 90 miles behind the Iron Curtain, that is, in the Soviet Zone but, unlike Berlin where Allied sectors were in wedges, those in Vienna were interspersed. For example, we lived in the III *Bezirk* (district) yet the II and IV were Russian. Naturally, we could move around in the Soviet sectors but not enter the Soviet Zone which surrounded the city. There had been two Field Security Sections in Vienna, 20 FSS in Hietzing near Schönbrunn Palace and 291 FSS in Sebastianplatz, the Viennese equivalent of Belgravia, but in 1950 all sections lost their numbers. As with all sections, we lived in comfortable private residences served by civilian cooks and cleaners.

After arriving I spent a short time tapping Soviet military telephone lines, but then went on to interrogating Illegal Frontier Crossers (IFCs) and, ultimately, working for 'The Firm' [MI6], which was located in the embassy. These IFCs were the men and women who had fled Hungary and Czechoslovakia through the frontier obstacles of ploughed fields, mines, patrols, barbed-wire and booby-traps, via the Soviet Zone and had been arrested by the Austrian Gendarmerie in the western sectors. Our job was to interrogate them to ascertain they were not infiltration agents (I am sure not always successfully), sap them of all military and industrial information they might have and then smuggle them past the infrequent Red Army patrols on the Semmering Pass, whence they would be picked up by Field Security Styria and placed in a Displaced Persons' camp. Eventually they would be transported to

Genoa and thence by ship to Australia, Canada, UK or USA. A short interrogation would last three or four days as it would start on the day the interrogatee was born until he or she was sitting in front of me. Everyone had information of some use. A housewife would have had relatives doing their National Service and so locations and types of unit were of value.

Details of unit locations would be sent to the Military Attachés in Budapest and Prague from Int Org in Schönbrunn Barracks. After questioning a housewife, although she did not realise it, I sent a note, 'Probable newly arrived Soviet artillery regiment 16 kilometres south of Pecs' (in central Hungary). Some three weeks later the reply came back, in clear, 'Bang on, ta' – which must have given the *AVO* [30] decoders a headache for months.

It must have been in the late spring of 1953 that a Czech deserter was brought to me. Jan Mašek was a lance-corporal and had been a clerk in the HQ of an armoured division stationed south of Olomouc in Slovakia. A simple basically-educated country lad but his earlier employment meant he had seen things on a relatively broad basis. After some four or five days of questioning, I sent a synopsis of his story up to Int Org who, to my initial surprise, reacted with alacrity. The reason was in 1945 the US Army had ended up in Czechoslovakia and, in accordance with the Yalta Agreement, withdrew to their allocated zone of Germany. The Sherman tanks in their units had been driven, for the most part, all the way from France and were worn out and it was not worth their while taking them back. They were left in Czechoslovakia and were incorporated in the post-war Czech army. Mašek described how in the summer of 1952 the entire division was confined to barracks, their Sherman tanks were taken away and replaced with Soviet-built

---

30 *Allamvedelmi Osztaly,* Hungarian Intelligence Service.

T34-35s – incidentally, one of the best tanks in the Second World War and the first AFV (Armoured Fighting Vehicle) with a diesel engine, so they did not 'brew up' when hit, unlike the Allied ones. It was this information which excited Int Org as it was the first concrete confirmation that the Czech Army was being Sovietised. It was just a pointer that could indicate that Moscow was preparing for a push westwards, in that, by having all satellite forces armed with common weapons etc., the supply of ammunition and parts was greatly simplified. The interest in Int Org was such that two fairly senior people were sent to sit in on my interrogation of Mašek for several days. The difficulty with such interrogations is that the subject being simple minded had seen and heard matters of importance to us but these still resided in the inner recesses of his mind and one had to ease them out by patient questioning. To add to this, Mašek was a very willing interrogatee and was offering information which he clearly invented in order to play the part. Fact and fiction had to be diplomatically sifted. In all the interrogation lasted for two and a half weeks and my report to Int Org comprised some forty-five typed pages including appendices.

So, I thought, we would smuggle Jan Mašek down to Field Security Styria and, as a priority, he would be sent to Australia, his chosen destination. But there was an unexpected turn of events.

I was one of three Field Security chaps working almost full-time for 'The Firm' and was involved in running line-crossers into Hungary and Czechoslovakia … and getting people out via my own means. Frequently I was present at the final briefing of the agent in a safe house the day before he went eastwards. Under my bed in my flat, I had a suitcase full of automatics which I would carry to a safe-house and, like a door-to-door salesman, offer our man a choice of them. Incidentally, when first given the weapons I stripped and cleaned them, most were German, and after obtaining permission from the adjutant, tested them all on the small arms range in Schönbrunn Barracks on the other side of Vienna. Whilst doing this I was approached by a, naturally, curious sergeant-major, it was an odd sight someone with twenty assorted German automatics banging away. He accepted my assurance I was there with the correct permission – 'heard about you Intelligent Corpse people'. He was understanding. I often spent the last night in the flat with the agent, not only because I had recruited them from the IFCs who passed through our hands ('do a couple of trips and we promise you will go to the country of your choice in no time') but also they nearly always became nervous and had doubts, such as, 'I know I'll not come back this time,' and I would attempt to reassure them and give them encouragement – a tall order for someone in his early twenties. I remember one Joseph ('Seppi') Prinz, a very brave man with at least three trips behind him, cried in his sleep before his last journey. He was surrounded just inside the border and shot himself with the chromed .45 automatic I supplied. It was advisable not to be captured by the *ŠtB* [31] or the *AVO* for obvious reasons.

It is no reflection on these people's bravery to mention their nervousness; it was a natural reaction. A colleague, Bill de May, was with 64 Field Security Section, one of the SOE sections, during the Second World War and he related how, occasionally, when over the DZ [Drop Zone] in France, if the agents had second thoughts and refused to jump, they would literally throw them out of the plane as the lives of the reception party were at risk. Bill was convinced that, once on ground, steadfastness would return to these doughty men and women.

Returning to the turn of events, a member of 'The Firm'

---

31   *Státní Bezpečnost*, Czechoslovak Intelligence Service.

informed me that a radio had urgently to be taken into Czecho-slovakia and the only person available was Mašek, the rest of the agents being either still behind the wire or killed. I vehemently pro-tested. I knew Mašek better than anyone; I understood his thought processes. I knew how he would react to certain situations. I had delved into the back of his mind and he was not of the calibre we required for someone for such an operation. Also, I had already told him that he was practically on his way to Australia. He had, after all, given the West information of prime importance. I was overruled as I was but a spear carrier. It was pointed out to me that, as I knew, the frontier obstacles were almost impenetrable and Mašek clearly knew a weakness, ergo, he could go in at the same place as he had come out. I was most unhappy as I felt we were sending this soft, simple country lad to a slow painful death. It was not a case of 'My country right or wrong.' To boot, I was told I had to do the dirty work.

I spent several hours explaining to Mašek the importance of the trip which I do not think he really understood. However, I con-vinced him enough for him to agree to go. Now, Mašek came from a small village in Slovakia and had been brought up by his mother, a single parent. She had fallen ill and he had gone AWOL [absent without leave] to see her, and it was because, as a result, he was awaiting a court-martial that he had deserted. At the final briefing I drummed into him that, after burying the radio at the appropriate spot, he was immediately to return and, under no circumstances, visit his mother. Clearly, his presence in the village would be noticed and the *ŠtB* informed.

As it transpired, he did precisely that. Word later trickled back. The *ŠtB* gave him a 'going over' and he was hanged in front of his regiment '*pour encourager les autres…*'

No. Before he went, I did not offer him a gun. He would not

have used it, either on himself or on anyone else. He was too nice a human being.

∞∞

Extracted from a collection of similar stories by those who worked in the Field Security Sections entitled *FSS: Field Security Section* edited by Bob Steers (available for purchase from Intelligence Corps Museum, Chicksands, Shefford, Bedfordshire, SG17 5PR)

A BRIEF HISTORY OF GEORGE SMILEY

JOHN LE CARRÉ

This is the first appearance, in 1961, of the man who replaced James Bond in the public perception as the perfect British spy. The creation of George Smiley, by John le Carré (former MI5 and MI6 officer David Cornwell) transformed our expectations of spy novels and our views of MI6 officers. Smiley lived in a more realistic, more easily recognised world, where spies lived relatively normal lives. Maybe not mundane, actually never mundane in Smiley's case, but he was not a trained killer with a fictitious 'licence to kill', he was someone who used brain rather than brawn to win his Cold War battles. (Although it ought to be said that there is more than a suspicion that the death of journalist spy Jerry Westerby was the result of an MI6 hit which must at least have been sanctioned, if not ordered, by Smiley, and surely he knew that Jim Prideaux would be bound to kill Bill Hayden?)

'A Brief History of George Smiley', which appears at the very beginning of John le Carré's first novel *Call for the Dead*, reeks of authenticity, not least in the political manoeuvring of career civil servants using the Service to make a name for themselves. At the time, and for most of the period during which Smiley featured in le Carré's writing, it was widely accepted among intelligence historians that MI6 had done little if anything inside Germany during the Second World War, so mention of Smiley's undercover work there, and he did have real-life counterparts, is to be welcomed.

Most fiction editors would have an apoplectic fit if a first-time author gave away the protagonist's complete back-story at the start of their novel, but since le Carré used it as a base from which to build an entire world revolving around the shabby offices of 'the Circus' and peopled only by very real, fully rounded characters, the editor of *Call for the Dead* deserves the gratitude of Smiley aficionados everywhere.

WHEN LADY ANN Sercomb married George Smiley towards the end of the war she described him to her astonished Mayfair friends as breathtakingly ordinary. When she left him two years later in favour of a Cuban motor racing driver, she announced enigmatically that if she hadn't left him then, she never could have done; and Viscount Sawley made a special journey to his club to observe that the cat was out of the bag.

This remark, which enjoyed a brief season as a *mot*, can only be understood by those who knew Smiley. Short, fat, and of a quiet disposition, he appeared to spend a lot of money on really bad clothes, which hung about his squat frame like skin on a shrunken toad. Sawley, in fact, declared at the wedding that 'Sercomb was mated to a bullfrog in a sou'wester'. And Smiley, unaware of this description, had waddled down the aisle in search of the kiss that would turn him into a Prince.

Was he rich or poor, peasant or priest? Where had she got him from? The incongruity of the match was emphasised by Lady Ann's undoubted beauty, its mystery stimulated by the disproportion between the man and his bride. But gossip must see its characters in black and white, equip them with sins and motives easily conveyed in the shorthand of conversation. And so Smiley, without school, parents, regiment or trade, without wealth or poverty, travelled without labels in the guard's van of the social express, and soon became lost luggage, destined, when the divorce had come and gone, to remain unclaimed on the dusty shelf of yesterday's news.

When Lady Ann followed her star to Cuba, she gave some thought to Smiley. With grudging admiration she admitted to herself that if there were an only man in her life, Smiley would be he. She was gratified in retrospect that she had demonstrated this by holy matrimony.

The effect of Lady Ann's departure upon her former husband did not interest society – which indeed is unconcerned with the aftermath of sensation. Yet it would be interesting to know what Sawley and his flock might have made of Smiley's reaction; of that fleshy, bespectacled face puckered in energetic concentration as he read so deeply among the lesser German poets, the chubby wet hands clenched beneath the tumbling sleeves. But Sawley profited by the occasion with the merest of shrugs by remarking *partir c'est courir un peu*, and he appeared to be unaware that though Lady Ann just ran away, a little of George Smiley had indeed died.

That part of Smiley which survived was as incongruous to his appearance as love, or a taste for unrecognised poets: it was his profession, which was that of intelligence officer. It was a profession he enjoyed, and which mercifully provided him with colleagues equally obscure in character and origin. It also provided him with what he had once loved best in life: academic excursions into the mystery of human behaviour, disciplined by the practical application of his own deductions.

Some time in the twenties when Smiley had emerged from his unimpressive school and lumbered blinking into the murky cloisters of his unimpressive Oxford College, he had dreamed of Fellowships and a life devoted to the literary obscurities of seventeenth-century Germany. But his own tutor, who knew Smiley better, guided him wisely away from the honours that would undoubtedly have been his. On a sweet July morning in 1928, a puzzled and rather pink Smiley had sat before an interviewing board of the Overseas Committee for Academic Research, an organisation of which he had unaccountably never heard. Jebedee (his tutor) had been oddly vague about the introduction: 'Give these people a try, Smiley, they might have you and they pay badly enough to guarantee you decent company.' But Smiley was annoyed and said so. It worried him that Jebedee, usually so precise, was so evasive. In a slight huff he agreed to postpone his reply to All Souls until he had seen Jebedee's 'mysterious people'.

He wasn't introduced to the Board, but he knew half of its members by sight. There was Fielding, the French medievalist from Cambridge, Sparke from the School of Oriental Languages, and Steed-Asprey who had been dining at High Table the night Smiley had been Jebedee's guest. He had to admit he was impressed. For Fielding to leave his rooms, let alone Cambridge, was in itself a miracle. Afterwards Smiley always thought of that interview as a fan dance; a calculated progression of disclosures, each revealing different parts of a mysterious entity. Finally Steed-Asprey, who seemed to be Chairman, removed the last veil, and the truth stood before him in all its dazzling nakedness. He was being offered a post in what, for want of a better name, Steed-Asprey blushingly described as the secret service.

Smiley had asked for time to think. They gave him a week. No one mentioned pay.

That night he stayed in London at somewhere rather good and took himself to the theatre. He felt strangely light-headed and this worried him. He knew very well that he would accept, that he could have done so at the interview. It was only an instinctive caution, and perhaps a pardonable desire to play the coquette with Fielding, which prevented him from doing so.

Following his affirmation came training: anonymous country houses, anonymous instructors, a good deal of travel and, looming ever larger, the fantastic prospect of working completely alone.

His first operational posting was relatively pleasant: a two-year appointment as *englischer Dozent* at a provincial German University: lectures on Keats and vacations in Bavarian hunting lodges with groups of earnest and solemnly promiscuous German students. Towards the end of each long vacation he brought some of them back to England, having already earmarked the likely ones and conveyed his recommendations by clandestine means to an address in Bonn; during the entire two years he had no idea of whether his recommendations had been accepted or ignored. He had no means of knowing even whether his candidates were approached. Indeed he had no means of knowing whether his messages ever reached their destination; and he had no contact with the department while in England.

His emotions in performing this work were mixed, and irreconcilable. It intrigued him to evaluate from a detached position what he had learnt to describe as 'the agent potential' of a human being; to devise minuscule tests of character and behaviour which could inform him of the qualities of a candidate. This part of him was bloodless and inhuman – Smiley in this role was the international mercenary of his trade, amoral and without motive beyond that of personal gratification.

Conversely it saddened him to witness in himself the gradual death of natural pleasure. Always withdrawn, he now found himself shrinking from the temptations of friendship and human loyalty; he guarded himself warily from spontaneous reaction. By the strength of his intellect, he forced himself to observe humanity with clinical objectivity, and because he was neither immortal nor infallible he hated and feared the falseness of his life.

But Smiley was a sentimental man and the long exile strengthened his deep love of England. He fed hungrily on memories of Oxford; its beauty, its rational ease, and the mature slowness of its judgements. He dreamt of windswept autumn holidays at Hartland Quay, of long trudges over the Cornish cliffs, his face smooth and hot against the sea wind. This was his other secret life, and he grew to hate the bawdy intrusion of the new Germany, the stamping and shouting of uniformed students, the scarred, arrogant faces and their cheapjack answers. He resented, too, the way in which the Faculty had tampered with his subject – his beloved German literature. And there had been a night, a terrible night in the winter of 1937, when Smiley had stood at his window and watched a great bonfire in the university court: round it stood hundreds of students, their faces exultant and glistening in the dancing light. And into the pagan fire they threw books in their hundreds. He knew whose books they were: Thomas Mann, Heine, Lessing and a host of others. And Smiley, his damp hand cupped round the end of his cigarette, watching and hating, triumphed that he knew his enemy.

Nineteen thirty-nine saw him in Sweden, the accredited agent of a well-known Swiss small-arms manufacturer, his association with the firm conveniently backdated. Conveniently, too, his appearance had somehow altered, for Smiley had discovered in himself a talent for the part which went beyond the rudimentary change to his hair and the addition of a small moustache. For four years he had played the part, travelling back and forth between Switzerland, Germany, and Sweden. He had never guessed it was possible to be frightened for so long. He developed a nervous irritation in his left eye which remained with him fifteen years later; the strain etched lines on his fleshy cheeks and brow. He learnt what it was never to sleep, never to relax, to feel at any time of day or night the restless beating of his own heart, to know the extremes of solitude and self-pity, the sudden unreasoning desire for a woman, for drink, for exercise, for any drug to take away the tension of his life.

Against this background he conducted his authentic commerce and his work as a spy. With the progress of time the network grew, and other countries repaired their lack of foresight and preparation. In 1943 he was recalled. Within six weeks he was yearning to return, but they never let him go.

'You're finished,' Steed-Asprey said: 'train new men, take time off. Get married or something. Unwind.'

Smiley proposed to Steed-Asprey's secretary, the Lady Ann Sercomb.

The war was over. They paid him off, and he took his beautiful wife to Oxford to devote himself to the obscurities of seventeenth-century Germany. But two years later Lady Ann was in Cuba, and the revelations of a young Russian cypher-clerk in Ottawa had created a new demand for men of Smiley's experience.

The job was new, the threat elusive and at first he enjoyed it. But younger men were coming in, perhaps with fresher minds. Smiley was no material for promotion and it dawned on him gradually that he had entered middle age without ever being young, and that he was – in the nicest possible way – on the shelf.

Things changed. Steed-Asprey was gone, fled from the new world to India, in search of another civilisation. Jebedee was dead. He had boarded a train at Lille in 1941 with his radio operator, a young Belgian, and neither had been heard of again. Fielding was wedded to a new thesis on Roland – only Maston remained, Maston the career man, the wartime recruit, the Ministers' Adviser on Intelligence; 'the first man,' Jebedee had said, 'to play power tennis at

Wimbledon.' The NATO alliance, and the desperate measures contemplated by the Americans, altered the whole nature of Smiley's Service. Gone for ever were the days of Steed-Asprey, when as like as not you took your orders over a glass of port in his rooms at Magdalen; the inspired amateurism of a handful of highly qualified, under-paid men had given way to the efficiency, bureaucracy, and intrigue of a large government department effectively at the mercy of Maston, with his expensive clothes and his knighthood, his distinguished grey hair and silver coloured ties; Maston, who even remembered his secretary's birthday, whose manners were a by-word among the ladies of the registry; Maston, apologetically extending his empire and regretfully moving to even larger offices; Maston, holding smart house-parties at Henley and feeding on the success of his subordinates.

They had brought him in during the war, the professional civil servant from an orthodox department, a man to handle paper and integrate the brilliance of his staff with the cumbersome machine of bureaucracy. It comforted the Great to deal with a man they knew, a man who could reduce any colour to grey, who knew his masters and could walk among them. And he did it so well. They liked his diffidence when he apologised for the company he kept, his insincerity when he defended the vagaries of his subordinates, his flexibility when formulating new commitments. Nor did he let go the advantages of a cloak and dagger man *malgré lui*, wearing the cloak for his masters and preserving the dagger for his servants. Ostensibly, his position was an odd one. He was not the nominal Head of Service, but the Ministers' Adviser on Intelligence, and Steed-Asprey had described him for all time as the Head Eunuch.

This was a new world for Smiley: the brilliantly lit corridors, the smart young men. He felt pedestrian and old-fashioned, homesick for the dilapidated terrace house in Knightsbridge where it had all begun. His appearance seemed to reflect this discomfort in a kind of physical recession which made him more hunched and frog-like than ever. He blinked more, and acquired the nickname of 'Mole'. But his debutante secretary adored him, and referred to him invariably as 'My darling teddy-bear'.

Smiley was now too old to go abroad. Maston had made that clear: 'Anyway, my dear fellow, as like as not you're blown after all the ferreting about in the war. Better stick at home, old man, and keep the home fires burning.'

Which goes some way to explaining why George Smiley sat in the back of a London taxi at two o'clock on the morning of Wednesday 4 January on his way to Cambridge Circus.

Extracted from *Call for the Dead* by John le Carré (first published by Gollancz in 1961 and reproduced here with permission of Curtis Brown Group Ltd, London, on behalf of le Carré productions)

WHEN PHILBY
MET HOLLIS
KIM PHILBY

Kim Philby, the so-called Third Man in the Cambridge spy ring, was the Cold War's most infamous traitor, a Soviet spy at the heart of British intelligence. He came down from Cambridge in 1933 determined to become a communist. At the time, this was not unusual. The effects of the deep recession of the '30s and the overwhelming power of the British class system led many people, particularly among the educated younger generations, to believe that Stalin's Soviet Union offered a different, brave new world.

Philby went to Austria where he worked as a courier for communist activists engaged in running street-battles with right-wing government forces and was talent-spotted by the Russian secret service, then known as the NKVD. When he returned to the UK he was recruited as a Soviet agent and sent by his Soviet control to Spain under cover as a journalist covering the Civil War, with the original orders that he was to find a way to assassinate the right-wing leader General Francisco Franco. On his return to the UK, he succeeded in getting himself recruited into MI6, eventually taking charge of a new department, Section IX, set up in anticipation of the Cold War to track down Soviet spies.

This report is written in October 1944 when in this new role Philby visited the MI5 anti-Soviet section, then based at Blenheim Palace in Oxfordshire. It was headed by Roger Hollis, later Director-General of MI5 and notorious for repeated claims that he was a long-term Soviet agent. The evidence against him was subsequently found to have been too 'insubstantial' to have merited investigation but the claims have refused to go away. In truth, it is difficult to believe that a man who spent a large part of the '30s in China associating with long-term Soviet agents like Agnes Smedley and Richard Sorge was not in some way involved in the espionage world, although given that he was working for British-American Tobacco, which frequently provided cover for MI6 officers, it is by no means a foregone conclusion that he was working for Moscow. Philby's account of their meeting includes an interesting reference to Millicent Bagot, who bears a striking resemblance to George Smiley's Russia expert Connie Sachs. Despite the claims about Hollis, Philby's reference here to future collaboration refers of course to that between MI5 and MI6.

I HAD A long interview with Hollis at his request, in order that we might discuss our future collaboration.

Hollis began by explaining that his Division of MI5 (F Division) was a wartime creation. Before the war, all the present work of F Division had been done by B Division. Indeed, work against Communism and the Soviet Union had been the principal task of B Division. As the war got under way, however, it became convenient to split B Division into two, one dealing with enemy espionage and sabotage, the other with subversive political movements and Soviet espionage. Thus F Division was born.

Hollis said that he had recently moved up to London from Oxford that section of F Division which deals with right-wing movements,

Fascists, etc.; that section is under Shelford. His anti-Communist section, however, remains at Oxford.

F Division is divided into three sections: F1 under Shelford is a new section set up to deal with British renegades captured on the continent, e.g.: William Joyce, P. G. Wodehouse etc. F2 deals with left-wing movements. F3, under Mitchell,[32] deals with right-wing movements.

The anti-Communist section is divided into three sub-sections. F2A, under David Clark, deals with left-wing political parties; F2B, nominally under Hugh Shillito but in practice run by Miss Millicent Bagot, deals with foreign Communists in the UK; F2C under Hugh Shillito deals with Soviet espionage. (Shillito was given a vague supervisory role in respect of F2B because it was thought better to have a man nominally in charge!)

F2A consists of eleven officers of whom about half are women. Its function is to study and investigate the activity of the Communist Party of Great Britain (CPGB). Hollis claims that MI5 have a really good knowledge of the organisation, personnel and activity of the CPGB: Curry[33] later substantiated this claim.

Clark, who obtained a first-class degree for economics in Cambridge, was employed in peacetime in a research institute of the Conservative Party. He is about thirty. According to Hollis, Clark is a really good intelligence officer, and is gifted in particular with a photographic memory.

F2B consists of Miss Bagot, and three women. Its function is to study foreign Communists in British territory, and to do this she must necessarily make a study also of Communist activity abroad.

---

32   Graham Mitchell, Hollis's Deputy Director-General, who was himself falsely accused of working for Moscow.

33   John Curry, a senior MI5 counter-espionage expert. He led F Section temporarily before Hollis and Section IX, again temporarily, before Philby.

Hollis declares that Miss Bagot is a really outstanding character. She has been working on the Communist problem for over twenty years and has a positively encyclopaedic knowledge of the subject. From what Hollis said, I gathered that he considers her as the most valuable member of the whole Division.

F2C consists of Shillito, and is responsible for Soviet espionage. Hollis considers that he is very good at worrying at the intricacies of a case, and mentioned in particular that he had done exceedingly good work in tracking down Green[34], and in getting him to talk after his arrest. He said, however, that Shillito was less good at the broader, political aspects of the problem.

Hollis then gave me the following resumé of the sources at the disposal of MI5. He spoke first of MI5's close co-operation with Special Branch. He said that Special Branch supplied a great deal of local, but fairly low-grade information about Communist characters in their district. They in their turn received from MI5 periodical appreciations and directives. He said that the Special Branch people were in general too conspicuous to achieve really startling results. There is a great shortage of good people for shadowing and surveillance, and the quality of this work varies from district to district. He mentioned Liverpool as being a district where the watching was of particularly high quality, since it was usually done by inconspicuous, local people, who were chosen for being as dissimilar as possible to the usual policemen.

Hollis next mentioned Maxwell Knight's agents. Knight does not serve F Division alone. He provides agents for the whole of MI5. His agents, according to Hollis, are usually of high quality.

There appears from what Hollis told me to be another group

---

34 Oliver Green, a British Communist who ran a Soviet intelligence network in Britain during the Second World War.

of agents run by a man named Hunter.[35] Most of these are agents of long-standing, and Hollis's chief complaint about them is that they are getting old, and Hunter is unwilling to recruit new people, because he always compares them unfavourably to the 'Old Gang'. These agents attend Communist meetings, etc., and report on the people who attend them. Hollis claims that they know most of the Communist leaders by sight, and can be relied on to provide accurate, if not high-grade, information.

Hollis next mentioned information obtained from telephone checks. These, he said, did not yield much information directly, but, they were useful in that they gave information about the movements of various people. It could be discovered, for instance, which people would attend which meetings, where they habitually kept rendezvous, etc. Through these telephone checks, therefore, it was possible to plant informers in public-houses, etc., before the arrival of the people in whom MI5 are interested.

Postal censorship, according to Hollis, yields some, but not much, of interest. It is not possible to cover the Communist HQ in London completely because of the volume of correspondence reaching it. Hollis mentioned to me one curious fact that Communists appeared to regard themselves as safe from censorship in the case of incoming correspondence. While many Communists who know that they are on check take great pains with letters which they themselves write and despatch, they seem to show no alarm whatever at receiving compromising letters. The truth of course is that the incoming letters are always a source of much greater danger.

Hollis finally turned to his greatest source of information. F Division has derived a great deal of information about the CPGB from

---

35   Harry Hunter, head of MI5's B6 surveillance section known as 'the Watchers.'

the use of 'special facilities', i.e. microphones installed in the telephone apparatus at 16 King Street, and other headquarters of the CPGB. They receive about seventy pages of information on an average every day. This material gives them a close insight into the activity of the leaders of the Communist Party, the deliberations of the Politburo, etc.

He said in a voice of triumph that they had got King Street completely buttoned up, and that they obtained from that source a huge volume of high grade material. He claimed that by assiduous reading, Clark was extraordinary well-informed about the politics, dissensions, private affairs, etc. of leading Communists and that this source was equivalent in value to ISOS[36] in the German field.

In addition, F Division, besides relying on secret sources as above, also makes great use of overt sources such as the Press. Communist publications, such as *World News and Views*, are regularly bought, analysed and indexed.

He struck me as being a man with a remarkable knowledge of his subject and with a good sense of bureaucratic organisation and technique. He was 'broad-minded' on the subject of Soviet policy, and himself put forward the view that Soviet policy might well be designed to attempt to make the Anglo-Soviet pact a reality, and consequently to temper the revolutionary spirit of the Communist Party. (This was in marked distinction to Vivian's usual view, which is to see something directly sinister in everything the Soviet Union does.)

Hollis spoke briefly about Whitson, saying that he had been impressed by Whitson's scholarly approach to his subject. The principal point of contact between Hollis and Whitson had been

---

36 Messages between *Abwehr* (German secret service) agent-runners and their agents enciphered used hand ciphers and broken at Bletchley Park. ISOS stands for Illicit Signals Oliver Strachey. Strachey originally ran the section which dealt with these messages.

that they were able to discuss the technicalities of their work. Whitson, according to Hollis, is a careful thinker, and scrupulous in weighing evidence.

Hollis, in the course of his conversation, said that he did not think that the CPGB was still receiving money from the USSR. He said that they used to, in 1935–6, to the tune of some £46,000 per annum. Another item of information that he gave me was that a telephone check had been put on the Soviet Trade delegation in London.

For the last two years little material of an incriminating nature had been obtained; all the evidence pointed to the sincerity of the party's support for the war effort, and to the temporary abandonment of revolutionary activity. Hollis and Clark agreed that there appeared to be little or no contact between the Party and the Soviet Embassy, though the Party maintained relations with Tass news agency.

Hollis said that the buildings of both the Russian Embassy and of the Russian Trade Delegation were so situated that they were extremely difficult to watch. At the moment, no attempt was being made to shadow Soviet officials partly owing to the timidity of the Foreign Office. Hollis has hopes of inducing the Foreign Office to adopt a less timid attitude. He said that the Soviet diplomatic bags presented a very difficult problem indeed because the couriers never parted from them.

Clark told me that he was reasonably certain, though he had no definite proof, that Springhall[37] had been in contact with a member of the staff of the Soviet Military Attaché in London. He mentioned it as being possibly (though not necessarily) significant that Graur, who had previously got into trouble for espionage in Sweden, left the UK suddenly four days after Springhall's arrest. Clark is now on

---

37   Douglas Springhall, CPGB organiser, ran a Soviet intelligence network in the UK during the Second World War. Captain Ormond Uren of SOE was one of his agents.

the track of a collaborator of Springhall's named Gregory. He does not know which Gregory it is, but he mentioned a James Gregory and a Leslie Gregory as being possibilities.

Clark obtained the information leading to the arrest of Captain Uren from Helen Gresson, an Edinburgh Communist. He found in Springhall's notebook a reference to a meeting with Helen 'and a friend'. He went up to Edinburgh, and evidently impressed Helen with his intimate knowledge of Communist Party matters.

When he referred casually to the other person who had been present at the meeting, she blurted out: 'Oh you mean Ormond Uren!' Clark concealed the fact that he had never heard of Uren before, pretending to be perfectly familiar with the name; he thus got Helen to make a statement in writing which contained Uren's name correctly spelled. Helen, I believe, is a member of the Russia Today Society. I am not sure how her surname is spelt. It might be Grierson.

Clark told me that Uren might easily have got away scot-free if he had realised the scantiness of the knowledge in the possession of the British authorities. If he had maintained steadily that, although approached by Springhall, he had refused to supply him with information, the authorities could never have broken him. He was, however, unable to stand the strain of the interrogation, and ended up by confessing everything.

Shillito has no current Soviet espionage cases at the moment. He is, however, in contact with two NKVD officials who were captured by the Germans and have since been recaptured by the British. One is called Yegoreff. He does not want to return to the USSR. The other is a Volga German by origin (I do not know his name). He has been working for the Germans since about 1930, and is a real traitor. He does not want to go back either! These two have not been interrogated by the British, owing to their fear of political complications with the USSR. Shillito, however, is endeavouring to induce the British authorities to accept a 'voluntary statement' from either or both. One of the two, I cannot remember which, has told the British authorities that the Russians were responsible for the Katyn massacre[38]. I hope to get more details of these cases.

The above document is held at the SVR Archives in Moscow

---

38 The massacres of Polish nationals in the Katyn Forest in April and May 1940 were carried out by the NKVD, the Soviet secret service, and blamed on the Nazis. Moscow did not admit responsibility for the killings until 1990.

KIM PHILBY: THE UNKNOWN STORY OF THE KGB'S MASTER-SPY

TIM MILNE

This is another book which in theory remains banned. Kim Philby was already a Soviet spy when he joined Britain's secret service MI6 during the Second World War. He went on to head the section tasked with rooting out Russian spies before becoming the service's chief liaison officer with the CIA. He betrayed hundreds of British and US agents to the Russians and compromised numerous operations inside the Soviet Union.

Tim Milne, the nephew of A. A. Milne, was Philby's closest and oldest friend. They were at Westminster School together and when Philby joined MI6 he immediately recruited Milne as his deputy. Philby's treachery hit Milne as hard as anyone and after he retired from MI6, he wrote a highly revealing account of Philby's time in MI6 but he was told it must never be published.

Philby was forced to resign from MI6 in 1951 amid suspicion that he was involved in the defection of Guy Burgess and Donald Maclean, two other members of the Cambridge Spy Ring. He was named in Parliament as the 'Third Man' who had tipped them off but was exonerated by Harold Macmillan, the then Foreign Secretary. This gave his supporters within MI6 the excuse they needed to rehabilitate him and he was sent to Beirut under cover as a journalist. When it was finally confirmed that Philby was a Soviet spy, he named Milne as a possible fellow-agent, an allegation which was completely untrue. Philby had wanted to recruit Milne, but his NKVD controllers had refused to allow him to do so. Milne's account is remarkable for its complete lack of any rancour.

T HE WORST OF his bad time was now nearly over, but first the suspicions which had lain dormant for so long were to come into the open. The change began with an article in *The People* in September 1955 in which Vladimir Petrov, a Soviet defector of the previous year, asserted that Burgess and Maclean had been Soviet agents ever since their Cambridge days and had defected to avoid arrest.

The government was forced to issue a long-promised but not very informative White Paper on the two men. Fleet Street was full of rumours about a Third Man who had warned them. These culminated in Marcus Lipton's question in the House on 25 October, naming Kim openly for the first time. Marie and I were now on the point of leaving for Switzerland. We had a farewell dinner with Kim at a restaurant and drove him back to his mother's flat at Drayton Gardens, which had been under siege by reporters for some days. Kim asked us to drop him at the back of the building so that he could climb up the fire escape. For a man facing a supreme crisis in his life, he was remarkably calm and cheerful. We were already in Berne by the time Harold Macmillan made his statement in the Commons: 'I have no reason to conclude that Mr Philby has at any time betrayed the interests of this country.'

At first I did not regard the statement as making a radical difference, except that the press hunt was now called off. Nothing, as far as I knew, had come to light to remove any suspicions that MI5 or SIS might have entertained for the last four years; whatever evidence they had, for or against him, remained exactly the same. The government, forced to make a statement, had followed the principle of 'innocent till proved guilty'. But before long it appeared that the atmosphere had changed after the parliamentary statement, and that Kim, while certainly not restored to official trust and favour, was no longer considered a total outcast. In July, shortly after Colonel Nasser had nationalised the Suez Canal, I received an elated postcard from Kim: he was back in journalism and about to take off for Beirut as *The Observer*'s correspondent.

'What's the betting I'll be a war reporter again within six months?' And so he was, in half that time.

It was not until July 1957 that I saw him again. At the beginning of that year I had been brought back to a London post which involved much travelling. Fairly soon I found myself visiting Beirut. Kim and I had a pleasant and rather mellow evening together, slightly marred at the end by my speaking of Connie.[39] Though I did not know it, and indeed had never heard of her, he was already in love with Eleanor Brewer. Reminders of discarded lives were not welcome.

In December, Aileen [Philby's wife] died. Marie and I had last seen her only a month or so earlier, when the three of us took an assortment of children to the zoo. Kim came back for the funeral. Characteristically he insisted that the youngest children should not be told of her death before he arrived, as he wished to tell them himself; he was never one to shirk an unpleasant duty. He stayed in England a few weeks, clearing up family affairs. Marie and I went down for a final

---

39   Philby's former mistress.

weekend at Crowborough, not more than a fortnight after Aileen's death. It could hardly be described as a happy occasion, but the atmosphere was in a way almost light hearted. This was nearly the last time we were to see any of the children. Jo was growing up to be a very pretty girl. The two elder boys, John and Tommy, just turned fifteen and fourteen, were learning to drive. Kim and I took them out in the old car Aileen had been using, and Kim made each of them take the wheel for a mile or two on the public road. The boys drove just as well as any learners of legal age, but the incident surprised me – it was so out of keeping with the law-abiding Kim I had known.

He returned to Beirut, leaving the children in the care of a sister of Aileen's and other relatives. After twenty years I was once again following his career from the press, that is to say his despatches in *The Observer*. But one story came through on the grapevine which in its first bald presentation was most alarming. Kim, it was said, had tried to commit suicide by jumping off a high balcony, and had been restrained just in time. A later version was less dramatic: he had got very drunk at a party in a fifth-floor flat and had been seen with one leg over the balcony railing, saying he was sick of this bloody party and was getting out. Somebody pulled him back. Probably, if the story is true, he was too drunk to realise what floor he was on.

I had occasion to visit Beirut again in October 1958. This time Kim said, 'There's someone I want you to meet,' and presented Eleanor as his fiancée. That he should be marrying again was quite to be expected, but that it should be an American was not; however, Eleanor, if not *déracinée*, was at least somewhat internationalised by the travelling life she had led for many years. Whereas I had quickly got on terms with Aileen – and Lizy[40] for that matter – I

---

40 Lizy Friedman, Philby's first wife, a Communist activist whom he met and married while in Vienna in the early 1930s. Their involvement led to Philby being recruited as a Soviet agent.

cannot say that I ever came to know Eleanor. She gave the impression that she lacked personality; that her life was shaped for her by others. She seemed something of a lame duck. And yet her book on Kim reveals her as a sensitive, intelligent and sympathetic person. Obviously I missed most of this.

The two of them came to London in December of that year, but after an initial evening together Marie and I did not see or hear from them for some weeks. Then out of the blue Kim telephoned me at my office one Friday evening to ask me to be a witness the next morning at their wedding. I do not know why he left it so late. I had a slight feeling that he thought I would be reluctant to take it on. Anyway, at eleven the next morning Jack Ivens and I, together with Nina and Marie, were at the register office in Russell Square to see them on their way, for better or worse. I think there were no other guests at the ceremony, but a few dropped in at the Ivens's house afterwards. Douglas and Patsy Collins had lent the couple their London flat, a very smart place in Hertford Street where we were invited for a farewell drink before they left for Beirut. We arrived at about half past six to be met at the door by an extremely shaken Eleanor. Kim had passed out and was supine on his bed. Eleanor, Marie and I and the only other guests, the Ivenses, sat around talking uneasily for an hour or two until Kim finally made a brief and groggy appearance. I had scarcely ever known him get drunk in this way, without benefit of outside company. He and Eleanor had apparently had an alcoholic lunch and then gone on drinking.

This was the last time I was to see him for nearly three years. At the end of 1959, I was transferred to Tokyo. When I arrived back in London on leave in November 1961, it so happened that Kim and Eleanor were there on a short visit. The four of us met at our wartime favourite, the Unicorn in Jermyn Street. Kim mentioned – though I never heard more of this – that he might later be visiting

Tokyo with Eleanor on journalistic business. They had planned to return to Beirut the following Sunday, overland as far as Paris, and we arranged to have a last drink on the morning of that day at a pub in Strand-on-the-Green, near where we were staying with Kim's sister Pat. Regrettably we turned up very late, and the rest of the party – Kim, Eleanor, Pat, Jo and her fiancé – were already on their way back from the pub when we arrived. Kim was a little annoyed.

'We'd given you up and written you a note,' he said, and handed me one of his visiting cards, on the back of which he had inscribed in his unforgettable handwriting a message which ran like this: 'Nothing can excuse defection. God rot you all – but look after Jo.' Unaccountably the signature, still in Kim's writing, was 'Eleanor Philby'. Fussed at being late, we took little note of the message – which incidentally did not appear to be in any way private, even though Jo was there – and would no doubt have thrown the card away if we had not used it to take down Pat and Jo's telephone numbers.

We came across it nearly two years later when packing up before leaving Tokyo. By that time Kim had indeed defected. It is easy now to read all sorts of meanings into this card, but the only one I read into the first four words at the time was that we had let him down by being too late to say goodbye. It was natural, among people accustomed to intelligence jargon, to use a term like defection light-heartedly to mean some minor social dereliction. In any case 'Nothing can excuse defection', in the ordinary sense of the word, makes no sense in the context of his life. It is clear from his book that he had had an escape plan for many years. One might as well say 'Nothing can excuse a lifeboat' on an ocean liner.

After we had been a few minutes in Pat's house, the taxi arrived to take Kim and Eleanor to Victoria. The rest of us stood outside in the weak November sunlight to say goodbye. With a last genial touch of *Schadenfreude*, Kim exclaimed:

'Why Tim, you're going grey!'

A moment later they were off. I never saw or heard from him again.

Early in March 1963 I was having a quick lunch at home in Tokyo before going back to the embassy. Marie, glancing through the *Japan Times*, came across a four-line news agency item on an inside page which I had missed at breakfast. The Foreign Office had asked the Lebanese government for information about Harold Philby, a British journalist in Beirut, who had disappeared towards the end of January. No more than that; but it did not take much thought to realise that if he had been missing for several weeks without trace, he had almost certainly vanished deliberately. Behind the Iron Curtain? With all that had happened before, it seemed likely enough. But why? I knew nothing at all of his life since he had returned to Beirut – the new suspicions that had fallen on him, the confrontations with an investigator from London and the growing mental strain.

One or two improbable scenarios went through my mind in the next few days. Even then I was looking for less disastrous explanations than the obvious. Some weeks later came the news that Kim was in Russia, and had been a Soviet agent for many years. In the world civil war we were now on opposite sides forever.

<hr>

Extracted from *Kim Philby: The Unknown Story of the KGB's Master Spy* by Tim Milne (published by Biteback in 2014)

THE HUMAN FACTOR

GRAHAM GREENE

Describing any espionage novel as the best every written is always likely to lead to strong debate. Any such judgement must of course be highly subjective. Many readers will regard le Carré's *Tinker Tailor Soldier Spy* as the ultimate in spy fiction, although for my part I prefer the stealthy control of *Smiley's People*. But one spy novel towers above even these two masterpieces. It is hardly surprising that one of the best writers of the twentieth century, a man who spent the war years in MI6, where he worked alongside Philby and Milne, should produce such a book. He adds a note of authenticity by having one of the characters refer to a fellow officer using the standard MI6 five-figure designator employed during his own time in the Service. The designation he uses is 59800, his own from his time as the MI6 representative in Sierra Leone.

Like le Carré, Greene gives his protagonist, Maurice Castle, the most ordinary of lives. Intelligence work is rendered almost boring. When he is called in to see the MI6 security officer Colonel Daintry in what is supposedly a routine check, Castle appears in complete control, even toying with Daintry. It is a mirage. Castle was forced to co-operate with the KGB in order to get his black wife out of South Africa. He is the traitor for whom Daintry is searching. Castle's reaction to the investigation sees

Greene at his very best, expertly using the most minor detail of Castle's apparently mundane home life to depict the internal terror of the traitor who fears he is about to be discovered.

$\diamond$

C ASTLE WAS ON the point of descending the four stone steps into Piccadilly when the porter said to him, 'Brigadier Tomlinson wants to see you, sir.' 'Brigadier Tomlinson?' 'Yes. In room A3.'

Castle had only met Brigadier Tomlinson once, many years before, more years than he cared to count, on the day that he was appointed – the day he put his name to the Official Secrets Act, when the brigadier was a very junior officer, if he had been an officer at all. All he could remember of him was a small black moustache hovering like an unidentified flying object over a field of blotting paper, which was entirely white and blank, perhaps for security reasons. The stain of his signature after he had signed the Act became the only flaw on its surface, and that leaf was almost certainly torn up and sent to the incinerator. The Dreyfus case had exposed the perils of a wastepaper basket nearly a century ago.

'Down the corridor on the left, sir,' the porter reminded him when he was about to take the wrong route.

'Come in, come in, Castle,' Brigadier Tomlinson called. His moustache was now as white as the blotting paper, and with the years he had grown a small pot-belly under a double-breasted waistcoat – only his dubious rank remained constant. Nobody knew to what regiment he had formerly belonged, if such a regiment indeed existed, for all military titles in this building were a little suspect. Ranks might just be part of the universal cover. He said, 'I don't think you know Colonel Daintry.'

'No. I don't think … How do you do?'

Daintry, in spite of his neat dark suit and his hatchet face, gave a more genuine out-of-doors impression than Davis ever did. If Davis at his first appearance looked as though he would be at home in a bookmakers' compound, Daintry was unmistakably at home in the expensive enclosure or on a grouse moor. Castle enjoyed making lightning sketches of his colleagues: there were times when he even put them on to paper.

'I think I knew a cousin of yours at Corpus,' Daintry said. He spoke agreeably, but he looked a little impatient; he probably had to catch a train north at King's Cross.

'Colonel Daintry,' Brigadier Tomlinson explained, 'is our new broom,' and Castle noticed the way Daintry winced at the description. 'He has taken over security from Meredith. But I'm not sure you ever met Meredith.'

'I suppose you mean my cousin Roger,' Castle said to Daintry. 'I haven't seen him for years. He got a first in Greats. I believe he's in the Treasury now.'

'I've been describing the set-up here to Colonel Daintry,' Brigadier Tomlinson prattled on, keeping strictly to his own wavelength.

'I took Law myself. A poor second,' Daintry said. 'You read History, I think?'

'Yes. A very poor third.'

'At the House?'

'Yes.'

'I've explained to Colonel Daintry,' Tomlinson said, 'that only you and Davis deal with the Top Secret cables as far as Section 6A is concerned.'

'If you can call anything Top Secret in our section. Of course, Watson sees them too.'

'Davis – he's a Reading University man, isn't he?' Daintry asked with what might have been a slight touch of disdain.

'I see you've been doing your homework.'

'As a matter of fact I've just been having a talk with Davis himself.'

'So that's why he was ten minutes too long over his lunch.'

Daintry's smile resembled the painful reopening of a wound. He had very red lips, and they parted at the corners with difficulty. He said, 'I talked to Davis about you, so now I'm talking to you about Davis. An open check. You must forgive the new broom. I have to learn the ropes,' he added, getting confused among the metaphors. 'One has to keep to the drill – in spite of the confidence we have in both of you, of course. By the way, did he warn you?'

'No. But why believe me? We may be in collusion.'

The wound opened again a very little way and closed tight.

'I gather that politically he's a bit on the left. Is that so?'

'He's a member of the Labour Party. I expect he told you himself.'

'Nothing wrong in that, of course,' Daintry said. 'And you...'

'I have no politics. I expect Davis told you that too.'

'But you sometimes vote, I suppose?'

'I don't think I've voted once since the war. The issues nowadays so often seem – well, a bit parish pump.'

'An interesting point of view,' Daintry said with disapproval. Castle could see that telling the truth this time had been an error of judgement, yet, except on really important occasions, he always preferred the truth. The truth can be double-checked. Daintry looked at his watch. 'I won't keep you long. I have a train to catch at King's Cross.'

'A shooting week-end?'

'Yes. How did you know?'

'Intuition,' Castle said, and again he regretted his reply. It was always safer to be inconspicuous. There were times, which grew more frequent with every year, when he day-dreamed of complete conformity, as a different character might have dreamt of making a dramatic century at Lord's.

'I suppose you noticed my gun-case by the door?'

'Yes,' said Castle, who hadn't seen it until then, 'that was the clue.' He was glad to see that Daintry looked reassured.

Daintry explained, 'There's nothing personal in all this, you know. Purely a routine check. There are so many rules that sometimes some of them get neglected. It's human nature. The regulation, for example, about not taking work out of the office…'

He looked significantly at Castle's briefcase. An officer and a gentleman would open it at once for inspection with an easy joke, but Castle was not an officer, nor had he ever classified himself as a gentleman. He wanted to see how far below the table the new broom was liable to sweep. He said, 'I'm not going home. I'm only going out to lunch.'

'You won't mind, will you…?' Daintry held out his hand for the briefcase.

'I asked the same of Davis,' he said.

'Davis wasn't carrying a briefcase,' Castle said, 'when I saw him.'

Daintry flushed at his mistake. He would have felt a similar shame, Castle felt sure, if he had shot a beater. 'Oh, it must have been that other chap,' Daintry said. 'I've forgotten his name.'

'Watson?' the brigadier suggested.

'Yes, Watson.'

'So you've even been checking our chief?'

'It's all part of the drill,' Daintry said.

Castle opened his briefcase. He took out a copy of the *Berkhamsted Gazette*.

'What's this?' Daintry asked.

'My local paper. I was going to read it over lunch.'

'Oh yes, of course. I'd forgotten. You live quite a long way out. Don't you find it a bit inconvenient?'

'Less than an hour by train. I need a house and a garden. I have a child, you see – and a dog. You can't keep either of them in a flat. Not with comfort.'

'I notice you are reading *Clarissa Harlowe*? Like it?'

'Yes, so far. But there are four more volumes.'

'What's this?'

'A list of things to remember.'

'To remember?'

'My shopping list,' Castle explained. He had written under the printed address of his house, 129 King's Road, 'Two Maltesers. Half pound Earl Grey. Cheese – Wensleydale? Or Double Gloucester? Yardley Pre-Shave Lotion.'

'What on earth are Maltesers?'

'A sort of chocolate. You should try them. They're delicious. In my opinion, better than Kit Kats.'

Daintry said, 'Do you think they would do for my hostess? I'd like to bring her something a little out of the ordinary.' He looked at his watch. 'Perhaps I could send the porter – there's just time. Where do you buy them?'

'He can get them at an ABC in the Strand.'

'ABC?' Daintry asked.

'Aerated Bread Company.'

'Aerated bread … What on earth…? Oh well, there isn't time to go into that. Are you sure those – teasers would do?'

'Of course, tastes differ.'

'Fortnum's is only a step away.'

'You can't get them there. They are very inexpensive.'

'I don't want to seem niggardly.'

'Then go for quantity. Tell him to get three pounds of them.'

'What is the name again? Perhaps you would tell the porter as you go out.'

'Is my check over then? Am I clear?'

'Oh yes. Yes. I told you it was purely formal, Castle.'

'Good shooting.'

'Thanks a lot.'

Castle gave the porter the message.

'Three pounds did 'e say?'

'Yes.'

'Three pounds of Maltesers!'

'Yes.'

'Can I take a pan-technicon?'

The porter summoned the assistant porter who was reading a girlie magazine. He said, 'Three pounds of Maltesers for Colonel Daintry.'

'That would be a hundred and twenty packets or thereabouts,' the man said after a little calculation.

'No, no,' Castle said, 'it's not as bad as that. The weight, I think, is what he means.'

He left them making their calculations. He was fifteen minutes late at the pub and his usual corner was occupied. He ate and drank quickly and calculated that he had made up three minutes. Then he bought the Yardley's at the chemist in St James's Arcade, the Earl Grey at Jackson's, a Double Gloucester there too to save time, although he usually went to the cheese shop in Jermyn Street, but the Maltesers, which he had intended to buy at the ABC, had run out by the time he got there – the assistant told him there had been an unexpected demand, and he had to buy Kit Kats instead. He was only three minutes late when he rejoined Davis.

'You never told me they were having a check,' he said.

'I was sworn to secrecy. Did they catch you with anything?'

'Not exactly.'

'He did with me. Asked what I had in my mackintosh pocket. I'd got that report from 59800. I wanted to read it again over my lunch.'

'What did he say?'

'Oh, he let me go with a warning. He said rules were made to be kept. To think that fellow Blake (whatever did he want to escape for?) got forty years freedom from income tax, intellectual strain and responsibility, and it's we who suffer for it now.'

'Colonel Daintry wasn't very difficult,' Castle said. 'He knew a cousin of mine at Corpus. That sort of thing makes a difference.'

Extracted from *The Human Factor* by Graham Greene (first published by Bodley Head in 1978 and later by Vintage Classics, with whose permission this has been reproduced)

GREAT OPPORTUNITIES
OPEN UP
GUY BURGESS

When Kim Philby was recruited by Soviet Intelligence, he was asked to compile a list of people he had known at Cambridge who might be willing to spy for Moscow. He wrote down the names of a number of fellow students with Donald Maclean at the top. At the bottom of the list, almost as an afterthought, was Guy Burgess.

History hasn't been kind to Burgess. He is usually regarded as the least important of the Cambridge Spy Ring, but there is no real justification for this. Although there were long periods when he was not in a position to produce high-level intelligence that all changed in 1947. For the next four years, as personal assistant to the influential Foreign Minister Hector McNeil, he was able to provide Moscow Centre with details of British attitudes not just towards the Russians, but just as crucially at a difficult time for Anglo-US relations, the attitude of the Labour government towards the Americans. During this critical period, which included the Berlin Blockade, the British transfer of power in the Indian sub-continent and the start of the Korean War, Burgess was providing as much high-grade intelligence as any member of the Cambridge Spy Ring. He was also regarded by his

NKVD contacts as a model spy who would actively seek out the intelligence they asked for and actually produce the goods, something that is far rarer in an agent than one might assume.

When Burgess was initially offered the job as McNeil's personal assistant, he was out of contact with the Russians. Konstantin Volkov, an NKVD officer based in Turkey, had attempted to defect to the British. He promised details of a Soviet spy in charge of a counter-espionage section in London. Despite being one of the most obvious potential suspects, Philby was told about Volkov's claims. He volunteered to go to Turkey to talk to Volkov and then played for time allowing the NKVD to remove the unfortunate Volkov to Moscow where he was interrogated and then executed.

The NKVD's London *Rezidentura* responded by cutting off contact with Philby and Burgess on security grounds. Burgess took the isolation badly and was evidently eager to resume contact, seeing his new job working for McNeil as a means of returning to a role he clearly loved, as an NKVD spy inside the British establishment.

9.12.46

I have been offered the post of 'Personal Assistant to the Minister of State' (Hector McNeil). This offer has been made officially and for that reason and since it is I think not only an important promotion but one that can be put to valuable use I shall accept it.

It should be said that this transfer is not yet finally completed from the purely bureaucratic angle. The situation is that the Personnel Department of the Foreign Office has been consulted and has agreed to recommend it but that final Treasury approval for what is a rather rapid and sensational advance in my status has not yet been obtained. It is not anticipated that this will cause much difficulty.

It can and should be pointed out that before Foreign Office

approval was given, my personal record and file was necessarily examined and therefore we are now justified in saying that it is certainly the case that there can be no suspicions of any kind against me, otherwise such central and confidential appointment would not have been sanctioned (as it has been) by the Foreign Office.

What is the nature of the job?

The best definition is in the title and it is clear that to some extent the actual duties will depend on what is aimed at by McNeil and also, I hope, myself.

McNeil in conversation has said that routine office work will continue to be looked after by the Private Secretaries and that my duties will be to assist him in the formulation of policy by the study of documents and by personal contacts and conversations with other officials and also with politicians, both British and foreign. There will also be opportunities for direct communication with the Secretary of State's office. He also wishes me to spend a certain amount of time in the House of Commons.

It would I think be wrong if I did not say that in my opinion great opportunities are opened to us by this transfer. Apart from telegrams which I shall continue to see I shall hope to be able to see those minutes and private letters (e.g. from and to ambassadors) which describe the inception and formulation of policy and to be present at, or aware of, conversations in which future decisions are canvassed and discussed before being arrived at. I believe the Minister of State usually (and certainly a Minister of State who is on such close personal terms as Hector is with Bevin[41]) is informed of all Foreign Office transactions and if he is, then I hope to be. As is known we are on excellent, indeed very close, personal terms.

I should add that it has not been forgotten that while civil servants

---

41   Ernest Bevin, Foreign Secretary from 1945 to 1951.

are permanent, politicians are not and that though this promotion is regular and authorised it is also to some extent a personal choice by Hector, with which incidentally Bevin, who has been consulted, agrees. Therefore I have tried to secure a way of retreat back to the News Department in the event of Hector falling and this resulting in me being transferred abroad.

As I say, I think this appointment is to one of the most desirable central positions in the Foreign Office and I should welcome any instructions as to how to make the fullest use of it and in what manner it can be turned to our best advantage.

6.1.47

Dear Max![42]

I have had the splendid news from Fred (NKVD note: i.e. Johnson)[43] that there is every possibility that our contact will soon be resumed.

I have only been in my new post for a week and I am sticking to instructions which, I believe, would hold were I to meet you – not rushing and behaving cautiously. The institution's rules are themselves new to me, and although there are documents which I would like to hand over to you (along with other things, cabinet protocols are filed in the secretaries' room) these documents would, of course, have to be returned and I know that you are unable to do that at present. Guided by security rules, I am unable to make copies of them in the room, where three other people are working.

---

42 Max was Boris Kreshin, Burgess's handler within the London *Rezidentura*, the NKVD station.

43 NKVD covername for Anthony Blunt, one of the other members of the Cambridge Spy Ring.

At the moment, I am studying the possibility of whether it is possible to take documents home for the night, but it is still too early to say whether this will be possible.

I enclose two documents from the Russia Committee, which you may keep. There is no need to return them. They are duplicates I made in my old post; moreover they were removed after I left for the new job, so this operation should be doubly secure.

I have to report the following general aspects:

In the near future Bevin will be asking the cabinet to decide on whether to extend Great Britain's present hostile relations with the governments of the countries which he calls Soviet satellites (Poland, Bulgaria, Romania) and whether Great Britain should maintain its present policy of support for the opposition or whether the time has come to recognise Soviet influence and cease the fight against it.

The way the question will be posed will be characterised not by the fact that Bevin will advocate one decision in preference to another, but by the fact that he will dispassionately set out the arguments and ask for a decision.

Should it be decided not to counter Soviet influence, this decision will, of course, apply only to political issues. British commercial and economic policy will remain unchanged.

McNeil is sure that in Yugoslavia, where political opposition to Tito inside the country has, to a greater or lesser extent, been left to its own devices, constant economic and commercial factors over the course of time will have a corresponding influence on Yugoslavia's political orientation towards the USSR and he is confident that Anglo-American influence will be restored through commerce and so on.

Sir R. Stevenson has made the suggestion that it is now a favourable moment to make an attempt to renew and refine the Anglo-Soviet treaty. This topic was discussed at the conference of the Russia

Committee and was the subject of a memorandum from the Northern Department sent to the Minister of State. For the time being I am unable to send copies of them.

As far as I know, no final decision has yet been made. In accordance with this idea, the corresponding proposal is to be made during the Molotov-Byrnes-Bevin[44] conference on the German question. I think the Americans have not yet been informed of the plan.

It has been decided to propose to the French government that the Harvey talks on the union which ended in disaster last summer be resumed. The proposal is to be made at the first convenient opportunity. The difficulty lies in determining when that convenient opportunity will present itself. The French Socialist Party has told McNeil of its hope that this will be done now. They said that this step would make their position easier in the future government, and this means that they reckon to be an effective force in the newly-formed government. Sir Orme Sergeant (Permanent Under-Secretary to the Foreign Secretary) told McNeil in an official note on this that, although he welcomes the talks with France and thinks that the treaty should be concluded, he does not agree, firstly, that now is a suitable time and, secondly, with the conclusion of the French Socialist Party on their influence in the future government. He expressed the desire to wait for 'a suitable moment'.

The British government has discovered that the American government has allegedly received from their ambassador in Teheran a report saying that KAVAM[45] told him that he would be able and

---

44 Vyacheslav Molotov, Soviet Foreign Minister; James F Byrnes, US Secretary of State; and Ernest Bevin, British Foreign Secretary.

45 Ahmad Qavām, Iranian Prime Minister.

intended to influence a majority of deputies in the *Majlis* to come out against giving the USSR the oil concessions they had promised in Southern Persia.

The British government has not received this information from KAVAM. It does not know if the American government information is good and how it is evaluating this report. The British envoy is to be informed (if he has not already been informed) that if KAVAM asks his opinion, he must reply that Great Britain is not opposed to oil being offered to the USSR on terms which are financially profitable and do not undermine Persia's independence.

The British are inclined to suspect American subterfuge in this whole business. I talked to McNeil and, although he is of the view that the concessions should not be given to the USSR, I do not believe he will prevail. I hope to be of some service by influencing McNeil a bit on this matter. In Washington and in the Foreign Office there is a widely-held view, according to which it is essential to prevent Soviet reconstruction by all possible means, including refusing to supply oil. McNeil and Bevin do not support that view. Of course, their motives have nothing to do with altruism in respect of the Soviet Union. They simply want no unpleasantness over British concessions in Southern Persia.

While in America, (according to personal secretaries):

1. Bevin was greatly alarmed by the parliamentary rebellions (hence the 'conciliatory' tone of his radio address)

2. Bevin increased his hostility and contempt for Byrnes (which was present even in Paris, where he preferred to work with Vandenberg[46]); McNeil was not afraid of the rebels and to some extent his confidence reassured Bevin;

3. British troops are now expected to be withdrawn from Greece

---

46   Arthur H Vandenberg, Chairman of the Foreign Relations Committee.

at the same time that, under the peace treaties, Soviet troops are withdrawn from the Balkans.

4. A representative of an Arab state in Moscow (I don't know precisely who) informed Frank Roberts[47] that comrade Molotov had persuaded the Egyptian ambassador in Moscow to insist to his government on the handover of its affairs to the UNO and promised full support from the USSR on this.

20 February 1947

<><><><><><><><><><><><><><><><><><><><><><><><><><><><><><><><><><><><><><><><><><><><>

The above reports from Burgess are held at the SVR Archives in Moscow

---

47   Bevin's Private Secretary.

THE WATCHERS' HANDBOOK

HARRY HUNTER

Anthony Blunt was recruited into the Cambridge Spy Ring by his close friend and one-time lover Guy Burgess. Blunt initially went into the Intelligence Corps before joining MI5 where he specialised in collecting intelligence from a variety of diplomatic sources based in London.

Blunt's main role within the Cambridge Spy Ring was ensuring that MI5 was not on the trail of the other members, and warning of any risks, but he did provide a substantial amount of information on various aspects of British counter-espionage operations against the Russians. He was in charge of intelligence collected from the interception of the diplomatic bags and telephone calls of the London-based embassies and ran a number of foreign diplomats as agents. He was also the main liaison officer in London for the MI5 anti-Soviet section based at Blenheim Palace in Oxfordshire.

One of the targets Blunt was assigned by Moscow was to find out how the 'Watchers' of MI5's B6 surveillance section operated, so that KGB officers operating in London could work out how best to avoid surveillance. The Watchers were run by Harry Hunter, a long-term MI5 officer who had been in MI5 since the First World War and was the main author of *The Watchers' Handbook* which Blunt handed over to his NKVD controller.

OBSERVATION

Observation is a very onerous and exacting profession. Screen sleuths of the secret service thriller or detective novel appeal to the uninitiated, but in actual practice there is little glamour and much monotony in such a calling as 'observation'. A successful watcher is a rarity and though 'many are called, few are chosen', even then not more than a very small proportion of those engaged in such work can be considered first class.

After many years experience of watching and following, the writer is forced to the conclusion that the ideal watcher is born and not made, and unless he has a natural flair for the work he will never rise above a mediocre standard. At various times hundreds of men have been interviewed as prospective trainees but very few have been accepted, for the reason that when tried out they are found to lack the one essential qualification, viz., patience, and to have engaged them would have been unfair to tried men who would be called to carry passengers every time a tricky spot of watching became necessary.

The ideal watcher should not be more than 5ft 7ins or 5ft 8ins in height, looking as unlike a policeman as possible. It is a mistake to use men who are too short as they would be just as conspicuous as tall men. A watcher should be a rather nondescript type: good eyesight is essential, also good hearing as it is often possible to overhear a suspect's conversation. He should be active and alert, as it frequently occurs that a suspect hastily boards, or alights from a fast-moving vehicle. Above all a watcher must be a quick thinker, capable of acting on the spur of the moment.

A watcher must adapt himself to the locality in which he is called upon to keep observation, e.g., he must wear old clothes, cap, muffler, etc., in the slum quarters, and be better dressed for the West End where he frequently has to enter hotels, blocks of residential flats or office buildings. In short, it is the watcher's job to carry on in such a manner as not to bring undue notice to himself from local residents.

The use of facial disguise is not recommended. It may be considered essential in secret service films but in practice it is to be deplored. A false moustache or beard is easily detected, especially under the high lights of a restaurant, pub or in a tube train.

In many cases, close observation is the only means of discovering a suspect's contacts and obtaining the essential evidence for prosecution. BUT the watching must be conducted with care in every case. Careless watching is not only useless but may result in serious harm to an important case. Unskilful observation is of the greatest benefit to the suspect when he is aware he is under observation, for, if he is clever, he will cover his tracks by assuming the actions and demeanour of an innocent person, and as a consequence the chance will be lost of obtaining incriminating evidence. On the other hand the accurate reporting of a suspect's movements has sometimes reacted to his advantage at his ultimate interrogation, when, in any case, it will be realised much reporting is essential for testing the accuracy of the suspect's statements.

OBSERVATION TIPS AND WRINKLES

Picking up the suspect from his address: If a full description is available together with a recent photograph the job is simplified. If there is no description then one must adopt a process of elimination to find the right person from among all the residents – often a long procedure.

A spots him coming – walks on apace,
B crosses over to take up the chase

Take up a position some distance from the address, on the same side if possible, or some distance away on the other side. Be careful to be out of view of the suspect's rooms.

Following in the street, keep about 25–30 yards behind the quarry and when on the move by foot it is preferable to keep on the opposite pavement, except in very busy streets.

Whenever possible have two watchers, one on the same side of the street, and the other on the opposite.

Shorten the distance from the suspect before reaching a corner, and at the corner take a detour, wide if possible, in order to avoid the suspect if he halts suddenly and turns around.

S turns the corner, B takes the lead, A watches B till it's safe to proceed

Be prepared for the suspect to board a moving vehicle such as a bus, tram or train, or hailing a cruising taxi, or any other such device to shake off a 'tail'.

The watcher must be prepared to think and act one jump ahead of the suspect, and if the latter does board a bus and mounts to the top, one watcher should take a seat or stand just inside the platform. If the suspect goes inside a bus one watcher should take a seat immediately behind him if possible, even at the risk of being noticed, and the second watcher should then be prepared to cover the first and carry on alone if the first is obliged to drop out.

ON THE UNDERGROUND

When travelling by Underground and booking a fare, if the suspect's destination cannot be overheard, take a ticket from a slot machine and have plenty of spare change ready at the other end to pay the excess if necessary. Pay the collector a little extra rather than argue with him and lose your suspect. On escalators, especially where they lead directly on to platforms or street exits, gradually close up on the suspect. When he is suspicious, a subject will often board a train just before the doors close, making himself the last one on the train, or he may alight at the last moment; so do not give him any rope on such occasions.

ENTERING BLOCKS OF FLATS OR OFFICES

When entering buildings or blocks of flats again use common sense. If possible precede the suspect, enter the lift and take a position at the back: do not accompany a suspect in a small lift, or where it is worked automatically, but judge the floor he uses from the action of the lift and the place at which it stops by making a rapid mounting of the stairs. A subsequent observation with the knowledge thus acquired will often get the suspect housed.

Wherever he's listed, top floor or basement, take care he can't peep at you down on the pavement.

IN A RESTAURANT

If a suspect uses a restaurant or cafe it is essential to see his contacts. If he feeds alone then entry and exit should follow each other rapidly. If he makes a contact then a full description of the person should be memorised with a view to subsequent picking up from such a description. If it is necessary to remain in a hotel, restaurant or café, be sure to be in a position to make a hurried exit – have such exits watched, have the bill ready for payment with plenty of loose change – don't be delayed at the cash desk.

HOUSING SUSPECTS

When housing contacts of suspects be certain of the number, name of the road or street, and the district – this is not easy in these days of blackout. Ascertain if possible whether the contact entered by key, knocking or ringing, or by communal doorway, as this may give some indication whether he resides at or visits this address: be prepared to take up observation early next day to confirm your suspicions. If the address is in a quiet street, observation has to

This is too small a lift so better beware. S asked for his floor, you'd best use the stair

be maintained from a distance, so be in a situation to keep watch on a definite mark or be able to get a silhouette of anyone leaving the doorway.

FOLLOWING BY TAXI

If a taxi is used to follow a suspect or contact, then it is desirable immediately to take the number of the cab being followed. Choose, if possible, a modern cab for following and enthuse a little extra activity into the driver in order that he may avoid the suspect's detecting the following cab in mirrors or from the rear window. Keep your driver keen at traffic lights or traffic congestion and generally co-opt his help. Concoct a suitable tale which may go down well with the cabby, such as a divorce case, absconding husband or wife and promise the driver a good tip.

TRAVELLING BY TRAIN

Travel by train in wartime is difficult, but much the same procedure should be adopted in the free and easy times. If possible, overhear the suspect's destination when he books and be guided accordingly as to booking a ticket, position to be occupied in the train and the tactics to be used at the destination. Close or free observation will depend on the circumstances of travel, but invariably it has been found that close observation on the heels of the suspect produces the best results.

If the suspect gets away or has to be picked up by a relief at his destination, take note of the time of departure of the train, its scheduled time of arrival, how the suspect is travelling, e.g., what class, how near from the front or rear, his baggage, whether light or heavy and any other encumbrances: and a full description of him, including his dress.

IN THE POST OFFICE

There are excellent opportunities for investigation, which may have important bearing on the case. If the suspect goes to a writing desk it is often possible to get a brief glance at the addresses should the suspect write a telegram, address a letter or postcard. If he goes to the counter, the watcher can learn a lot if he gets close behind him.

POSTING A LETTER

Immediately after he posts a letter take a loosely folded newspaper and thrust it through the aperture of the letter-box in such a way that it will open out as it falls on the letters that have been posted; this will facilitate the identification of the correspondence posted by the suspect.

OBSERVATION REPORTS

The utmost care should be exercised in writing up observation reports. It cannot be too strongly emphasised that success or failure of a case depends in great measure on the exact times of a suspect's meetings with contacts, and the time spent in his or her company.

In instructions to watchers the following points should be brought out for their daily reports.

The hours when observation was commenced, interrupted, and finished.

All incidents, etc. however trivial.

The addresses of people contacted – these are important.

Suspect's demeanour under observation.

Full description of contacts.

Follow-up enquiries as soon as possible after locating a contact.

The daily reports should be written out at the first opportunity after the duty has been completed. When two watchers are employed on the same case they must compile their reports without collaboration.

AVOIDING RECOGNITION BY SUSPECTS

Perhaps to wind up, it would be as well to mention the best methods experience has found to counter observation. Frequently a watcher has been 'dogged' and here once again a watcher will use his common sense. He will probably walk home, walk round a block, return home, leave again and start off in another direction from his most direct route. He will know his own neighbourhood intimately and use such knowledge to alternate his means of conveyance by bus, tram or train, but always gradually making towards his objective and ascertaining at the same time if he has a 'tail'. If he finds he has, then it is his best plan to act normally but not to go anywhere near to his particular 'job'. A good watcher will change his clothes daily if possible; change his route to and from home frequently; will not form habits such as that of drinking in one public house at a particular time; will not frequent a particular restaurant or café; will be discreet on the telephone and will not mention names or addresses unless told to do so; he will make his notes with care and above all will cultivate a good memory.

Finally REMEMBER.

Observation cannot be mastered from textbooks or lectures. Hard practical training in the street is the only way to bring out a man's aptitude for the job – generally a long process.

DON'T BELITTLE THE PERSON YOU ARE FOLLOWING. IF HE DOES APPEAR SIMPLE APPEARANCES ARE OFTEN DECEPTIVE.

<hr />

Extracted from *The Watchers' Handbook* by Harry Hunter (held in Anthony Blunt's file at the SVR Archives in Moscow)

SLINGSHOT

MATTHEW DUNN

We close with two contrasting styles of spy novel from former MI6 officers. If Alan Judd, whose *Uncommon Enemy* follows this extract, is the natural
successor to John le Carré, then Matthew Dunn is the new Ian Fleming. A
former MI6 agent runner who has operated in numerous hostile environ-
ments around the world, Dunn's extensive experience in missions where
his life was at risk are reflected in those of his protagonist Will Cochrane,
a man with the familiar characteristics exhibited by 007.

MI6 likes to insist that its officers are not James Bond types and that
they do not carry guns. It is true that most intelligence work does not
involve weapons, but they are certainly available, indeed in many theatres
where MI6 has operated in recent years, the Balkans, Iraq, Afghanistan,
east Africa, they are a necessity. You can tell your own officers that they
must resist using weapons at all costs, you can tell them they don't have a
licence to kill, but you can't dictate the rules of the game to the opposition.

All new MI6 officers are taught to fire guns at their Fort Monckton
training base in Hampshire by an ex-special forces sergeant-major and
for many years now former special forces soldiers have been employed
by MI6 to provide the heavyweight firepower, and operational nous, when
difficult missions turn nasty. Originally, they were hired by the day, but the

Treasury soon realised it was cheaper to employ them on staff. Here they are referred to as the Q team although, as befits a latter-day Bond, Will Cochrane has more than enough nous of his own to run the operation.

A Russian spy who is defecting to the Poles is due to arrive in Gdansk on board a freighter, the *Paderewski*, which is being tracked by a small Polish search and rescue boat. Unknown to the Poles, the Russian secret service, the SVR, has sent in a team to kill the defector. The Poles are also unaware that Cochrane and his Q team are waiting to intervene. Cochrane is confident they can control the situation. What he doesn't know is that someone else is also after the defector.

WILL RAN EAST along Na Ostrowiu. Within five seconds, he was crossing the river. Within ten seconds he was on the large island. The place was silent; sea mist hung thickly over the security lit warehouses, moored cargo ships, jetties, cranes, small factory units, roads, and the waterways around the island. He slowed to a jog and began moving across the island toward the canal containing the target vessels. He saw no movement of any sort and heard nothing beyond the distant foghorn. The whole island seemed deserted.

'Delta 1. The *Paderewski*'s slowing down.' The Q operative's voice was a near whisper. 'It's about two-thirds of the way along the canal. Speed now about five knots. Four locals near us, all of them holding handguns.'

'Received.' Will dashed along a narrow gap between two warehouses, gripping his handgun tightly with one hand, searching for glimpses of the canal. But so far all he could see were more industrial shipping units. The air was even colder here; the whole place felt eerie. He ran alongside a stack of big freight containers before reaching a small road. On the other side of it were two large warehouses, between them an alleyway. Lights were visible at the far end of the gap. He entered the gap, nearly fell as his feet struck loose girders on the ground, staggered to stay upright, and continued sprinting. The lights belonged to lamps straddling the broad canal.

'Delta 1. The *Paderewski*'s now at a crawl and so is the search-and-rescue boat.'

Will slowed to a walk. Sweat from his exertions felt cold against his skin. He held his gun high with both hands, searching for sight of Russians or the local intelligence operatives. Reaching a road by the side of the canal, he stood still and looked left. Cargo boats were moored on either side of the waterway, derrick cranes beside them; a row of warehouses was adjacent to the road, larger ones on the other side of the canal. But here the icy mist seemed thicker and was moving slowly along the canal toward him. He was blind to anything beyond a 40-yard radius of his location. 'I'm in position.'

'There's a man who's emerged onto the deck of the search-and-rescue boat.' Delta l's voice was still a whisper, but urgent. 'Tall, athletic, dressed in overcoat and suit, hand inside his jacket.'

Will saw lights draw closer along the canal.

The *Paderewski*.

'The tall man moves across the boat's deck, he faces the island bank, he looks at the *Paderewski*, he looks back at the bank, he runs forward, jumps, and lands on the island. He pulls his hand out of his jacket. He's holding a pistol.'

Will looked sharply away from the encroaching *Paderewski* toward the road he was on. The big Russian was somewhere in the darkness ahead of him.

'The *Paderewski*'s pulling alongside the island. Four Polish sailors are on deck.'

Will watched the ship. 'What's the search and rescue boat doing?'

'It's still right on the ass of the *Paderewski*. No sign of any other men coming out of it though.'

'They're waiting. Everyone: stand by.'

'Delta 1. We've got two locals moving across the southern crossing onto the island. Their handguns are out. My men are following them.' Silence. 'The *Paderewski*'s stationary. Two of the sailors are on the island, roping the ship to the berth. Four Delta and four locals are now on the east bank of the canal, close to the two vessels. Our locals have still got their guns trained on the search and rescue boat. Another man on the deck of the *Paderewski*. He's not dressed like the sailors.'

Will took five quick paces toward the ship, but could not distinguish anything beyond the bow of the vessel. 'That could be our defector.'

'Men emerging on the search and rescue boat's deck! Four of them, now six, now ... now eleven! All armed with assault rifles.'

Pistol shots rang out.

'The Poles have opened fire!'

The sound of machine gun fire was deafening. 'Russians are returning fire. Some of them are jumping onto the island.'

'Take them down!' Will ran along the road toward the gunfight.

Four shots came from his left. One of the bullets ripped through the front of Will's overcoat, narrowly missing his body. He spun to face the direction of the shots, saw two Poles emerge from the darkness pointing their handguns at him, dived to the ground as they fired again, rolled, got to his feet, and sprinted as they kept shooting. The noise of a different handgun came from behind the Polish operatives. Will looked in that direction while continuing to run, caught a brief glimpse of a man wearing a baseball cap and pointing his gun at the sky, knew that man had to be a Delta operative, saw the Poles spin around to face the Q man, and then saw him dash away into the fog. The Poles spun back to face Will, but the Delta operative's distraction had enabled Will to get farther away from them and out of their sight.

He reached the side of the *Paderewski*. Two sailors were lying on the ground, immobile and moaning in pain. He was about to move to them when he felt a tremendous force on his shoulder blade. He collapsed to his knees in agony. A man emerged from behind him. He was tall and dressed in an overcoat and suit – he had to be the SVR officer. Will tried to raise his arm to shoot him, but winced in pain from the movement and involuntarily lowered it. The Russian ignored him, walking quickly to the sailors. He grabbed one of them, hauled him onto his shoulder, carried him 20 yards away from the boat, lowered him onto the ground, and then did the same with the other sailor.

Over the sound of near continuous gunfire, Delta 1 screamed, 'The defector's jumped onto the island. He's somewhere close to you.'

Gritting his teeth, Will forced himself onto his feet, this time managing to keep his arm moving upward. Pointing his gun at the Russian, he saw the man turn to face him. He was holding something in his hand.

A detonator.

Four explosions happened in quick succession to his right, causing Will to twist and fall back to the ground. Shards of metal flew through the air; smoke and fire seemed to cover everything. Will covered his head and lay flat on the ground, feeling small pieces of debris fall over him. He turned his head, his ears ringing from the explosions, and saw that the *Paderewski* was ablaze and beginning to sink.

He looked at the Russian. The man was facing Will and firing, but not at him. The SVR officer began running and by the time he passed Will's prone body he was at full sprint while still shooting. Will rolled onto his side, ignored the intense heat from the fire in the canal, saw an unarmed man disappear down the road and saw the Russian chasing him. He looked back and frowned as he saw that the two sailors had not been hurt by the explosion because the man who had blown up the boat had moved them out of harm's way.

Getting to his feet, he began running after the Russian, but after a few paces he heard a hail of machine-gun fire. He threw himself sideways onto the ground and rolled away until he was behind the cover of a warehouse. More bullets hit the wall by his side, causing chunks of brick to fly off it.

Will clutched his mic against his throat. 'Delta 1: I'm going after the big SVR guy. He's pursuing an unarmed man who is almost certainly the defector.'

'Delta 1.' The Q man was screaming over the sound of gunfire. 'Men have just taken out my two Poles. There're six of them, and they're firing at us as well. But they're not the Russian SVR men.'

'What?'

Delta 1 did not answer, and before Will could speak again, another voice shouted in his earpiece. 'Delta 9. My two locals have just engaged four SVR men on the island. I'm going to get on their flank and assist the Poles with … What the hell?'

Will shouted, 'Delta 9? What's happening?'

The noise of automatic gunfire was continuous.

'Delta 9: my locals and the SVR men are dead. Killed by the other team. I can see you, Zulu. I'm 30 yards behind you.'

Will got to his feet just as the Q operative got alongside him. Both men began running east, in the direction of the big SVR officer and the defector, their guns pointing at the darkness and fog ahead of them. Muzzle flashes were visible coming from the other side of the canal on their left.

'No, no!'

Will grabbed his throat mic. 'Delta 1?'

Nothing.

'Delta 1?'

'Delta 1: They're … They're dead.'

'Who?'

'The Russians, the Poles, my men. Fucking everyone!'

Incredulity struck Will. 'Get onto the island! Head west. We're pursuing the defector.'

Will and Delta 9 suddenly stopped. In the distance ahead of them they could see the long road that led over the western bridge. Lights straddled it, and easily visible were three men running at full speed toward the crossing. The defector, the SVR officer, and the last remaining Polish operative.

Will raised his gun and moved its muzzle so that it was pointing slightly in front of the Russian's body. Tensing, he pulled back the trigger. But the moment his gun fired, the SVR officer stopped. Will's bullet passed in front of him. Will looked beyond the officer to the far side of the bridge. A van was heading fast toward the defector. The Polish operative and the SVR officer began firing at the oncoming van.

Will and Delta 9 sprinted and fired at the front windows of the vehicle. As they did so, they saw the SVR officer raise his gun and fire one bullet. The defector stumbled, then carried on moving toward the van, one of his legs limping. Nine men poured out of the van. They were dressed in fire-resistant black combat overalls, upper body and head armour, and night-vision goggles, and were carrying sub-machine guns.

Some of them fired at the SVR officer and the Polish operative behind him; others fired toward Will and Delta 9. Whatever hand-gun the SVR officer was carrying, it was obviously much more powerful than those being carried by Will and his team. The officer fired two rounds at two of the hostiles and dropped them both. Will dodged left and right, fired three times at three of the hostiles, and saw his bullets simply glance off their body armour.

'Delta 1: I'm pinned down! Centre of the island.'

Will looked toward the end of the bridge. Three of the hostiles ran along the crossing, passed the defector, and fired their automatic weapons at the Russian and Polish operatives. Both men remained stock still, firing their handguns at the hostiles. Two other men ran to the defector, grabbed him, pulled him toward the van, and bundled him into the vehicle. Then five of the hostiles started slowly walking along the bridge, firing their weapons continuously. Will stopped. He felt useless. The hostiles knew that they controlled the ground. The Polish operative fell down as one bullet struck him in the face. The Russian's powerful handgun boomed, flipping one of the hostiles off his feet and backward. The Russian then turned, looked at the prone Polish officer, looked back at the encroaching force, fired a couple more shots toward them, and ran to the stricken Pole.

Will watched the hostiles move back to the van and enter the vehicle. The van quickly reversed. Within seven seconds it was off the bridge, out of sight, and heading west away from Gdansk.

The defector had been kidnapped.

◇◇

Extracted from *Slingshot* by Matthew Dunn (published by HarperCollins, with whose permission this has been reproduced)

UNCOMMON ENEMY

ALAN JUDD

Our collection of the best writing by British spies on spies ends pretty much as it began, with an intelligence service that is only interested in the quick fix. Alan Judd, a former army officer who went on to serve in MI6, created Charles Thoroughgood in what, one suspects, was occasionally fairly close to a mirror image.

The first novel, *A Breed of Heroes*, written before Judd left MI6, had Thoroughgood serving in the army in Northern Ireland. But once Judd left the Service, Thoroughgood was free to join it. In *Uncommon Enemy*, Thoroughgood is no longer in MI6 but has been called back to deal with one of his old agents now deemed to have gone rogue. It swiftly becomes clear that all is not as it seems. MI6 has been amalgamated with GCHQ and MI5 to form an amorphous Single Intelligence Agency. The newly created SIA has moved away from the unique atmosphere of MI6 to make itself more like the rest of the modern British Civil Service, adopting pseudo-business procedures and business-speak to cover for its own weaknesses.

In this particular passage, Thoroughgood meets up with the former agent, Martin Worth, codename *Gladiator*, who confirms his suspicions that all is not well within the Service he once loved.

T HE SKY WAS grey, a damp wind buffeted the grass and there was snow on the Welsh mountains to the west. In the deep valley to his right a red Dinky-toy tractor was carrying hay to sheep, white blobs on a green handkerchief. A hawthorn hedge marked a gentler slope to his left but there was no sign of the gap he sought, only a sheep's skull and rabbit holes in the bank. He followed the hedge down the other side of the hill until eventually he saw a rusty metal gate and in the grass beside it a broken and faded footpath sign.

From there he followed a thinner and more neglected hedge across two fields. Eaten out by sheep and worn through by their tracks, it was decades since it had served any purpose. Probably not since the days when farms had workers whose winter jobs were hedging and ditching. Those might also have been the days when the single-roomed ruin they called Templewood had functioned as – as what? A shepherd's hut during the lambing? Too substantial for that and, anyway, they would have lambed lower down or in the barns. Something to do with the water supply? He recalled an iron relic in the stone floor. Or someone's folly, a summerhouse for picnicking and enjoying the views, built during a burst of prosperity and romantic naturalism. Whatever its origin, the overgrown ruin had provided a good hide from which to log the comings and goings of the unsuspecting Valley Farm below. That it was also cold, wet and hospitable to vermin was so much the better. Train hard, fight easy, the army used to say. He wondered when MI6 had last used the place. The new SIA would find it incompatible with health and safety.

But he had yet to find it at all. From the end of the hedge he could see the farm, a scattering of grey stone buildings in varying states of disrepair, roofed with slate and corrugated iron and surrounded by the scruffy detritus of old working farms – tyres, rusty implements, bits of tractor, discarded axles, fence posts, wire netting, the

skeleton of a van, dilapidated hen-houses and a moss-grown cara-
van with an incongruous blue roof and dirty net curtains. A few
chickens were scratching about and a collie was sniffing a pile of
logs. The only change was that they had started to convert one of
the barns to accommodation, and then abandoned it.

The ruin must be nearby, since it offered virtually the same view,
but the wind-warped undergrowth looked too sparse to conceal
it. Charles began circling the rim of the valley from the field side,
peering down into twisted thorn and stunted scrub oak. Thinking it must be lower than he remembered, he made his way down
through the trees. As he slithered and caught himself on a branch
he heard a man's distant voice, a single gruff shouted word. The
dog turned and trotted back to the house. He froze: they wouldn't
spot him among the trees but they might notice movement.

It was as he stood holding the branch that he became aware of
the hide above and behind him, to his right. He must have moved
below and across it after entering the trees. Dug into the hillside
and facing across the dell, it was concealed from above and on both
sides by undergrowth, concealed also from the dell by tree growth.
There was an entrance with no door, a rotting door frame with the
lintel missing, the stonework around it cracked and sagging. The
windows were dark misshapen rectangles, sprouting weeds, and
the tiled roof was holed and uneven, its timbers exposed.

If Martin was there he would have seen Charles arrive, but there
was no sound. Charles remained still, neither frightened nor uneasy,
but wondering if he should be. Martin was an unknown quantity
now; what he was doing, what he thought, what he wanted was a
mystery. It was possible he had returned to kill his former case officers; Charles had once run an agent who had done just that to the
officer of a liaison service. Perhaps he really had become an extrem-
ist as Nigel Measures wanted everyone to believe, or perhaps he

wanted to revenge himself on anyone from the service that had sent him back to Afghanistan. Well, he could do it here and now easily enough. The only sound was the cawing of rooks.

Treading carefully on the loose earth, Charles climbed the few yards to the hut, stepped in and paused to let his eyes adjust to the gloom. It felt damp, there were leaves on the broken stone floor and weeds coming up through the cracks. In the middle, about knee-height, was the iron relic he remembered. It looked like the remains of a water pump. He had forgotten there was a boarded ceiling, sagging and holed in places. Some of the boards had rotted and fallen to the floor.

'Welcome back to Templewood. Glad you came alone.'

Martin spoke quietly, from somewhere very close.

Charles felt a slight spasm in his throat.

'Don't worry, I'll come to you,' said Martin.

There was slithering and creaking overhead. Charles remembered now that the actual hide was between the roof and a reinforced section of ceiling, entered from the bank behind via an enlarged hole in the tiles, hidden by bushes. Martin would have slid in on his belly from the field and could be heard now, pushing his way back out through the thicket.

Charles stepped outside the door to await him, shielded by branches from the farm below. After a minute or so Martin appeared without a sound from the other side of the hide, a tall man with reddish-brown stubble. He wore camouflage kit and the kind of green woollen hat the army used to call a cap comforter. He carried a green rucksack in one hand and held up his other like a policeman stopping traffic.

'Come no closer. I probably smell worse than the last time you picked me up from this place.'

Charles stepped forward. 'We can chance a handshake.' Martin's grip was strong and his hand hard. His face was dirty and his green eyes looked tired.

'How long have you been here?' asked Charles.

'Long enough. Sarah passed the message, then? She assured me she could. Mrs Measures, I should say.' He laid heavy emphasis on her married name. 'How is she?'

'Well, I believe. I saw her a couple of weeks ago.'

'Still married?'

Charles nodded. 'Where shall we talk?'

'Here. Nowhere's safe.'

'From what?'

'From your friends. Your employer, if you're still employed. From the organisation you got me into many years ago and which right now is trying to kill me.'

They squatted on the earth, leaning against tree trunks. Martin's speech was quiet and controlled, as if long thought about, or even rehearsed. He would have had time to rehearse, thought Charles, lying day and night in that damp hide.

'You sent me to Afghanistan to target the Taliban. Or al-Qaeda. It wasn't clear which, but that didn't matter. No longer the PIRA, anyway. I'd done that crusade. I was keen and d'you know what? – I loved it, every frozen, boiling, tedious, gruelling, exciting, awful, wonderful, boring minute of it. Away from my own country, I found I loved war. It surprised me, I thought I'd be appalled by the suffering and want to help but instead I found the struggle of man against man the most exhilarating thing I knew. Better than sex, religion, climbing Everest, better than anything. It may seem a dreadful thing to say, but I never felt more fully alive than when killing. I did a lot more of that than I ever let on to you or your successors.'

He paused, looking for a response. This was a more expressive

Martin than Charles remembered. He's been saving it for a long time, he thought. He nodded. 'I always suspected you did.'

'That wasn't why you sent me, I knew that. But they were so appealing, those Afghans, it was impossible not to get involved. Their fierce simplicity, their courtesy, their manners, their pitilessness, their fantastic loyalty and treachery, their bravery. I love them for it. I know it's said that you don't buy an Afghan, you rent him, but that doesn't make him any less brave or even less loyal, provided you know the rules he lives by. For him, life is fighting and striving; for us it's security and comfort. Colours are vivid for him, for us they're blurred. Life for him is crueller, and clearer. I couldn't be with them and not be one of them. I was young, I guess. That's why I stayed on after 9/11.'

'You found a cause.'

'I found a mission. I stayed to help. Schools, medicine, roads, whatever I could. Mainly schools, because without education you can't do anything; but if they've got that they can do the rest themselves. For a while it was fine; so much to do, and no one seriously trying to stop you. But when the security situation worsened and the warlords fell out with one another everything changed. I became a Muslim, as perhaps you know. That kept my head on my body, at least. It also helped my education mission. It was never a question of belief – I no more believe in the Prophet than in the Pope or the Reverend Ian Paisley, for Christ's sake. Not that there aren't some fine things in Islam. Like most religions, it's a good enough way to live if you don't believe very much, or take it literally. It's just that accepting faith means giving up on questioning, which is how we learn, how we move on. So I pretended.'

'You had a lot of time for thinking,' said Charles.

'A lot of time sitting cross-legged and talking. Conversion was not only a way of showing where my sympathies lay, it was also a way of getting beneath the skins of a people and culture that intrigued me. Not that the Afghans are very religious, most of them. Unlike AQ – which I could've joined, by the way, if I'd sworn allegiance to UBL and all that.' There was another shout from the farm below. He glanced down the hill towards it. 'Going deaf, that dog. But love dies, doesn't it? That's the trouble. Dwindles, fades, anyway. I fell out of love with the office and in love with the Afghans, the non-Taliban ones. But when the stability they were promised after 9/11 never happened, it became more and more difficult for me to do my work. Down in the south where the Taliban were regaining control the only way for me to survive would have been to join them, and I didn't want to kill my own. At least not then.'

'You do now?'

'Don't worry, not you. So far as I know.' Martin's smile showed a broken tooth and made him look younger than his thirty-five years. 'So, I moved back here full time and built up my practice, my legal practice, largely in the Pakistani community where my languages help. I travelled out there quite a lot. I kept my hand in with Afghan work, when I could, though there wasn't much scope for legal process there.'

'But you were still an agent, weren't you, still working for the office?'

Martin picked a strip of bark from the ground and turned it over the fingers of both hands, his arms around his raised knees.

'Off and on, gradually more off than on. We sort of drifted apart. It was mutual, I guess. They used to be pretty good at keeping in touch in your day, didn't they? Just that – keeping in touch, we're here if you want us, we haven't forgotten you. They'd never forget; and if you were ever lost they'd always, always find you. That's what you felt. But not nowadays. It's changed since your time. Now everything's immediate, current; either a quick win or forget it, waste of time. I did get in touch a couple of times because I came across people in my charity work. People who might have been useful in future, with a little cultivation, gentle and early. But no one's got time for that now, it's all wham-bam-thank-you-ma'am. You miss a lot of good agents that way.'

Martin broke off a small piece of bark and flicked it away.

'And then one day the phone rings again. What about getting back into harness for a while, scouting things out, re-visiting some old contacts who might help us win the great War on Terror without their knowing it? Only this time I had two case officers, younger than me, which was a first, a man and a woman. Nice couple, good, keen; didn't know much about Afghanistan but that's not their fault, they'll learn. So I did a couple of trips to Pakistan for them, which I could combine with genuine business, and I made contact with one or two people. Came back each time with a few snippets which they raved over – and which suggests to me the SIA doesn't have much coverage out there these days. Does it?'

Charles shrugged. 'I don't see current stuff. They asked me back to find you.'

'Tell me about it. In a minute. So, after the last trip I get this summons to go back in a great hurry. It came by an unusual route, suggesting there was something urgent they wanted my help with. Looked fishy to me, not the normal way of my friends over there. They like to play things long – if it doesn't happen this time, then next if Allah wills, and if he doesn't it still doesn't matter, because their timelines are millennial. No performance indicators for them.'

Extracted from *Uncommon Enemy* by Alan Judd (published by Simon & Schuster, with whose permission this has been reproduced)

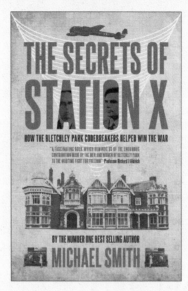